Transition Ahead: Lesson Plans for Life Beyond High School

A Resource Created By:

Dr. Annette Diane Anderson Fields

of

Living & Learning Unlimited, LLC

Copyright (2019) - All Rights Reserved

Transition Ahead: Lesson Plans for Life Beyond High School

Copyright © 2019 by:

Dr. Annette Diane Anderson Fields of Living & Learning Unlimited

ISBN # 978-0-578-65840-7

Copyright Registration: # TXu002186120 / 2020-02-21

Printed in the United States of America

L & L Publication House
Saint Louis, Missouri

PREFACE

Transition Ahead: Lesson Plans for Life Beyond High School has been created to provide an added tool to enhance service delivery of special education teachers who are preparing students as they transition to life after high school. It consists of various lessons related to post-secondary academic preparation, career development, and quality of adult living.

Transition planning is a legal requirement for students receiving services related to disabilities. Transition services are noted in student Individual Educational Plans. The Individuals with Disabilities Education Act (United Stated Department of Education, 2004) specifies that transition services are a coordinated set of activities to assist students with disabilities in moving from high school to life after high school.   Consideration of individual strengths, preferences, and interests are to be taken into account as plans are made to help students prepare for post-secondary education, employment, and independent living. One means for addressing transition, according to this act, is by the **provision of instructional activities.** This compilation of lesson plans is designed to be used as part of the effort to provide transition-related guidance and instruction to students who have disabilities.

Special educators are in place to help prepare students to eventually function as independently as possible and to the greatest extent possible as they exit high schools and enter post high school living. This may or may not include going to college. Topics were generated during a qualitative research study utilizing special educators from multiple school districts. The topics were later developed into lesson plans, peer reviewed, and then field-tested by special education practitioners who coordinate community-based transition programs and amended as needed.

The lessons stemming from my research are inclusive for those who have disabilities but not considered as functioning within lower levels of cognitive ability. Lessons in this book can be used with a wide spectrum of ability levels and can be modified to be more or less complex based upon the populations being taught. Since transition plans are required for **all students who receive special education services,** this resource intentionally stretches across diverse ability levels as well.   This resource can be used as a tool that embraces the Self Determination Learning Model of Instruction which teaches students to problem solve and use self-awareness to create, pursue, and self-monitor the attainment of personal goals (Little, 2012).

Opportunities to provide transition-related instruction can take place in multiple settings. Lessons or parts of them can be completed as a enrichment activity that accompanies or precedes the semester(s) work experience is provided. Lessons can take place prior to group departures for work or by instructors at the worksites. Special workshops can be offered at school as part of a transition or career fair or as an inhouse field trip. Advisory/homeroom time could sometimes be utilized as well. These scenarios are examples of opportunities that allow students who are not in functional academics classes to not be excluded and also benefit from transition-related instruction.

DEDICATIONS & ACKNOWLEDGEMENTS

Welcome to Transition Ahead: Lesson Plans for Life Beyond High School. This book is dedicated to all who co-labor with me in the field of transition. Thank you for your valuable contribution to society as you continue to help prepare young people to move from the realm of life in high school to adult living that takes place after high school. In addition, I am grateful for those who serve within these ranks who participated in generating many of the topics incorporated in this curriculum. This was facilitated by serving as interview participants during the qualitative research conducted as part of my doctoral dissertation completed at Saint Louis University.

There were those who, like myself, are site coordinators/transition teachers of off-campus transition programs in the Saint Louis Public Schools. Thank you, Glenda Lee, Verdene Walls, Iris Robinson Riddle, and Wilma Jones, who field-tested and provided feedback in regard to the lessons that were created. Your professional opinions, encouragement, and support during the development of this curriculum mattered.

Expressions of acknowledgement and gratitude are being given to The Council for Exceptional Children. This international organization has widened my network of professional affiliations in the field of special education, and has provided opportunity for sharing expertise and knowledge. It has been a valuable support system to me as I embarked upon and completed this writing project.

I am grateful for the additional flavor added to this production by the colorful downloaded images purchased from Shutterstock for the purpose of integrating them into this production. These images helped to set the stage for the content within the various sections as well as add to the attractive quality of the book cover.

I dedicate this book to my family members who have encouraged and supported me through the development of this project. To my husband, Johnnie Fields, my children, Jeremi, Kottia, Florence, and Johnnie Jr., thank you! To my big sister, Jan, and little brother, John Patrick, thank you! To my mother and father, Florence and John H. Anderson and my big brother, Raoul, who have passed on from this life into eternity, thanks for all of your encouragement to excel as evidenced by this book writing journey. To my extended family in the Saint Louis Public Schools and at Harris-Stowe State University, thank you! Most of all, I thank God for giving me the vision, direction, and drive to accomplish this task.

ABOUT THE AUTHOR

DR. ANNETTE DIANE ANDERSON FIELDS

Dr. Annette Diane Anderson Fields, a native of Saint Louis, Missouri, has served in the field of special education at the high school level in the Saint Louis Public Schools for more than thirty years. Her motto is: "Empowerment for Life Through the Acquisition of Knowledge." Prior to her current position of Site Coordinator/Transition Teacher of the Saint Louis Public Schools at Harris-Stowe State University Transition to College, Work, and Adult Living Program, she held other special education positions. She was a teacher assistant, and a certified special educator teaching science in a self-contained as well as in co-teaching classrooms. She also provided guidance to several students who won awards at the city-wide science fair. During that time, she served as Assistant Science Fair Coordinator at Roosevelt High School.

She was later promoted and assumed leadership as a special education department head. This position included her management of special education faculty, related service provision, and special education compliance for Soldan International Studies High School. She has also overseen

v

special education processes at Metro Academic & Classical Academy High School as well as Collegiate School of Medicine and Bioscience. Her tenure working with populations from those schools include students considered as twice exceptional. In addition, she provides mentoring support to new high school special education department heads. Facilitating district-wide professional development sessions has allowed her to share knowledge regarding policy, procedure, and strategies with other teachers. She also assists with various district compliance-related projects.

Dr. Fields' primary position, however, is at Harris-Stowe State University where she facilitates weekly transition-related seminars and supervises work experiences for twelfth grade college-bound students with disabilities from various high schools in the Saint Louis Public Schools. Students earn elective course credit toward meeting high school graduation requirements, while at the same time receive transition-related instruction and supervised work experiences on campus. This is a program that she marketed, pioneered, and has continued to develop and refine.

Dr. Fields takes pride in being a lifelong learner. She maintains membership with the Council for Exceptional Children. Not only has she regularly attended their annual international conferences to expand her knowledge in the field of special education, but has also had opportunities to share her expertise as part of panels on best practices to consider when providing transition-related instruction. In addition, she presented her transition-related research at their Division on Career Development and Transition Conference.

Her educational credentials include:

- **Bachelor of Science / Administration of Criminal Justice** - University of Missouri St. Louis
- **Initial Missouri State Teacher Certification** – Harris-Stowe State University through the Pathways to Teaching Careers Program
- **Master of Arts in Teaching / Science** – Webster University
- **Doctor of Education** – Saint Louis University

While completing her doctorate, Dr. Fields was inducted into the Alpha Epsilon Lambda Honor Society that is specifically designated for distinguished graduate and professional school students.

Her motto as she serves students and fellow educators while continuing to develop professionally is, "Empowerment for Life Through the Acquisition of Knowledge." High School and Beyond reflects this motto. Her goal is that this body of lesson plans and resources will empower both those providing instruction as well as the students who will be better equipped for life after high school.

TABLE OF CONTENTS

METHODS OF USING TRANSITION AHEAD

The content of these lesson plans can be used in part or in whole for enrichment activities or as a component of a transition-related class. Content can be covered during one class or can be spread across multiple class sessions as desired.

The following are included for each lesson:

- Topic to be addressed
- Goal(s) and objectives related to the topic
- Sample of types of content standards related to lesson
- Related vocabulary and terms
- Explicit instruction and practice activities
- Key pieces of information that should be shared with students (Points to Make)
- Suggested online media resources

Transition Ahead includes a variety of interactive, reflective, and writing activities. Lessons are grouped by transition-related category (post-secondary education, employment, and independent living) for the purpose of being user-friendly as well as correlating with major categories listed on student Transition Plans located within the Individualized Education Plans. **Permission is granted by the author of this book for the copying and use of activity worksheets contained within it for student instructional purposes only.**

Online subject-related websites and videos are suggested within each lesson to provide a current electronic library of resources. Websites can be accessed by utilizing your chosen internet search engine and searching by name of article and author. Suggested online videos can be accessed through YouTube at www.YouTube.com and typing the name of the chosen video within its search box while confirming the source that has been indicated.

Emphasis has been placed on exposing students to and/or expanding their knowledge of transition-related vocabulary and phrases/terms that may encounter or have to interact with as young adults. A dedicated section has been included that lists and defines vocabulary and terms that are part of the lesson plans provided. This section can be referenced as part of the lessons or used in other ways that have been determined by the instructor to clarify transition-related subject content.

CHAPTER ONE

POST-SECONDARY ACADEMIC PREPARATION

For the transitioning student, high school life will soon end and if more education and training is desired, planning and preparation must take place. It was found in The National Longitudinal Study-2 that, "Of young adults with disabilities, sixty percent were reported to have continued on to postsecondary education within eight years of leaving high school." (Newman, et al, 2011). This set of lessons involves self-reflection on personal career interests, what type of education or training is needed to qualify, and what steps should be taken between the present and enrollment in appropriate post-secondary institutions. In addition, various scenarios that take place as part of the college/post-secondary training experience will be visited to help students develop personal plans of action.

LESSON #1 – PREPARING TO GO TO COLLEGE

GOAL: Students will learn about how to prepare for changes that will happen when they leave high school and go to college.

OBJECTIVES: Students will

1. Realize how available special education services may change.
2. Explain how their levels of responsibility will change.
3. Identify the items they will need if going away to school vs. what will be needed if commuting.
4. Identify the schools they have chosen, the preparations they have made to attend, and contact information for the office that facilitates disability accommodations.

SAMPLE CONTENT STANDARDS: Apply information to revise and implement a personal educational plan.

VOCABULARY & TERMS: self-advocacy, commute, accessibility, self-identification, prioritizing, student support services, major, minor, financial aid, qualifications, living arrangements, scheduling conflicts

CONCEPT SUMMARY: Students have a sequence of events that must be completed prior to beginning college coursework. Deadlines must be adhered to for many of these tasks.

EXPLICIT INSTRUCTION AND PRACTICE:

- Discuss personal plans for getting ready to attend college.
- Review vocabulary and terms and elaborate upon them.
- Compare and contrast preparing to attend high school with preparing for college entry.
- Identify relevant services for students with disabilities and how to access them.
- Consider how time-sensitive tasks can be accommodated in personal schedules.
- Compare personal educational goals to ideals of others.
- Explore website that addresses preparing for college.
- Review and discuss video that addresses getting ready for college life.
- Discuss video that provides advice on what to pack and carry to college.
- Participate in a question/answer session in regard to the online resources viewed.
- Reflect upon steps that need to be taken to prepare for college.

- Complete the worksheet that lists preparatory tasks and then sequence the tasks on the flowchart provided.
- Complete personal "to-do lists" that can be monitored and amended as one moves toward his/her first day of college coursework.

POINTS TO MAKE:

- It is important to get time-sensitive tasks completed in order to get accepted and enrolled in school and coursework.
- Different colleges have different cut-off dates related to enrollment and registration for coursework.
- Personal deadlines should be created that allow extra time to adhere to college deadlines and allow room for the unexpected.
- In order to receive disability accommodations in college, it is up to students to self-identify with the appropriate office that helps to facilitate accommodations.
- Preparing to attend a college includes requirements such as completing FAFSA forms for financial aid, completing college applications, and securing financial aid.
- Decisions should be made to choose the most appropriate school that meets personal needs by first narrowing down one's choices and then enrolling in the preferred choice.
- Arrangements for placement testing to assess if any remedial classes are required will take place prior to entering college coursework.
- After acceptance and enrollment in a college, a meeting with an academic advisor occurs to create an appropriate course schedule.
- Student housing applications and deposits rendered should be submitted on time for on-campus housing.
- Arrive on campus during freshmen move-in dates. a
- Be guided by personal preferences, availability of desired programs and support systems, and availability of funding.
- Although advice, insight, and counsel are helpful, college choice should not depend upon others to make decisions for you without personal input.
- Students will no longer have Individualized Education Plans (IEPs) or modified lessons to help facilitate the completion of college degrees.
- Some college disability accommodations may help provide better access to meeting college requirements but needs to be initiated by student request through the Disability Office.
- Disability offices on college campuses require verification of disability such as the most recent evaluation or Individualized Education Plan.

- Special written permission must be on file with the college if students desire that academic progress be shared with their parents.

INSTRUCTIONAL RESOURCES:

Suggested Website(s):

Title: A Big College To-Do List
Created or Produced by: about education
Web Address: http://collegelife.about.com/od/beforeyouarrive/a/todolist.htm
Brief Summary: Includes links related to specific tasks and adjustments that may be helpful as one prepares to go to college

Suggested YouTube Video(s):

Title: Advice about Transitioning from High School to College

Creator/Producer: Christian Rafan
Running Time: (6 minutes 39 seconds)
Format: mini-lecture
Brief Summary: A young adult shares insight on topics pertaining to how to make a smooth transition into college life as well as the type of thought processes that are helpful during that time

Title: Packing for College: Dos and Don'ts

Creator/Producer: Lisa Ferg / Think Tank
Running Time: (5 minutes 46 seconds)
Format: mini-lecture
Brief Summary: Advice on what should be brought to college if living in the dorms as well as things that have dual purpose, thus eliminating the need for certain items

MOVING TOWARD THAT FIRST DAY OF TAKING COLLEGE CLASSES

Place the following activities in the correct sequence on the flowchart on this sheet:

- **Fill out financial aid application (FAFSA).**
- **Start taking classes.**
- **Research your college of interest to see if this is a good personal choice.**
- **Meet with an academic advisor to be advised of required coursework matching personal academic interests.**
- **Complete a college admissions application.**
- **Confirm acceptance of the financial aid package the college is offering.**
- **Register for classes.**

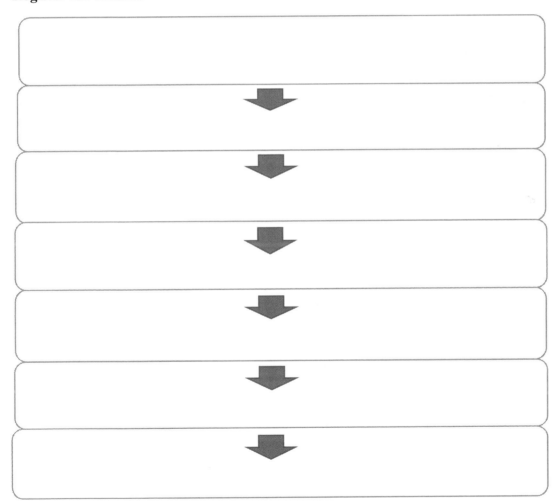

LESSON #2 – STAYING ON CAMPUS VS. COMMUTING TO COLLEGE

GOAL Students will personally make plans on how to successfully move into the realm of participating in the college experience.

OBJECTIVES: Students will

1. Decide upon what things they need to do to prepare for attending college.
2. Establish timelines for getting their business in order to either move on campus or to commute back and forth.
3. Compare and contrast scenarios as they pertain to commuting vs residential students.
4. Create a "needs vs. wants" list of things that they will need when they attend college.

SAMPLE CONTENT STANDARDS: Use decision making skills to make safe and healthy life choices

VOCABULARY & TERMS: commute, campus community, room and board, off campus housing, housing regulations, flexible scheduling, self-discipline, self-advocacy, housing deposit, shared space, personal vs. communal

CONCEPT SUMMARY: On-campus housing and off-campus housing have their pros and cons. Living arrangements and housing payment practices as well as convenience and campus access may also differ when comparing both options.

EXPLICIT INSTRUCTION AND PRACTICE:

- Discuss who plans to move on campus or move in town to access his/her college choice, and why.
- Describe factors that influence housing choice(s).
- Review vocabulary and terms and relate them to housing choices.
- Create a timeline to establish residency on or off campus.
- Review and discuss material from suggested website and videos.
- Weigh requirements for commuting vs. living on campus.
- Address the pros and cons of both options on the provided worksheet.

POINTS TO MAKE:

- Examples of student housing include living in dorms, sharing apartments, and rooming in reputable people's homes.
- Many students choose to commute from home instead of making other living arrangements when attending college.
- When sharing living space with other students, one must respect the property, personal space, and privacy of those resided with.
- Some living arrangements cost more and are riskier than others.
- Off-campus student housing can be furnished or unfurnished.
- Housing on campus is usually furnished.
- When living off-campus, students must also budget for meals, utilities if not included in the rent, furnishings that are needed, and transportation to and from school.
- Living on campus is paid for by the semester.
- Campus room and board can be budgeted as an expense when securing financial aid.
- The price of living on campus often includes meal plans.
- Payment for off-campus housing is documented in the housing or rental agreement.
- Living off-campus requires allocating time in one's schedule to commute.
- Doing laundry on and off-campus can be an additional expense.
- A housing deposit is required to hold a space for anyone who intends to move in and is held until the occupants move out (unless the occupants have damaged the property, in which case the deposit may be forfeited).
- Housing deposits are not returned to students when they move out if the place they have resided in is not left in the same condition that it was in when they moved in.
- Housing deposits must be returned to occupants when they vacate a property if nothing has been damaged and housing fees have been paid and are current.
- If damages are discovered by student housing, some or all of the deposit is retained when moving out to make repairs and restorations.
- There are rules that must be abided by or the occupants risk being evicted.
- Students sharing off-campus housing can be evicted if they get too far behind on their rent.
- If one or more people leave the off-campus housing residence during a lease term, those who remain are responsible for finding a way to cover the total rent payment.
- On-campus housing requires payment from individual students that has been agreed upon for the semester and that amount does not change due to a roommate moving.

INSTRUCTIONAL RESOURCES:

Suggested Website(s):

Title: Living On-Campus vs. Off-Campus: A List of Pros and Cons
Created or Produced by: Caroline Eaton – Lee University
Web Address: http://www.thecollegetourist.com/living-on-campus-vs-off-campus-a-list-of-pros-and-cons/
Brief Summary: Lists and explanations comparing living on vs. commuting to college

Suggested YouTube Video(s):

Title: Living on Campus vs. Off Campus
Creator/Producer: Jacy Buchholz
Running Time: (3 minutes 8 seconds)
Format: Pictures show some of the comparisons that are being narrated through the video.
Brief Summary: Compares and contrasts both college living arrangements

Title: What To (and NOT To) Bring to College / College Survival Guide
Creator/Producer: Kara Lyn
Running Time: (12 minutes 7 seconds)
Format: mini-lecture with dorm room background
Brief Summary: A college student is transparent on what she found that she actually needed and what she could have done without and why

LIVING ON CAMPUS VS. NOT LIVING ON CAMPUS

In the space provided below, compare and contrast living on campus vs. commuting back and forth to campus by listing the pros and cons of each option.

PROS OF LIVING ON CAMPUS	PROS OF NOT LIVING ON CAMPUS

CONS OF LIVING ON CAMPUS	CONS OF NOT LIVING ON CAMPUS

LESSON #3 – THE COLLEGE APPLICATION AND FUNDING PROCESS

GOAL: Students will complete pre-requisite college paperwork.

OBJECTIVES: Students will

1. Complete federal financial aid applications.
2. Complete college applications online for schools they qualify for which have their anticipated majors.
3. Request application fee waivers if available and needed.
4. Explore what additional financial aid opportunities they may qualify for at the institutions of their choosing.

SAMPLE CONTENT STANDARDS: Set post-secondary goals for themselves and take actions that are required to attend post-secondary institutions

VOCABULARY & TERMS: FAFSA, financial aid, loans, grants, scholarships, work-study, deadlines, college application, major, letter of recommendation, entrance requirements, college essay

CONCEPT SUMMARY: Along with choosing colleges of interest, one must complete application procedures as well as follow through and apply for financial aid within established timelines.

EXPLICIT INSTRUCTION AND PRACTICE:

- Identify colleges of interest.
- Review and discuss vocabulary and terms.
- Discuss what funds would be needed to cover college expenses.
- Compare various financial aid options at institutions of interest.
- Digest website and suggested videos that address the college application process.
- Research information on their colleges of interest, document the requested information, and compare and contrast on the worksheet that has been provided.
- Complete the College Application Processes Worksheet listing considerations related to personal college choices.
- Complete online college applications and request application fee waivers as needed for colleges of choice if entrance requirements are met.
- Complete FAFSA forms for financial aid.
- Request parent(s) to fill out the parental section.

POINTS TO MAKE:

- Student financial aid applications must be completed yearly to help determine what type and amount of monetary assistance should be granted for student expenses.
- Parental income and student income are considered when granting financial aid to students who are still dependents to help determine the amount of assistance required.
- Scholarships can be granted based upon academic achievement, need, affiliation with various groups or populations, or talent that the college plans to utilize.
- Scholarships can often be renewed if one continues to meet the criteria designated for the particular scholarship.
- Scholarships are limited, and therefore everyone who qualifies may not necessarily receive one.
- College work study allows students to perform work on campus in exchange for some of the expenses of attending that college or university.
- Grants are monies awarded for school-related expenses by the government or various foundations that do not have to be repaid and are based upon eligibility criteria.
- Installment plans are agreements between colleges and students that allow paying for tuition to be spread out during a semester.
- Tuition reimbursement is a form of financial aid where an employer will help to pay an agreed upon percentage of school expenses after satisfactory grades are earned.
- A student loan is a form of financial aid where the student borrows money to pay for school and agrees to pay it back to the source of funding.
- College applications are completed and submitted to institutions of higher learning along with other verification of student performance as part of the review and acceptance process.
- Sometimes a fee is charged to apply; sometimes the charge is waived.
- Colleges often require that applications be made online prior to established deadlines.
- Review factors such as grade point average, ACT scores, and high school transcripts help colleges make decisions on which students will be accepted.
- Entrance requirements vary from college to college.
- Consider the majors offered, financial aid available, the location and setting, and entrance requirements when choosing a college.

INSTRUCTIONAL RESOURCES:

Suggested Website(s):

Title: Applying to Schools
Created or Produced by: United States Department of Education
Web Address: https://studentaid.ed.gov/sa/prepare-for-college/applying
Brief Summary: Steps that need to be taken when applying to colleges including various links for handling specific tasks

Suggested YouTube Video(s):

Title: College Application Dos and Don'ts
Creator/Producer: ABC15 Arizona
Running Time: (4 minutes 17 seconds)
Format: interview on news show
Brief Summary: Interview of Tim Desch, sharing best practices for going through the college application process and the choices that are involved

WHAT IS REQUIRED FOR MY COLLEGE CHOICES?

Research three of your colleges of interest and record information related to going to those schools in the chart below.

	COLLEGE NAME	COLLEGE NAME	COLLEGE NAME
ENTRANCE REQUIREMENTS			
TUITION			
ROOM AND BOARD			
APPLICATION DEADLINE			

THE COLLEGE APPLICATION PROCESS

What do you plan to major in when you go to college? _____

Do you plan to attend college full time or part-time? _____

What are the top five (5) things that you are looking for in a college?

    1. _____

    2. _____

    3. _____

    4. _____

    5. _____

Have you taken the ACT Test yet? _____

What areas on the ACT test do you need to spend the most time on in order to help meet ACT Test Score requirements for the schools you are interested in applying to?

_____

_____

LIST THE COLLEGES YOU ARE APPLYING TO

Name of College: _____

Why did you choose this school? _____

_____

··

Name of College: _____

Why did you choose this school? _____

··

Name of College: _____

Why did you choose this school? _____

_____

LESSON #4 – COMPLETING THE "TO DO LIST" BEFORE COLLEGE CLASSES BEGIN

GOAL: Students will prepare to go to college by creating plans for tasks that need to be accomplished before college matriculation begins.

OBJECTIVES: Students will

1. Create "to do" lists of what tasks need to be completed and when, prior to taking college coursework.
2. Check off the items that have already been completed.
3. Add to or amend the lists as needed.

SAMPLE CONTENT STANDARDS: Develop plans that will address personal goals based on current interests, strengths, and limitations

VOCABULARY & TERMS: FAFSA, college application, housing deposit, scholarship applications, school/dorm supplies, freshmen orientation, course scheduling, placement tests, disability access office

CONCEPT SUMMARY: Students will reflect upon steps that have already been completed and add additional tasks to complete prior to beginning college coursework.

EXPLICIT INSTRUCTION AND PRACTICE:

- Review vocabulary and terms and how they related to preparation for college.
- Brainstorm about and list tasks that need to be accomplished prior to starting college.
- Break listed tasks into smaller tasks if possible.
- Introduce and dialogue all of the points to make that are listed.
- Review created lists and check off what has already been completed.
- Establish priority of tasks to be completed.
- Create personal deadlines for tasks and place them on "to do lists".
- Review and discuss suggested website and video.
- Revisit, check off, and amend "to-do lists" as needed.

POINTS TO MAKE:

- Timelines need to be created and met for tasks to be completed before college.
- College applications should be made during the first semester through the beginning of the second semester of the senior year in high school.

- Student financial aid forms should be completed no later than February during the year the high school senior is graduating.
- Scholarship application deadlines vary by institution, but many are due no later than the first few weeks of the second semester during the senior year in high school.
- Housing deposits, for those who will reside in student housing, are usually due the spring before the academic year that one will begin attending college.
- College acceptance should be confirmed with the college that has approved your enrollment by the deadline the college has established.
- Placement tests are taken prior to officially registering for college classes in the fall to determine if any remedial courses are required.
- A meeting with academic advisors should take place prior to registering for classes in order to help assure that appropriate courses are being taken during the first semester.
- Immunization and health information and verification should be shared with student health services before college begins .
- Those who have Individualized Education Plans (IEPs) and desire accommodations in college need to self-identify with the disability office before school begins.
- The disability access office shares student accommodation needs with their respective professors.
- ACT and/or SAT test scores are taken and sent to colleges that are designated by the student to help validate qualifications for being accepted.
- College applications must be completed and submitted by specific deadlines in order to be considered for admission.
- Financial aid applications should be filed by deadlines in order to secure funding to help with tuition and related expenses.
- Financial aid packages are put together for students based upon information on the FAFSA form.
- Financial aid packages include the different forms and amounts of financial aid that will be provided to select students to assist with college related expenses.
- High school transcripts must be sent when requested, to assist the college in accepting or rejecting the application.
- Students must respond to acceptance letters from schools they have applied to by required deadlines in order to enroll in coursework during the upcoming semester.
- Deposits must be turned in on time in order to guarantee placement in requested student housing.
- In the event that one desires to share student housing space with someone in particular, those wishes should be expressed ahead of time, prior to room assignments.

- One should gradually purchase personal items to increase one's comfort and convenience in student housing if one decides to not commute to college from home.
- Secure a personal laptop and/or tablet, if able, to take to school so that one can have increased accessibility to research and/or type assignments when time permits.
- After officially enrolling in the college of choice, initiate a meeting with an academic advisor to receive guidance on choosing appropriate coursework.

INSTRUCTIONAL RESOURCES:

Suggested Website(s):

Title: College Preparation Checklist
Created or Produced by: United States Department of Education
Web Address: https://studentaid.ed.gov/sa/sites/default/files/college-prep-checklist.pdf
Brief Summary: Extensive list of things to do to prepare for attending college that can be utilized as a checklist

Suggested YouTube Video(s):

Title: Back to School/Preparing for First Day of College Classes and Organization Tips
Creator/Producer: Jayla Elisha
Running Time: (12 minutes 35 seconds)
Format: mini-lecture with pictures to demonstrate what she is sharing
Brief Summary: College student shares helpful tips for getting and remaining organized in college

Title: Where Am I Going to College?! (College Application Tips)
Creator/Producer: Brooke Miccio
Running Time: (14 minutes 32 seconds)
Format: mini-lecture
Brief Summary: High school senior shares her process of filling out multiple college applications after deciding upon her personal needs and considerations made when deciding upon which one to enroll in

LESSON #5 – THE COLLEGE COMMUNITY

GOAL: Students will increase their knowledge about what a college community consists of.

OBJECTIVES: Students will

1. Identify the location of various departments located on college campuses.
2. Describe some of the types of activities on campus that may help students meet their academic and social goals.
3. Explain what a college community consists of.
4. Compare and contrast some ways that the community of a small college may differ from a large university.

SAMPLE CONTENT STANDARDS: Develop strategies for integrating into an environment

VOCABULARY & TERMS: campus security, student housing, Greek life, student support services, athletics, faculty, staff, university administration, student activities, food services, student population, student demographics

CONCEPT SUMMARY: People, places, and activities contribute to what exists within specific college communities. Some types of communities are more favorable than others with respect to individual desires and personal needs.

EXPLICIT INSTRUCTION AND PRACTICE:

- Identify and list specific types of familiar campus places and their purposes.
- List additional major places/departments and their purposes on the board as they are recalled.
- Introduce and define vocabulary and terms.
- Watch virtual tours of a small, mid-size, and large college campus.
- Isolate campus website information about those colleges including student population numbers, demographics, as well as student activities and organizations.
- Compare and contrast different sized campuses for similarities and differences.
- Address the concept "community" and discuss how the characteristics of the observed campuses contribute to the campus community.
- Identify people other than instructors and students who make up a college community.
- Review and discuss the suggested website and video that convey the concept of college community.
- Provide evidence of how preferred colleges will meet their personal needs.

POINTS TO MAKE:

- The number of students attending a college/university could have an impact on the school atmosphere.
- Every individual on a college/university campus plays a role in contributing to the atmosphere.
- The amount and type of student organizations and activities can vary from school to school.
- Academics on college campuses extend beyond the classroom and can continue informally at other places on campus.
- Community implies that many features within an area combine to create an atmosphere and environment.
- Those who reside together on college campuses can serve as temporary extended families who benefit by assimilating and co-existing within their environment.
- Student demographics may matter with some students if they want to be educated and/or housed with others from similar backgrounds.
- Larger student populations often mean larger teacher/student ratios and less individualized attention.
- A benefit of small universities and colleges: many students get to know each other and their instructors, well.
- Universities with larger student populations often provide a greater variety of student activities.
- Universities with smaller student populations are often more likely to have communities where a larger percentage of the students know each other.

INSTRUCTIONAL RESOURCES:

Suggested Website(s):

Title: What Will College Life Be Like?
Created or Produced by: Collegedata
Web Address:
http://www.collegedata.com/cs/content/content_magarticle_tmpl.jhtml?articleId=10103
Brief Summary: A brief introduction to a typical college day experience

Title: Discovering College Life
Created or Produced by: Virginia Commonwealth University
Web Address: http://www.going-to-college.org/campuslife/discovering.html
Brief Summary: Describes how school life changes when leaving high school and then attending college

Suggested YouTube Video(s):

Title: A Day in the Life of a College Student
Creator/Producer: Guthrie Collins
Running Time: (4 minutes 32 seconds)
Format: demonstration through videography with music background
Brief Summary: A walk-through of a typical college day from getting up in the morning through going to bed in the evening

LESSON #6 – COLLEGE COURSEWORK AND DEGREE COMPLETION

GOAL: Students will realize how completed college courses accumulate to fulfill degree requirements.

OBJECTIVES: Students will

1. Explain the different formats through which college coursework is offered.
2. Create a compatible course schedule.
3. Describe a method of getting additional help with coursework outside of the classroom setting.
4. Self-monitor academic progress and consider advice from an academic advisor.

SAMPLE CONTENT STANDARDS: Develop and monitor personal educational plans

VOCABULARY & TERMS: pre-requisite, required courses, electives, lab classes, lecture classes, online classes, academic support, course catalog, full time student, part-time student, registration, balanced course load, course sections

CONCEPT SUMMARY: College coursework can be completed in various ways.

EXPLICIT INSTRUCTION AND PRACTICE:

- Review vocabulary and explain the differences between types of class formats.
- Verbally compare and contrast various class formats.
- Identify a course schedule that is balanced and based upon current course offerings found online.
- Explain how the amount of credit hours taken per grading period has an impact on how long it may take to graduate.
- Consider reasons why schools offer several sections of the same course.
- Provide examples of means and places that students can get additional academic assistance.
- Review college websites to identify the academic requirements for completing degrees of interest.
- Investigate upcoming course offerings, compare to academic requirements, and create compatible course schedules.

POINTS TO MAKE:

- A number of courses within various categories must be successfully completed in order to obtain college degrees.
- Elective courses are classes that don't have to fit within a certain category or type of class but count toward credit hours needed to graduate.
- Pre-requisite courses are classes that must be completed before one is allowed to take certain higher-level classes must be taken.
- Lab courses are classes that allow the student to do hands on activities to help facilitate learning of content.
- Lecture courses are classes in which the instructor provides information to students and elaborates upon and clarifies course concepts orally.
- Online courses are completed via the internet and include online discussions, viewing lectures, literature review/reflection, and uploading assigned work.
- A course catalog lists courses and descriptions of courses being offered by a college during a given semester.
- A separate listing of the same course that is taught at a different time of day or day of the week or by another instructor is considered as a class section of the course.
- Academic support such as writing and math labs on college campuses are free sources of assistance with math concepts and writing projects/assignments.
- Professors have office hours during which one can make appointments to get additional assistance.
- Some larger classes have assistants assigned to them who also provide additional support to students.
- Students often form study groups to help one another by sharing and solidifying their understanding of course content as well as drilling each other for upcoming tests.
- Formal tutors are sometimes provided by colleges in support centers but at other times must be contracted as private tutors who are paid for their time.
- A part-time student is a college student who is taking less than twelve credit hours during a given semester.
- A full-time student is a college student who is taking at least twelve credit hours.
- Registration is the process of signing up for classes.
- After a student has registered for classes, he/she may drop or add courses prior to designated deadlines.
- Registration is voided if a student does not pay for the courses he/she has chosen to take for the semester.
- Once one registers for a class and quits attending without officially dropping the class an F will be received for that course, and refunds will not be provided.

- Failed classes can be repeated but require payment of a second registration fee.
- If one is failing a course and drops it by the designated deadline, he/she will not receive an F for that class but must pay for it again in the future to retake it.

INSTRUCTIONAL RESOURCES:

Suggested Website(s):

Title: What is the Purpose for Taking General Classes for a College Degree?
Created or Produced by: Fitzalan Gorman
Web Address: http://classroom.synonym.com/purpose-taking-general-classes-college-degree-1136.html
Brief Summary: Explains why some college coursework is not directly related to one's major

Suggested YouTube Video(s):

Title: Students Advising Students: General Education Courses
Creator/Producer: University of California – Santa Cruz
Running Time: (2 minutes 5 seconds)
Format: interview excerpts from various students
Brief Summary: College students share why general education courses are important as a part of pursuing degrees

Title: College 101: Credits, Degrees, Majors
Creator/Producer: Kira Kennedy
Running Time: (3 minutes 46 seconds)
Format: mini-lecture
Brief Summary: College students share basic information in regard to pursuing college coursework including types of degrees

LESSON #7 – STUDY SKILLS

SUBJECT: Study Skills

GOAL: Students will review and apply strategies for studying coursework material.

OBJECTIVES: Students will

1. Organize information to facilitate studying.
2. Describe methods of reviewing materials for tests.
3. Identify good study habits.
4. Explain the benefit of studying material in increments.

SAMPLE CONTENT STANDARDS: Synthesize and organize information for personal use

VOCABULARY & TERMS: crash studying, study buddies, main ideas, undivided attention, creating connections, personal application, idea clustering, mnemonic, flow chart, Venn diagram, Frayer model, concept maps, paraphrasing ideas, repetitive review

CONCEPT SUMMARY: Studying information requires processing and making sense of the material by connecting it to prior knowledge and then integrating key information into one's extended personal knowledge.

EXPLICIT INSTRUCTION AND PRACTICE:

- Differentiate reading, observing, and studying.
- Address the importance of making personal connections to course concepts throughout the study process.
- Review and discuss the vocabulary and terms.
- Discuss how to organize materials and time for study.
- Examine various graphic organizers and how they are used to organize information.
- Consider the benefit of gradually studying material repeatedly and in increments.
- Locate examples of good note taking.
- Describe and provide examples of the form and function of note taking
- Practice connecting supporting information to main ideas when note taking.
- Demonstrate strategies for memorizing key information.
- Explore the concept of collaborating to study material.
- Discuss ways to avoid getting overwhelmed while studying such as taking breaks or focusing on one small section at a time.
- Review suggested website and videos for this lesson.
- Share which study tips will be added to personal practices.

POINTS TO MAKE:

- New information is better remembered when it is connected to information that one is already familiar with.
- Venn diagrams are graphic organizers designed to compare and contrast ideas.
- Flow charts are graphic organizers designed to help in sequencing activities.
- Frayer models are graphic organizers designed to bring clarity to vocabulary words and what they are as well as what they are not.
- Concept maps are graphic organizers designed to group related ideas and show how they are grouped.
- Once difficult information is understood, rephrase and/or rewrite the information in one's own words and then confirm the accuracy with someone else.
- Teaming up with others who desire to study together can be helpful to confirm one another's interpretation of material taught by the instructor.
- Study buddies can be resources for sharing content that may have been missed during the note-taking process.
- Study buddies can collectively process what was taught in class and they can help one another review for tests.
- Make lists of concepts that are not clearly understood when reading assignments and then seek clarity with the instructor.
- Approach instructors to clarify understanding of material either before or after class or during his/her office hours.
- Take the first letter of related concepts and make a word out of them to help recall.
- Effective studying requires alertness and concentration.
- Choose a location that minimizes the amount of distraction during study time.
- Create designated study times as part of one's schedule.
- Repeated study of specific concepts will help one remember the information.

INSTRUCTIONAL RESOURCES:

Suggested Website(s):

Title: Top 10 Study Skills
Created or Produced by: Lynchburg College
Web Address: http://www.lynchburg.edu/academics/tutoring-academic-support/top-10-study-skills/
Brief Summary: List of strategies to use when studying

<u>Suggested YouTube Video(s):</u>

Title: How to Study: Positive vs. Active Studying
Creator/Producer: Clarissa
Running Time: (3 minutes 35 seconds)
Format: mini-lecture
Brief Summary: A nursing student shared some of her strategies for studying in preparation for tests and the advantages related to "active studying"

Title: The 9 Best Scientific Study Tips
Creator/Producer: AsapSCIENCE
Running Time: (3 minutes 25 seconds)
Format: visual illustrations to accompany study methods that are explained
Brief Summary: Strategies on preparing for exams that compare and contrast methods

LESSON #8 – SELF-MONITORING OF ACADEMIC REQUIREMENTS

GOAL: Students will develop skills to maintain awareness of their progress toward meeting academic requirements and will use strategies for making sure that they remain on course.

OBJECTIVES: Students will

1. Identify sources that list academic requirements for available majors/minors.
2. Distinguish academic needs that have been met from those which have not been met.
3. Identify multiple paths of meeting specific academic requirements.
4. Recognize when a change in course schedule may be beneficial.

SAMPLE CONTENT STANDARDS: Exhibit self-management skills necessary to meet post-secondary goals

VOCABULARY & TERMS: personal academic plan, pacing, pre-requisite course, alternative coursework, course substitution, frequency of course offering, check-off sheet, course preference

CONCEPT SUMMARY: One must be aware of requirements to meet academic goals and to stay on track and meet them

EXPLICIT INSTRUCTION AND PRACTICE:

- Review and discuss vocabulary and terms.
- Compare and contrast some of the academic requirements found on various college websites for offered degrees.
- Examine how various majors overlap in academic requirements.
- Locate different types of courses that fulfill the same requirement.
- Explain the concept of prerequisite courses and the purpose for counting those toward academic requirements.
- Describe a method for keeping up with which requirements have already been met and what is still needed for degree completion.
- Explain the purpose and benefit of course substitutions.
- Identify situations when a course change could benefit the student.
- Review requirements for a specific degree, identify courses that fulfill one of the requirements, and then choose which one is personally preferred.
- Weigh factors that should be considered when choosing which courses to register for.

- Review and discuss suggested website and video.
- Create an eight semester schedule for a specific major using an online course catalogue along with a list of degree requirements.

POINTS TO MAKE:

- Academic advisors on college campuses are able to provide lists of course requirements for completing various degrees.
- Three credit hours are awarded for most college courses.
- It is important to find out what courses are offered at the college attended that fulfill various categories of required credit hours.
- Be willing to choose among available courses to best meet one's personal interests and needs when options are available.
- Some specific courses require related lower-level courses related to them be taken first.
- There are cases when alternative, but related courses can be substituted for those normally required for particular degrees.
- Sometimes special permission for course substitution needs to be gained prior to enrolling in the alternative courses.
- Take infrequently offered required courses when they are available to avoid postponing graduation.
- Consider course difficulty and other persona responsibilities when deciding how many credit hours to take during a given grading period so that workload will be manageable.
- Students should set personal goals for each semester in college and amend long range plans as necessary.
- An academic advisor can help a student monitor his/her own academic requirements and fulfillments.

INSTRUCTIONAL RESOURCES:

Suggested Website(s):

Title: What Exactly is a College Credit? (And How Many Do I Need to Graduate?)
Created or Produced by: Susan Orr
Web Address: http://collegedegreecomplete.com/what-exactly-is-a-college-credit-and-how-many-do-i-need-to-graduate
Brief Summary: Explanation of how requirements may vary from program to program

Suggested YouTube Video(s):

Title: 14 Tips For Surviving Freshman Year of College
Creator/Producer: Erkita Beauty
Running Time: (14 minutes 24 seconds)
Format: mini-lecture
Brief Summary: College student shared strategies that helped her to assimilate into the college environment during freshman year.

LESSON #9 – SELF-AWARENESS OF LEARNING STYLES, STRENGTHS, AND WEAKNESSES

GOAL: Students will review their Individualized Education Plan (IEP) documents to help confirm their strengths as well as strategies to compensate for their challenges.

OBJECTIVES: Students will

1. Identify types of information on the Individualized Education Plan (IEP) related to learning style and disability that indicate helpful strategies to use in school.
2. Express strategies and supports that have been helpful in obtaining successful outcomes in school.
3. Consider areas that were identified as areas of academic weakness and share what helped with personal growth.

SAMPLE CONTENT STANDARDS: Develop self-management skills necessary for educational achievement

VOCABULARY & TERMS: auditory learner, visual learner, hands-on learner, prior knowledge, scaffolding, integration of ideas, supplemental learning, personal application, repetition of concepts

CONCEPT SUMMARY: When students are aware of what they are able to do as well as their challenges, they are able to create personal goals that capitalize upon their strengths while also diminishing their weaknesses.

EXPLICIT INSTRUCTION AND PRACTICE:

- Brainstorm examples of different ways that people learn.
- Review and discuss the vocabulary and terms.
- Visit website and discuss the personal relevance of it.
- Complete a brief learning style inventory contained in the website link.
- Watch and discuss the video about learning styles and studying.
- Consider strategies related to learning styles that have helped with academics.
- Identify a strategy that will be added to personal study practices.
- Review accommodations found on Individual Education Plans and how they contribute to learning.
- Discuss other factors on the IEP that may continue to influence personal goals.
- Share observations of personal growth in school and led to it.

POINTS TO MAKE:

- Connecting prior knowledge and understanding to new related information helps the learning process.
- Successful strategies for integrating new information into long-term memory should be utilized and practiced when striving toward academic success.
- Student IEPs contain clues from case managers in regard to strategies that have improved retention and mastery of academic content.
- Personal study skills for tests should include methods for retaining information that have already been successful.
- Students should add to the strategies that have helped them learn.
- A variety of strategies can increase learning such as:
- Making flash cards to study
- Collaborating with other students to review course material
- Creating graphic organizers to show connections between important information
- Analyzing pictures and illustrations related to the academic content
- Reviewing audiovisual material to reinforce lessons
- Discussing academic content in and outside of class
- Using soft music or movement if helpful
- Studying in areas with minimal distraction
- Drawing connections between material covered in class and one's personal life
- Paraphrasing class content will aid in remembering the information.
- Choosing the best time of day to study
- Classes and study times should be scheduled, if possible, to be compatible with one's personal body clock as it pertains to alertness and attentiveness
- Learning can be facilitated through auditory, visual, kinesthetic, and tactile modalities.

INSTRUCTIONAL RESOURCES:

Suggested Website(s):

Title: Got Style? Understanding Your Own Way of Learning
Created or Produced by: West Virginia Department of Education
Web Address: https://wvde.state.wv.us/counselors/links/students/documents/9.8.1-Learning_styles_assessment.pdf
Brief Summary: Addresses learning styles and includes a brief assessment

<u>Suggested YouTube Video(s):</u>

Title: How to Study for Your Learning Style
Creator/Producer: HACC Central Pennsylvania's Community College
Running Time: (4 minutes 21 seconds)
Format: mini-lecture with pictorial illustrations
Brief Summary: Provides strategies that will help in preparing for tests and based upon personal learning styles

LESSON #10 – SELF-ADVOCACY IN COLLEGE

GOAL: Students will increase their knowledge about when, where, and how to self-advocate in college.

OBJECTIVES: Students will

1. Identify situations that may occur in college that require self-advocacy.
2. Recognize the academic chain of command within a college setting.
3. Conclude that student disability access offices and student affairs offices can help students with success in college.
4. Consider self-advocacy involves others in the college community.

SAMPLE CONTENT STANDARDS: Exhibit self-management skills necessary for educational achievement

VOCABULARY & TERMS: window of opportunity, academic advisor, disability access office, faculty office hours, dean, student affairs office, compatible scheduling, persistence, compromise, win/win

CONCEPT SUMMARY: Students in college must operate as young adults who look out for their personal interests and goals being attained. Sometimes others must be accessed on campus to assist with resolution of school-related problems.

EXPLICIT INSTRUCTION AND PRACTICE:

- Discuss problems that came up in high school and what steps were taken to resolve them.
- Review and discuss vocabulary and terms.
- Locate the names of various personnel and departments on college campuses that help students have positive college experiences.
- Relate the purpose of using the Disabilities Access Office on campus after self-identifying
- Accommodations are only provided in college classes after one has registered with the Disabilities Access Office on campus.
- Recognize that special education case managers are not assigned to college students, so advocacy needs to come from other sources including himself/herself.
- Review and discuss suggested website that addresses self-advocacy.
- Complete worksheet on personal strategies to resolve situations requiring self-advocacy.
- Watch suggested videos on transitioning to college life and isolate the main points.

43

POINTS TO MAKE:

- College students are expected to advocate for themselves at school.
- Self-advocacy includes knowing what campus resources are available and how to access those resources should a situation require intervention.
- Self-advocacy in college involves proactively avoiding problems that can't be controlled or are opposed to personal needs and desires to graduate and have positive experiences in college.
- Speaking up for oneself, avoiding unnecessary conflict, and knowing when and how to engage others who may need to provide assistance are all parts of self-advocacy.
- Although there are some accommodations available through the disability office on campus, students must meet the same academic requirements as those without disabilities in order to complete college degrees.
- Students should become familiar with key support systems on campus that can help resolve situations as well as facilitate satisfactory progress in school.

INSTRUCTIONAL RESOURCES:

Suggested Website(s):

Title: Top 5 Tips for Self-Advocacy
Created or Produced by: Dr. Scott Allen
Web Address: http://experiencecle.com/2013/09/top-5-tips-self-advocacy/
Brief Summary: Five main pointers including additional explanation and examples related to self-advocating

Suggested YouTube Video(s):

Title: Transitioning to College With a Disability
Creator/Producer: Rebecca Siton
Running Time: (4 minutes 43 seconds)
Format: role play dialogue
Brief Summary: Role play addresses student support that is available in college for students with disabilities

Title: 5 Tips for New College Students with Disabilities
Creator/Producer: AHEAD (Association for Higher Education Access and Disability)
Running Time: (2 minutes 10 seconds)
Format: mini-lecture with drawn captions
Brief Summary: Advises students about getting connected and becoming knowledgeable about services and people available to them who will help to make college more pleasurable and productive

LOOKING OUT FOR YOURSELF IN COLLEGE

Below, you will find some scenarios that may occur in college. Given each scenario, list steps that you could take to resolve the issues and follow-up steps in case you don't resolve your concern with the first and or second solutions. Share and discuss your answers..

SCENARIO #1 –   You don't understand the lesson the professor has taught and must use the content from the lecture to complete a project.

1st	
2nd	
3rd	

SCENARIO #2 – You share a dorm room with someone who keeps so much company and noise in the room that you have a difficult time studying.

1st	
2nd	
3rd	

SCENARIO #3 – You believe that you are being graded unfairly.

1st	
2nd	
3rd	

SCENARIO #4 – You have to meet with your academic advisor prior to signing up for next semester's classes and the recommended schedule is not compatible with your preferences.

1st	
2nd	
3rd	

SCENARIO #5 – You discover that your grades are falling.

1st	
2nd	
3rd	

LESSON #11 – CREATING AND FOLLOWING COLLEGE COURSE SCHEDULES

GOAL: Students will learn about creating course schedules that are compatible with their needs.

OBJECTIVES: Students will

1. Describe how they select and schedule specific courses that meet their academic needs.
2. Explain how to strategically integrate their personal schedules with their academic schedules.
3. Demonstrate how they will store and view their class schedules.

SAMPLE CONTENT STANDARDS: Employ strategies needed for educational progress and achievement

VOCABULARY & TERMS: flexible scheduling, balanced workload, schedule conflict, study time, leisure time, credit load

CONCEPT SUMMARY: College coursework scheduling should be a joint effort between the student and academic advisor keeping in mind preferences, personal schedules, and manageable workloads.

EXPLICIT INSTRUCTION AND PRACTICE:

- Examine current course schedules, what they include, and types of credit hours that are being earned.
- Discuss similarities and differences between high school and college course schedules.
- Review vocabulary and terms.
- Show how total college credit hours are earned for courses while the number of class meetings per week may vary.
- Observe that some courses are offered in multiple sections
- Select courses based upon what is offered and fits within one's personal and desired course schedule.
- Review online the courses that are being offered at different colleges.
- Find five courses that will be placed on a course schedule.
- Create a course schedule consisting of five classes (3 credit hours per class totaling 15 credit hours) including the dates and times and store it for future reference.

- Seek alternative classes that will go toward degree requirements if scheduling conflicts exist.
- Explain why certain courses and course times were chosen and how these choices help them to meet personal goals.

POINTS TO MAKE:

- College class times can be flexible and arranged to meet students' personal needs.
- Some classes meet once a week, twice a week, or three times a week regardless of the number of required hours needed for granting course credit.
- The more frequently a class meets, the less time spent in each session during each week to equal a set amount of credit hours for the course.
- The less frequently a class meets, the more time spent in each session during each week to equal a set amount of credit hours for the course.
- Many campuses offer morning, afternoon, evening, and weekend classes.
- There are classes that are held in campus classrooms, off-campus classrooms, some online, and others that combine class locations.
- Scheduling of classes should meet personal needs that may include how much time one desires to sit in a class and what time of day or day(s) of the week are preferred.
- Other things to consider are which instructors are preferred, which class times are compatible with other needs, and how much of a course load one wants to carry.
- Networking with other students who have already taken desired courses with specific instructors may be helpful in deciding which sections of classes to take.
- Courses with heavier amounts of reading can sometimes be taken simultaneously with courses not requiring as much reading to help balance one's academic workload.
- Students should review course offerings for the upcoming semester and determine what remains to complete degree requirements.
- Prior to registering for coursework, ask an academic advisor to review and provide feedback to what has been chosen.

INSTRUCTIONAL RESOURCES:

Suggested Website(s):

Title: Class Scheduling Dos and Don'ts for First-Year Students
Created or Produced by: Lori Murray
Web Address: http://www.collegeview.com/articles/article/class-scheduling-dos-and-don-ts-for-first-year-students
Brief Summary: Helpful tips to utilize when deciding upon creating personal college course schedule

Suggested YouTube Video(s):

Title: College Tip – Scheduling Classes
Creator/Producer: Bee's Beauty
Running Time: (3 minutes 15 seconds)
Format: mini-lecture
Brief Summary: Student shares thought processes that have worked for her when creating compatible course schedules.

Title: College Advice / Schedules and Teachers and Time Management
Creator/Producer: Asia Webb
Running Time: (20 minutes 24 seconds)
Format: mini-lecture
Brief Summary: Students share advice through being transparent with their own experiences on how to set up compatible course schedules as well as how to manage time for completing assignments.

LESSON #12 – TEST TAKING SKILLS

GOAL: Students will increase their use of strategies to prepare for and take tests.

OBJECTIVES: Students will

1. Review and highlight main points within assigned reading material.
2. Demonstrate various methods of grouping concepts for retrieval and study.
3. Use the process of elimination for choosing answers to questions.
4. Explain how to constructively participate in study groups.

SAMPLE CONTENT STANDARDS: Develop performance skills necessary to prepare for academic assessment

VOCABULARY & TERMS: review, grouping concepts, connecting concepts, study buddy/study group, acronym, acrostic, process of elimination, justification, thoroughness

CONCEPT SUMMARY: Test preparation requires becoming aware of major concepts being tested, and systematically identifying main ideas, grouping concepts, making meaningful connections and remembering relevant information.

EXPLICIT INSTRUCTION AND PRACTICE:

- Describe strategies that have been useful when preparing for and taking tests.
- Consider additional strategies to increase test-taking ability.
- Review and discuss vocabulary and terms.
- Review suggested websites and videos and add to the list of strategies.
- Model some of the strategies and steps discussed.
- Practice some unfamiliar strategies.
- Assess the extent to which the new strategy worked.
- Identify at least one new strategy to try when preparing for the next test.
- Examine samples of various test formats that have been constructed differently.
- Eliminate obvious incorrect distractors form a multiple choice test item.
- Create mnemonics to help recall a series of words that are related to a specific concept.
- Discuss the benefit of reviewing material repeatedly.
- Defend whether it is wiser to complete sections of tests in the order they appear as opposed to skipping sections or questions to do later.
- Recognize the need to pace oneself when tests are timed.
- Provide strategies to use when tests are timed.
- Practice isolating sub-parts of test questions in order to provide complete answers.

POINTS TO MAKE:

- Students should scan through a test and complete the answers they are sure of and then go back to the answers they are unsure of.
- When unsure of an answer to a multiple choice question, eliminate the answers that are obviously incorrect to narrow down choices.
- When a test questions requires a written response, be sure to answer all parts of the question.
- As each part of the question is answered, use a checkmark or other way to indicate it.
- When narratives are required, write down key words that should be used when answering the question and then make sure that they are included.
- Make sure that questions have been answered as completely as possible.
- When uncertain how to answer a question, temporarily skip it after circling or highlight it.
- Revisit skipped questions and attempt to answer them after completing the questions that one is more confident about.
- With true and false and multiple-choice questions, if any part of a given response would keep the answer from being correct, don't choose that response.
- For matching items, first complete the answers one is sure of to narrow down the range of choices for the remaining responses or terms.
- When studying lists, try to form a real or imagined word from the first letter of each item.
- When it is time to answer a respective question, list each letter that is part of the real or imagined word and try to remember the item that begins with these letters.
- Create flow charts or ladders to organize answers for sequential responses to test questions.
- Venn diagrams help to visually organize responses that require comparing and contrasting
- Leave no multiple choice or true or false answers blank. Sometimes the guess is the right answer.
- Create flashcards to drill one another when preparing to test on specific answers that go with specific questions.
- Keep reviewing the flashcards until answers are mastered.
- Convene several short study group sessions on likely test as opposed to relying upon overnight cramming sessions.
- Get a good night's sleep before a test to help avoid sleepiness and brain-fog while trying to remember information that must be used during the test.

- Make sure that hunger does not become a distraction while testing.
- When unsure how to answer a short essay question, provide an answer – even if it is incomplete and it may earn partial credit.

VOCABULARY & TERMS: review, grouping concepts, connecting concepts, study buddy/study group, acronym, acrostic, process of elimination, justification, thoroughness

INSTRUCTIONAL RESOURCES:

Suggested Website(s):

Title: Top Ten Test-Taking Tips for Students
Created or Produced by: Teacher Vision
Web Address: https://www.teachervision.com/study-skills-test-prep/top-10-test-taking-tips-students
Brief Summary: List of Best Practices

Title: Ten Tips for Terrific Test Taking
Created or Produced by: Study Guides & Strategies
Web Address: https://www.studygs.net/tsttak1.htm
Brief Summary: List of strategies

Suggested YouTube Video(s):

Title: Test Taking Strategies / How to Pop an "A" on School Tests
Creator/Producer: Kantis Simmons
Running Time: (11 minutes 5 seconds)
Format: mini-lecture
Brief Summary: Shares and elaborates on strategies on what things that will be helpful when preparing for taking a test

Title: 7 Tips to Beat Exam Anxiety
Creator/Producer: AsapTHOUGHT
Running Time: (4 minutes 36 seconds)
Format: co-presentation
Brief Summary: A sharing of steps that should be taken mentally and physically to help diminish test-related anxiety

LESSON #13 – MANAGING SHORT AND LONG-TERM ASSIGNMENTS

GOAL: Students will learn how to manage assignments of different lengths.

OBJECTIVES: Students will

1. Explain the difference between short-term and long-term assignments.
2. Routinely break long-term assignments into manageable parts.
3. Complete short-term assignments while making progress on long-term ones.
4. Determine the priority status of assignments.

SAMPLE CONTENT STANDARDS: Develop skills necessary for educational achievement

VOCABULARY & TERMS: student planner, personal deadline, time-line, prioritizing, manageable sections, "to-do" lists pacing, instructor feedback, objectives

CONCEPT SUMMARY: Academic performance is related to the quality and timeliness of completed assignments. Some assignments are more complex and take longer than others and therefore self-management and regulation is needed to get all course requirements completed within given timelines.

EXPLICIT INSTRUCTION AND PRACTICE:

- Review and discuss vocabulary and terms.
- Share examples of long-term assignments and contrast them with short ones.
- Break one of the examples into smaller tasks that lead to the completed assignment.
- Explain how each part of an assignment can be considered as a different task.
- Differentiate essential from non-essential tasks and prioritize the essential ones.
- Create a timeline by placing essential tasks in order, working backwards from the deadline.
- Document the timeline on a recording document such as a planner or calendar.
- Discuss the importance of creating personal deadlines that come before the real deadlines in order to accommodate unexpected delays.
- Review and discuss suggested website and video.
- Analyze a sample long-term assignment; break it into smaller manageable steps, and then set personal and actual due dates.

POINTS TO MAKE:

- Large assignments involving multiple tasks can be broken into segments based upon the types and complexity of tasks that need to be completed.
- Breaking larger assignments into smaller segments provides multiple opportunities to experience the sense of completion.
- Smaller assignments that have been created allow gratification along the way to completing the major assignment.
- Deadlines should be created and listed on calendars as target completion dates for each segment of the assignment.
- Personal deadlines created for each segment of long term assignments should allow enough time for the total assignment to be assembled, edited, refined, and completed.
- Check with instructors after completing a portion of a segment for reactions and suggestions.
- One should not wait until the last minute to begin long-term assignments because unexpected delays and/or setbacks can occur.
- Time should be allowed for critique, guidance, and revision of each segment of long term assignments.

INSTRUCTIONAL RESOURCES:

Suggested Website(s):

Title: Time Management on Long Term Projects
Created or Produced by: California Polytechnic State University
Web Address: http://sas.calpoly.edu/asc/ssl/timemgmt-longtermprojects.html
Brief Summary: Strategies and suggested time allowances for completing various parts of long-term assignments

Suggested YouTube Video(s):

Title: How to Make Homework Less Work
Creator/Producer: Howcast.com
Running Time: (2 minutes 2 seconds)
Format: mini-lecture with video representations of strategies
Brief Summary: Stresses how to make the homework completion process more efficient

LESSON #14 – THE STRUCTURE OF COLLEGE CLASSES

GOAL: Students will learn more about the various formats that college classes follow and the pros and cons of them.

OBJECTIVES: Students will

1. Compare and contrast the basic structures of seminar, lab, lecture, online, and hybrid classes.
2. Identify some of the pros and cons of each of these class structures.
3. Consider some of the challenges in each of these class structures may present as well as potential work-arounds.

SAMPLE CONTENT STANDARDS: Apply knowledge of self to make informed decisions about post-secondary options

VOCABULARY & TERMS: lecture class, lab class, seminar, hybrid class, course sections, lecture/lab class, online class, mid-terms, final exams, class presentations, term papers, research assignments, reflection assignments, class projects, prerequisite class

CONCEPT SUMMARY: College classes consist of a variety of structures and expectations related to the type of class.

EXPLICIT INSTRUCTION AND PRACTICE:

- Articulate class structure preferences in terms of successful outcomes.
- Review and discuss vocabulary and terms.
- Discuss the basic structure of various types of classes and routine activities that comprise each.
- Compare class structures in term of personal pros and cons.
- Determine coping mechanisms to surmount class structure challenges such as sitting in front of large lecture halls.
- Discuss the content in the suggested website and video.
- Define vocabulary and terms in one's own words.
- Compare and contrast the basic components of different class formats (lab, lecture, hybrid, online, independent study) and indicate them by completing worksheet.

POINTS TO MAKE:

- Lab classes provide opportunities for hands-on activities to facilitate learning concepts.
- In lecture classes, the teacher orally shares concepts with students as students record notes for later study and reference.
- Seminar classes provide topical information sharing with classroom discussion and interaction pertaining to the topics.
- Some courses combine formats.
- Online classes provide information and interaction accessed by students on the computer by way of the internet or software.
- Hybrid classes combine classroom meetings and internet meetings.
- All class structures are amenable to reflection assignments which require students to read material and then share their beliefs in regard to what was read.
- Course grades in college depend largely on mid-term and final examination results.
- Major assignments in college include term papers, research papers, portfolio development, and classroom presentations.

INSTRUCTIONAL RESOURCES:

Suggested Website(s):

Title of Document: How is College Different from High School?
Created or Produced by: Southern Methodist University
Web Address:
https://www.smu.edu/Provost/ALEC/NeatStuffforNewStudents/HowIsCollegeDifferentfromHighSchool
Brief Summary: Compares and contrasts class structure and expectations in high school vs. college

Suggested YouTube Video(s):

Title: College 101: Professors, Classes, and Academics
Creator/Producer: Clancy Burke
Running Time: (8 minutes 0 seconds)
Format: information sharing through a student perspective
Brief Summary: College student speaks about strategies for doing well academically

A VARIETY OF COURSE OFFERING FORMATS

Indicate the basic and usual characteristics of the various formats of class offerings listed along the side of this chart by placing a "yes" or "no" in the appropriate boxes.

	TESTS	CLASS PRESEN-TATIONS	TERM PAPERS AND/OR PROJECT	CLASS TIME	ONLINE TIME	READING TEXTS, BOOKS, AND/OR ARTICLE
LECTURE CLASS						
LAB CLASS						
ONLINE CLASS						
HYBRID CLASS						
INDEPENDENT STUDY CLASS						

LESSON #15 – CHOOSING THE MOST APPROPRIATE COLLEGE PROGRAMS

GOAL: Students will acknowledge desirable characteristics for potential colleges and will search for institutions that intersect with their interests and qualifications.

OBJECTIVES: Students will

1. Identify schools that have their major of interest.
2. Elaborate upon the factors that contributed to the school choices.
3. Indicate the entrance requirements for the schools of interest and if qualifications have been met.

SAMPLE CONTENT STANDARDS: Synthesize career and educational information gathered from a variety of sources

VOCABULARY & TERMS: course offerings, majors, entrance requirements, campus life, demographics, activities, student population size, atmosphere, student housing, tuition, accessibility, support services, average class size, location, reputation, internships

CONCEPT SUMMARY: Multiple factors contribute to some colleges being of interest.

EXPLICIT INSTRUCTION AND PRACTICE:

- Brainstorm factors that make certain colleges different from other colleges.
- Use vocabulary and terms to describe factors that vary based upon the educational institution.
- Identify factors that are important when choosing which college to attend.
- Review and discuss the major points of the suggested websites and video.
- Research on the internet to discover if the colleges of interest have the characteristics that are important to them.
- Analyze if he/she is on track for meeting the entrance requirements.
- Compare college choices in terms of location, demographics, student/teacher ratio, activities, tuition, and available majors.
- Confirm if the colleges of interests are reasonable choices that reflect their interests and qualifications.
- Rank order college choices based upon findings.

POINTS TO MAKE:

- Some college programs have higher entrance requirements than others.
- Some college majors are not offered at every college.
- Tuition vs. financial aid availability may differ from institution to institution.
- Student housing options may differ from institution to institution.
- Some colleges are easier to get to using public transportation.
- Average student-teacher ratios vary from college to college.
- School environments vary.
- Some schools are located further away from home than others.
- Some colleges are more diverse than others.
- Involvement in certain student activities may be emphasized on some campuses more than on others.
- Some colleges have more social events of interest than others.
- Some colleges have more options for completing coursework than others.

INSTRUCTIONAL RESOURCES:

Suggested Website(s):

Title: The Pros and Cons of Community College
Created or Produced by: Scholarships.com
Web Address: https://www.scholarships.com/resources/college-prep/choosing-the-right-school/the-pros-and-cons-of-community-colleges/
Brief Summary: Brief narratives listing and elaborating upon the pros and cons of attending a community college

Title: 20 Bad High School Habits That Don't Belong in College
Created or Produced by: Study.com
Web Address: http://study.com/articles/20_Bad_Habits_That_Dont_Belong_in_College.html
Brief Summary: Old habits that need to change in order to increase the chances for success in college

Suggested YouTube Video(s):

Title: College Talk #6: Picking the Right College
Creator/Producer: Katizzletalks
Running Time: (14 minutes 40 seconds)
Format: mini-lecture
Brief Summary: Student shares what she has learned in regard to making informed choices when deciding upon a college to attend

Title: How to Graduate from College With a Job You Love and Less Debt
Creator/Producer: Julien Gordan at TEDxMidwest
Running Time: (12 minutes 10 seconds)
Format: mini-lecture
Brief Summary: Shares thoughts to consider when choosing to pursue certain college paths

Title: Community College vs. University / My Advice and Tips
Creator/Producer: Courtney Lundquist VLOGS
Running Time: (9 minutes 54 seconds)
Format: mini-lecture
Brief Summary: Student is transparent in regard to sharing what she believes what factors need to be considered when making a choice between going to a community college and a university

Title: The Differences Between Community Colleges and Universities
Creator/Producer: Omar DeBrew
Running Time: (3 minutes 10 seconds)
Format: mini-lecture
Brief Summary: Addresses basic differences between attending community colleges and universities and what factors may make one more favorable than the other

DECIDING FACTORS RELATED TO CHOOSING A COLLEGE

	COLLEGE NAME	COLLEGE NAME	COLLEGE NAME
ENTRANCE REQUIREMENTS			
STUDENT/TEACHER RATIO			
GEOGRAPHIC LOCATION			
STUDENT POPULATION SIZE			
STUDENT DEMOGRAPHICS			
FINANCIAL ASSISTANCE			
TUITION/ ROOM & BOARD			

LESSON #16– HIGH SCHOOL VS. COLLEGE

GOAL: Students will become more aware of how college differs from high school.

OBJECTIVES: Students will

1. Recognize the difference between modifications and accommodations.
2. Describe student roles in self-advocating.
3. Discuss the flexibility in scheduling coursework that will occur when attending college.
4. Consider the increased amount of independence that comes along with being college students.

SAMPLE CONTENT STANDARDS: Revisit current career and educational plan based on evolving and/or new interests, strengths, and limitations

VOCABULARY & TERMS: independence, accommodations, flexible scheduling, internships, tuition, academic advisors, dean, disability access office, placement testing, office of student affairs, full time/half time/part time, major, minor, credit hours, required course, elective course, course substitution

CONCEPT SUMMARY: Major differences between high school and college include factors related to disability services, confidentiality, course scheduling, and independence.

EXPLICIT INSTRUCTION AND PRACTICE:

- Identify how college and high school are similar.
- Distinguish how college will differ from high school.
- Anticipate changes that are expected and reasons how these changes will make life better or worse and in what ways.
- Determine how and when to make necessary changes.
- Discuss vocabulary and terms and provide examples.
- Explore what accommodations colleges generally provide.
- Review and discuss the suggested websites and videos.
- Visit a college class after receiving permission and summarize observations on the provided worksheet.

POINTS TO MAKE:

- Colleges do not create implement Individualized Education Plans (IEPs).
- High school students who have disabilities often have IEPs to document individual student challenges/needs and strategies to help facilitate students meeting goals.

62

- Students are considered to be adults in college and legally make their own decisions.
- Primary decision makers for non-adult aged high school students are their parents.
- Modifications to academic requirements can be made if needed to help students finish high school coursework.
- Students who have disabilities and attend college must meet the same entrance requirements and matriculation requirements as students who do not have disabilities.
- Accommodations in college help to facilitate access to the curriculum and facilities but do not change the content or mastery that is expected in classes that are taken.
- Students ages twenty-one or younger with disabilities have the right to a free and appropriate public education through the twelfth grade.
- Attending college is a choice if one is interested and qualifies, but is not a right.
- In high school. the school day starts and ends at certain times agreed upon by the school district, but in college, students create their own class/study schedules.
- In high school, students normally attend full time until completed, but in college, students are able to attend part-time and pace themselves based upon individual needs.
- In high school, student grades and records are shared with parents, but in college student information is confidential unless the student agrees otherwise and has documented this choice with the institution.

INSTRUCTIONAL RESOURCES:

Suggested Website(s):

Title: 20 Differences Between High School & College Life
Created or Produced by: Elizabeth Hoyt
Web Address: http://www.fastweb.com/student-life/articles/the-differences-between-high-school-college
Brief Summary: Parallel comparisons

Suggested YouTube Video(s):

Title: The Difference Between High School and College
Creator/Producer: Irene Fernandez
Running Time: (11 minutes 49 seconds)
Format: mini-lecture
Brief Summary: Student expresses how and why mindsets must change as more independence is expected in college

Title: High School Classes Versus College Classes
Creator/Producer: rm1695
Running Time: (9 minutes 55 seconds)
Format: mini-lecture
Brief Summary: Student explains how the amount of responsibility and structure changes when one begins taking college classes, including the amount and type of disability support

COLLEGE CLASS OBSERVATION EXPERIENCE

After choosing a college class that you are interested in and available to attend, please answer these questions to summarize your experience:

What is your anticipated college major?

_____

What are you interested in as your minor?

_____

What is the name of the class that you observed?

_____

Why did you choose this class?

_____

_____

How was the class different from high school classes that you have attended?

_____

_____

How was the class similar to high school classes you have attended?

_____

_____

What specific content covered in class increased your knowledge today?

_____

_____

Is this a course that you would consider taking when you attend college, and why?

_____

_____

Is there anything else that you would like to share about your college class observation experience?

_____

_____

LESSON #17 – NOTE-TAKING IN COLLEGE

GOAL: Students will refine strategies for taking notes in classes.

OBJECTIVES: Students will

1. Explain the importance of taking class notes.
2. Practice grouping important information based upon content.
3. Identify ways to gather missing information from notes that they have taken or have missed.
4. Describe how to abbreviate content they are documenting.

SAMPLE CONTENT STANDARDS: Review and build upon educational skills necessary to progress toward meeting academic goals

VOCABULARY & TERMS: abbreviations, main ideas, major points, recording, buddy system, highlighting, grouping concepts, organizing, Cornell notes, visuals

CONCEPT SUMMARY: There are effective ways to capture and organize information during instruction for later use and study.

EXPLICIT INSTRUCTION AND PRACTICE:

- Talk about the importance of quality notes that capture the main ideas being conveyed by the instructor.
- Review, discuss, and provide examples related to the vocabulary and terms.
- Provide different examples of note-taking related to the content of a short video.
- Visit the suggested website that suggests note-taking strategies.
- Review and discuss the suggested video.
- Practice taking notes during a mock lecture.
- Compare and contrast student notes.
- Verify if notes captured the main ideas.
- Provide suggestions to one another for improvement..

POINTS TO MAKE:

- Class notes should be dated.
- Notes from the same class should be sequenced and kept together.
- Words and terms that summarize major concepts given should be written by or under the concept.

- Notes reflecting major concepts should be underlined, highlighted, or circled to stand out.
- Flow charts/arrows are useful to provide visuals related to sequence.
- Abbreviations should be used in place of words or terms that are used repeatedly or on a regular basis.
- Create and use a form of shorthand instead of taking notes in complete sentences.
- Use technology when available by using cell phones or tablets to take pictures of instructor illustrations on the board. .
- Classmates can team up to share notes so everyone has a complete set.

INSTRUCTIONAL RESOURCES:

Suggested Website(s):

Title: Comprehensive Guide to Note-Taking in College
Created or Produced by: Sharon – Arizona State University
Web Address: http://www.collegefashion.net/college-life/comprehensive-guide-to-note-taking-in-college/
Brief Summary: Shows and explains different ways to organize information from college classes into notes

Suggested YouTube Video(s):

Title: How to Take Good Notes
Creator/Producer: Reese Regan
Running Time: (6 minutes 20 seconds)
Format: mini-lecture with demonstrations and examples
Brief Summary: Student shows and explains her system for taking notes and keeping them organized and strategies for deciding what should be included

Title: How to Use Mind Maps for Studying
Creator/Producer: Clarissa
Running Time: (3 minutes 29 seconds)
Format: mini-lecture with illustrations and examples
Brief Summary: Shares a strategy for note taking and connecting information that is documented

LESSON #18 – DOING RESEARCH FOR TERM PAPERS

GOAL: Students will be able to prepare for and complete term papers.

OBJECTIVES: Students will

1. Identify sources and collect information that can be used when writing papers.
2. Collect reference information and create citations related to them.
3. Write an outline to organize the information that will be placed in a paper.
4. Describe what plagiarism is and why it should be avoided.

SAMPLE CONTENT STANDARDS: Integrate multiple sources of information presented in diverse media or formats

VOCABULARY & TERMS: citation, references, bibliography, plagiarism, outline, draft, main ideas, supporting ideas, proofread, editing

CONCEPT SUMMARY: There are multiple sources that contain information to include in term papers, but sources need to be acknowledged properly.

EXPLICIT INSTRUCTION AND PRACTICE:

- Explain the purpose of term papers.
- Review and discuss the vocabulary and terms.
- Review steps that are needed to develop and complete college term papers.
- Identify useful sources for term paper content.
- Provide examples of how to organize the information that is collected from various sources for later use.
- View website related to writing term papers.
- Review examples of an outline for a term paper and explain the method of organizing it.
- Examine various citations, explain the purposes for them, and share what information should be included in them.
- Agree on reasons not to plagiarize
- Outline the main ideas for a hypothetical term paper.
- Create some citations that are based upon excerpts from reading materials.
- Explain the sequence of steps to capture, organize, and report the information that has been researched in the form of a term paper.

POINTS TO MAKE:

- Term paper preparation needs to be broken into smaller sequential tasks.
- Assign each task a personal deadline that is prior to the actual deadline to allow for any changes that may need to be made.
- Find out what the professor expects you to include when gathering information and completing your paper?
- Seek the advice of the librarian, when needed, to recommend resources that may provide information related to specified topics.
- Ask the professor how references should be formatted for the final paper.
- Select a narrow aspect of a topic to research for a term paper.
- Notes should have citation information recorded for later use (author, book/article name, year it was written, publisher, web address).
- Plagiarism is when another person's words or thoughts are placed in one's paper without formally giving that person credit.
- Plagiarism is considered academic dishonesty and can result in not getting credit for the assignment, failing the course the paper was submitted in, or expulsion from college.
- All references used should be cited at the end of the paper to avoid plagiarism.
- An outline should be created and include related sub-topics to guide research for the paper.
- Subject-related information collected online, at the library, or through some other source, should be sorted, recorded, and organized based upon the part of the topic it addresses.
- Organize paragraphs for each concept and then draft a topic sentence for each paragraph.
- Remember to create an introduction to begin the report as well as a conclusion/summary to end the report.
- Complete a draft copy early enough to allow time for final revisions and editing.
- Have someone else (known to be a good writer and thinker) read the draft for understanding and offer suggestions for improvement.
- Writing labs on campus can be utilized to assist students in making editing suggestions but must be accessed early enough to receive feedback so that final editing and paper submission deadlines can be met.

When completing a term paper, here are some of the things that could be included based upon what is relevant for the topic:

- What is the main topic?
- Why is the topic important?
- Where are the events taking place?

- Why are the events taking place?
- How are the events taking place?
- When are the events taking place?
- How is the topic related to mankind or society?
- What cause and effect relationships exist?
- What things contribute to the significance of this topic?
- How has the topic evolved over time?
- Are there significant variations that exist related to the topic that should be mentioned?
- What are your personal reflections regarding the information gathered during your research?

INSTRUCTIONAL RESOURCES:

Suggested Website(s):

Title: How to Write Term Papers
Created or Produced by: McGraw Hill Higher Education
Web Address: http://novella.mhhe.com/sites/0079876543/student_view0/research_center-999/research_papers30/how_to_write_term_papers.html
Brief Summary: Step by step instructions for developing a term paper from beginning to end

Title: MLA vs APA
Created or Produced by: University Writing Center
Web Address:
https://writingcenter.appstate.edu/sites/writingcenter.appstate.edu/files/MLA%20v%20APA%203-11.pdf
Brief Summary: Compares and contrasts two styles of documenting sources within academic papers that one drafts include gathering information or thoughts from other authors

Suggested YouTube Video(s):

Title: How to Write a Good Term Paper
Creator/Producer: WaysAndHow
Running Time: (5 minutes 54 seconds)
Format: mini-lecture with pictorial support for the information being covered
Brief Summary: Covers steps for choosing, drafting, and refining a term paper

Title: How to Write a Research Paper Fast
Creator/Producer: WaysAndHow
Running Time: (5 minutes 15 seconds)
Format: mini lecture that lists steps and then elaborates
Brief Summary: Provides strategies to make the most of one's time and complete a research paper efficiently

Title: How to Develop a Good Research Topic
Creator/Producer: K State Libraries
Running Time: (4 minutes 33 seconds)
Format: mini-lecture with written notes to go along with the presentation
Brief Summary: Provides suggestions of what should be considered when choosing a research topic and then steps to develop and report on the topic

LESSON #19 – ACCESSING UNIVERSITY SERVICES

GOAL: Students will learn more about how to utilize campus services and resources to assist them in reaching personal post-secondary goals.

OBJECTIVES: Students will

1. Determine availability of useful university services.
2. Explain appropriate circumstances to utilize various university services.
3. Commit to exercising self-advocacy to receive various university services.

SAMPLE CONTENT STANDARDS: Review and implement strategies to resolve problems and conflicts successfully

VOCABULARY & TERMS: math lab, writing lab, disability access office, student affairs, financial aid, student health, student counseling, student advising, career placement office, computer technology services, library, media lab

CONCEPT SUMMARY: Self-advocacy in college involves helping yourself get the attention and help you need. It sometimes includes getting others involved from various departments on campus to assist.

EXPLICIT INSTRUCTION AND PRACTICE:

- Discuss the function and purposes of major departments and offices found on typical college campuses while reviewing vocabulary and terms.
- Review the website that tells about resources on college campuses.
- Watch and comment on the suggested video.
- Consider various scenarios that may require intervention and assistance on college campuses and determine where one should go for help.
- Use the provided worksheet to match the type of need on college campuses with the type of department that helps to meet that need.

POINTS TO MAKE:

- The admissions office assists students who are seeking college acceptance as part of the application process.
- The academic advisor's office has staff who assist students in choosing and enrolling in appropriate classes needed to complete credit hours for various degrees.
- The financial aid / bursar's office assists students with securing funding to pay for school and school related expenses.

- The cashier's office is where students make tuition and parking pass payments or go to pick up refunds related to financial aid for expenses that exceed tuition and room and board.
- The registrar's office handles student records and transcripts.
- The disability access office is where students who have disabilities submit appropriate verification to the college to get reasonable accommodations.
- The dorm director's office handles housing issues related to living on campus.
- The dean's office handles academic concerns that have not been successfully resolved with various instructors who report to them.
- The technology (IT) department handles problems accessing computer technology on campus.
- The student health center has healthcare providers to assist with health conditions not requiring high levels of care while at school.
- Student health centers also maintain proper documentation of student vaccinations, required health screenings, and health insurance information.

INSTRUCTIONAL RESOURCES

Suggested Website(s):

Title: Eight Campus Resources Your College Student Should Know
Created or Produced by: Vicki Nelson, Founder of College Parent Central
Web Address: https://www.collegeparentcentral.com/2012/05/eight-campus-resources-your-college-student-should-know/
Brief Summary: Introduction to offices and services that college students may need to use on campus

Suggested YouTube Video(s):

Title: Transitioning to College with a Disability
Creator/Producer: Rebecca Sitton
Running Time: (4 minutes 42 seconds)
Format: role play dialogue
Brief Summary: A role play dialogue of a student sharing his hesitation to go to college because of a disability with another student who was attending college and receiving support through disability accommodations

HANDLING PERSONAL AFFAIRS ON COLLEGE CAMPUSES

Match the various departments found on college campuses with what is handled there.

Campus Offices:

(a) Student Affairs Office

(b) Student Health Services

(c) Disability Access Office

(d) Registrar's Office

(e) Cashier's or Bursar's Office

(f) Campus Public Safety Office

(g) Student Academic Support Services

(h) Dean's Office

(i) Internet Technology (IT) Office

(j) Admissions Office

(k) Academic Advisement Office

(l) Financial Aid Office

(m) Faculty Offices

(n) Student Counseling Office

_____ 1. The office for getting assistance in choosing the classes that meet your goals

_____ 2. The office for help with writing and math as well as receiving available tutoring

_____ 3. The office that records grades on student report cards and transcripts

_____ 4. The office that informs you about being accepted for enrollment at that college

_____ 5. The office where professors have posted hours and meet with students

_____ 6. The office where a nurse can treat and/or advise on a mild injury or illness

_____ 7. The office where you can discuss and sort through personal problems

_____ 8. The office that makes college-provided financial support decisions

_____ 9. The office that oversees accommodations for students who have disabilities

_____ 10. The office on campus that helps to make student events available

_____ 11. The office that mediates unresolved academic disputes

_____ 12. The office that helps to resolve campus computer access issues

_____ 13. The office that has personnel that help to maintain a crime-free environment

_____ 14. The office that handles the payment of student accounts

LESSON #20 – CONNECTIONS BETWEEN SCHOOL AND WORK

GOAL: Students will discuss how habits formed in high school can be carried over into the world of work.

OBJECTIVES: Students will

1. Compare and contrast a workday with a school day.
2. Describe positive habits that should be practiced in both places.
3. Identify skills learned in school that will help them when they engage in work experiences.
4. Determine the relationship between education and types of jobs that may be available to them.

SAMPLE CONTENT STANDARDS: Develop short- and long-term post-secondary career plans

VOCABULARY & TERMS: attendance, punctuality, task-completion, teamwork, effort, socialization, work quality, preparation, authority figures, cooperation, evaluation

CONCEPT SUMMARY: School and work have many overlapping practices and values. Good habits formed in school can contribute to good habits to be practiced on jobs.

EXPLICIT INSTRUCTION AND PRACTICE:

- Identify good school habits and then contrast them with poor school habits.
- Review vocabulary and terms and discuss related examples.
- Provide examples of how habits and competencies gained in school have the potential to spill over into practices at work.
- Discuss practices at school that have negative as well as positive consequences.
- Review and discuss suggested websites and videos.
- Complete provided Venn diagrams comparing school and work activities.
- Discuss positive and negative practices that can carry over from school to work.
- Discuss what types of jobs match the education and experiences being acquired.

POINTS TO MAKE:

- Attention to detail not only pertains to school assignments but work assignments as well.
- Adherence to timelines/deadlines is a habit in both school and work that will contribute to achievement.
- Perseverance is an attribute that drives people to persist at school and work even when facing challenges.
- Tenacity drives individuals to hold firmly to pursuits after experiencing obstacles and disappointments at school and work.
- Punctuality – being on time - is seen as a sign of enthusiasm and readiness to engage in the day's events at school and at work.
- Self-advocacy must be exercised to get one's personal needs met and be fairly treated at school and work.
- Reliability means that a person can be counted upon to get tasks completed at school and work.
- Social competence – getting along with others - developed while in school can have an impact on functioning in the world of work.
- Efficiency relates to getting tasks completed without expending extra unnecessary time and energy.
- Motivation is a reason or passion to accomplish a result.
- When desire and ability outweigh the challenges and probability of failure, then one can become and/or remain motivated at school and work.
- Flexibility is needed at school and work so that when situations change, one is still able to function and accomplish goals.

INSTRUCTIONAL RESOURCES:

Suggested Website(s):

Title: How Bad Study Habits Affect You Post-High School
Created or Produced by: Evie Sellers
Web Address: http://classroom.synonym.com/bad-study-habits-affect-posthigh-school-2084.html
Brief Summary: Covers factors related to habits that overlap from high school to the world of work

Suggested YouTube Video(s):

Title: The School and Work Connection
Creator/Producer: Rob McClendon – Oklahoma Horizon
Running Time: (6 minutes 42 seconds)
Format: interview
Brief Summary: Shows how K-12 educational experiences and coursework can contribute to the type of career a student later decides to pursue

SCHOOL AND WORK SIMILARITIES AND DIFFERENCES

List some of the activities that take place that differ between the work world and school world. Then list some of the activities that happen in both of them. Follow-up with identifying positive and negative habits related to activities that occur in both settings.

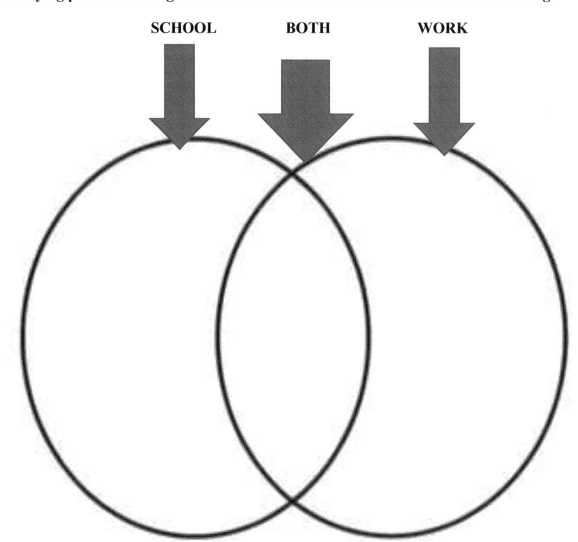

SCHOOL **BOTH** **WORK**

POSITIVE HABITS RELATED TO COMMON ACTIVITIES :

_____

_____

NEGATIVE HABITS RELATED TO COMMON ACTIVITIES::

_____

_____

LESSON #21 – CHANGING COLLEGES AND/OR MAJORS

GOAL: Students will have a greater awareness of the pros and cons of changing colleges and/or majors.

OBJECTIVES: Students will

1. Supply appropriate reasons for leaving one college to attend another.
2. Explain what happens during the credit transfer process.
3. Identify reasonable steps to take in order to change schools.
4. Identify some of the drawbacks related to changing college majors.
5. Minimize the number of wasted credit hours when changing majors or colleges.

SAMPLE CONTENT STANDARDS: Use knowledge of self, levels of functioning and interest, to guide career exploration and educational planning

VOCABULARY & TERMS: transfer credits, comparable program, personal compatibility, electives, required courses, substitute coursework,

CONCEPT SUMMARY: There are valid reasons for changing colleges and/or majors, but there are also pros and cons to making these changes.

EXPLICIT INSTRUCTION AND PRACTICE:

- Share prospective majors and institutions where students plan to get their degrees.
- Justify why these choices were made.
- Discuss factors that could cause changes in earlier choices.
- Determine justifiable reasons for makings changes as well as the pros and cons of making such changes.
- Review vocabulary and terms and practice using them correctly to make changes in major and/or college.
- Visit and discuss website on changing majors.
- Compare requirements between two majors and identify which courses will transfer into the requirements for the new major and which credit hours will not be usable.
- Review and discuss suggested videos on changing colleges.
- List steps to take to change colleges
- Pose reasons some people attend community colleges prior to transferring to four-year colleges or universities.

POINTS TO MAKE:

- Some colleges have different entrance requirements than others.
- When changing from one college to another, students must meet the entrance requirements of the new school.
- Some colleges have majors that others don't have.
- Receiving colleges have the right to determine which credit hours will transfer from sending colleges.
- It is helpful to know which courses can be taken at the current college that will transfer to the new college.
- Transferable credits help to minimize the amount of coursework required to graduate from the new school.
- Some credits may not be transferable when changing majors.
- Sometimes students change colleges due to the current college atmosphere or geographic region not being compatible with their personalities and interests.
- Changing majors may require changing colleges.
- When more support is needed to complete degrees than is offered at the current college, students may want to move to a college with more accommodating services.
- Increased availability of financial aid can be a contributing factor in moving from one college to another.
- More than one major may be pursued and graduate with a dual major.
- It may be hard to determine if a major is suitable before taking some of its required courses.
- Some required coursework may be overwhelming and the effort required may outweigh the interest in completing the major.
- If career interests change, it may be necessary to take more relevant courses.
- When interested in more than one major, and undecided, it is advisable to take courses that may be required by both in order to help avoid wasted credit hours.
- Some courses that were taken prior to changing majors may possibly be counted toward the new major as elective coursework.

INSTRUCTIONAL RESOURCES:

Suggested Website(s):

Title: 4 Things to Consider Before You Change Your Major
Created or Produced by: Odyssey
Web Address: https://www.theodysseyonline.com/4-things-consider-before-changing-major
Brief Summary: Explores timing and reasoning when deciding to change majors

Suggested YouTube Video(s):

Title: Tips on Transferring from Community College to a University
Creator/Producer: DominiqueVictoriaTV
Running Time: (13 minutes 24 seconds)
Format: mini-lecture
Brief Summary: Student shares strategies and steps for successfully transferring from a community college to a university

Title: Good and Sketchy Reasons to Transfer to a New College
Creator/Producer: Forster Thomas Educational and Career Consulting
Running Time: (3 minutes 55 seconds)
Format: mini-lecture
Brief Summary: Shares what one should consider when deciding if a college transfer should take place

LESSON #22 – STUDENT FINANCIAL AID

GOAL: Students will become better acquainted with student financial aid options.

OBJECTIVES: Students will

1. Explain how to qualify for various forms of financial aid.
2. Identify sources of financial aid that are renewable from year to year.
3. Distinguish between financial aid that must be repaid and that which does not need to be.
4. Identify ways that a person can lose the financial aid that has been awarded.

SAMPLE CONTENT STANDARDS: Use current interests, strengths, and limitations to guide career exploration and educational planning

VOCABULARY & TERMS: merit based scholarships, talent based scholarships, need based scholarships, group affiliation based scholarships, athletic scholarships, grants, student loans, employee tuition reimbursement, tuition installment plans, assistantships, college work-study

CONCEPT SUMMARY: College costs money and planning should take place to get funding to assist with expenses. Some forms of college funding one qualifies for don't have to be paid back and some require repayment.

EXPLICIT INSTRUCTION AND PRACTICE:

- Discuss student plans for financing college education and what needs to be paid for.
- Review basic types of financial aid and respective qualifications.
- Introduce and discuss vocabulary and terms.
- Explore and discuss websites and videos about completing financial aid paperwork.
- Complete FAFSA financial aid application forms online.
- Consider likely ability to repay aid received.
- Discuss the possibility of scholarships for expanding financial aid.
- Conduct online scholarship searches to complete on the worksheet provided.
- Follow-up with completing scholarship applications for which one qualifies.
- List ways that financial aid can be lost along with strategies to avoid that consequence.

POINTS TO MAKE:

- Grants and scholarships do not have to be paid back.
- Some employers reimburse employees for school expenses as a benefit after successful completion of classes.
- College work study requires that students perform work duties on campus in exchange for funds that will help to cover college expenses.

- A college assistantship is another form of college work study (often utilized in graduate school) where students are required to help professors in exchange for some of the tuition.
- Tuition installment plans require students to make down payments and then pay agreed upon amounts throughout the semester that will lead to the cost being paid in full.
- Merit based scholarships provide money to students to cover costs based upon high academic performance.
- Athletic scholarships are provided for some students who have made great athletic accomplishments in exchange for them sharing their talents on college athletic teams.
- Talent based scholarships are provided for those who have demonstrated talent in the performing arts in exchange for students continuing to perform in university groups.
- Group affiliation scholarships are provided by various organizations based upon the students or parents being members.
- A student loan is money supplied in advance that needs to be paid back with interest.
- Need-based scholarships are based upon students meeting as well as other established qualifying criteria.
- Students must maintain satisfactory academic progress in order to continue receiving funding from various scholarships and grants.
- Some scholarships give students a one-time amount, and others are renewable from academic year to academic year if appropriate steps are taken to remain eligible.

INSTRUCTIONAL RESOURCES:

Suggested Website(s):

Title: The FAFSA Process
Created or Produced by: United States Department of Education
Web Address: https://studentaid.ed.gov/sa/sites/default/files/fafsa-process.pdf
Brief Summary: Brief overview of steps needed to complete financial aid application

Title: How Long Does it Take to Apply for Financial Aid?
Created or Produced by: Edvisors
Web Address: https://www.edvisors.com/ask/faq/how-long-apply/
Brief Summary: Explains the process of seeking financial aid for college

Suggested YouTube Video(s):

Title: Filling out the FAFSA Application
Creator/Producer: College Sense
Running Time: (6 minutes 56 seconds)
Format: co-presentation
Brief Summary: Explains the process of filling out a FAFSA Application

Title: Top FAFSA Tips: How to Get the Most Out of Financial Aid

Creator/Producer: GoBankingRates

Running Time: (5 minutes 19 seconds)

Format: mini-lecture

Brief Summary: Explains the process of getting financial aid and how to help maximize what is received

COLLEGE SCHOLARSHIP SEARCH

Research three scholarships of interest and list information about them in the spaces below.

****

NAME OF SCHOLARSHIP:

_____

FUNDING SOURCE OF SCHOLARSHIP:

_____

QUALIFICATIONS FOR SCHOLARSHIP:

_____

APPLICATION DEADLINE: _____ # OF RECOMMENDATIONS NEEDED: ____

****

NAME OF SCHOLARSHIP:

_____

FUNDING SOURCE OF SCHOLARSHIP:

_____

QUALIFICATIONS FOR SCHOLARSHIP:

_____

APPLICATION DEADLINE: _____ # OF RECOMMENDATIONS NEEDED: ____

****

NAME OF SCHOLARSHIP:

_____

FUNDING SOURCE OF SCHOLARSHIP:

_____

QUALIFICATIONS FOR SCHOLARSHIP:

_____

CHAPTER TWO

CAREER DEVELOPMENT

Paid employment is a means of becoming as financially independent as possible. Some students have not entered the world of work. However, some high school students have already experienced employment opportunities, both as volunteers and as paid employees. Regardless of experience, all can stand to increase their knowledge as they pursue careers and employment stability. This set of lessons will cover how to seek, gain, maintain, and explore further employment. Various scenarios present how to contribute to a positive workplace. In addition, lessons explore how to avoid negative workplace outcomes that are within personal realms of control.

LESSON #23 – RESUME PREPARATION

GOAL: Students will become familiar with components of a resume and how to represent themselves within the confines of a resume.

OBJECTIVES: Students will

1. Describe the purpose of a resume.
2. Explain what contents should be included in a resume.
3. Organize personal information for inclusion in a resume..
4. Document academic and work experience including encompassing dates for each entry..

SAMPLE CONTENT STANDARDS: Integrate self-knowledge into seeking employment

VOCABULARY & TERMS: resume, recommendation, personal reference, experience, personal strengths, update, objectives, accuracy

CONCEPT SUMMARY: Resumes are created to highlight and market oneself as a potential employee. They should be well organized and information about accomplishments and work/skill-related experiences should be included to establish credibility.

EXPLICIT INSTRUCTION AND PRACTICE:

- Review and discuss media resources related to creating resumes.
- Explain what makes a resume different from a job application.
- Cite reasons for each section of a resume.
- Review vocabulary and terms as they relate to the job search
- Summarize personal information on the resume pre-writing worksheet.
- Show students how information can be placed on the Sample Resume Format sheet.
- Analyze examples of complete resumes and discuss how information on them has been organized.

POINTS TO MAKE:

- A resume gives a person the opportunity to present himself/herself as valuable to prospective employers.
- Resumes can include additional positive information about oneself might not be requested on a job application.
- Volunteer experience can be listed under work history.
- On-the-job training can be included under training and education.

- Resumes should be organized, accurate, neat, and concise
- Produce a resume with a type font that is crisp and legible (e.g. Times New Roman).
- Sections can be included that address accomplishments and transferable work skills.
- Resumes should be updated regularly so that the information is current.
- Resumes should be confined to as few pages as possible.
- Encompassing dates of work experience and education/training should be included.
- Resumes should be customized toward the type of position one is seeking.
- Resumes should be taken to and distributed at job/career fairs to perk the interest of potential employers.
- Resumes should include personal contact information including an email address.

INSTRUCTIONAL RESOURCES:

Suggested Websites(s):

Title: 44 Resume Writing Tips
Created or Produced by: Daniel Scocco
Web Address: http://www.dailywritingtips.com/resume-writing-tips/
Brief Summary: Best Practices

Suggested YouTube Video(s):

Title: Top 10 Resume Mistakes
Creator/Producer: Resume Review Services
Running Time: (1 minute 57 seconds)
Format: examples of mistakes and solutions with music being played in the background
Brief Summary: List of common mistakes and how to avoid them

Title: Resumes for Young People with No Experience
Creator/Producer: Gayle M. Howard
Running Time: (5 minutes 33 seconds)
Format: mini-lecture
Brief Summary: Supplies strategies to use and why they should be used when work experience is very limited

RESUME PRE-WRITING INFORMATION SHEET

CONTACT INFORMATION

Name:

_____

Mailing Address:

_____

Email Address:

_____

Telephone Number: Home _____   Cell: _____

WORK-RELATED
SKILLS_____

_____

_____

_____

MAJOR ACCOMPLISHMENTS IN SCHOOL AND/OR
COMMUNITY_____

_____

_____

_____

EDUCATION

High School: _____ **Anticipated Graduation Date:**_____

Post-Secondary Education/Training Plans:

_____

_____

_____

RESUME PRE-WRITING INFORMATION SHEET cont.

EMPLOYMENT OBJECTIVE:

Contribute to the field of _____ by providing efficient and effective services as a _____ while continuing to grow and develop/add to my skills. (example)

_____

_____

_____

WORK EXPERIENCES (Repeat this section as needed for additional work experiences.)

Place: _____   **Volunteer or Paid:** _____

Position: _____   **When:** _____

Duties:

_____

_____

_____

Place: _____   **Volunteer or Paid:** _____

Position: _____   **When:** _____

Duties:

_____

_____

_____

Place: _____   **Volunteer or Paid:** _____

Position: _____   **When:** _____

Duties:

_____

_____

_____

(SAMPLE RESUME FORMAT)

FIRST AND LAST NAME
STREET ADDRESS
CITY, STATE, and ZIP CODE
PHONE # / EMAIL ADDRESS

EMPLOYMENT OBJECTIVE: (What do you want to do and for what purpose?)

WORK-RELATED SKILLS:

- **Skill** _____

- **Skill** _____

- **Skill** _____

- **Skill** _____

WORK EXPERIENCE:

Beginning Date to Ending Date	**Place of Employment (Write the name)** **Position:** **Duties:**
Beginning Date to Ending Date	**Place of Employment (Write the name)** **Position:** **Duties:**
Beginning Date to Ending Date	**Place of Employment (Write the name)** **Position:** **Duties:**

SPECIAL ACCOMPLISHMENTS AT SCHOOL OR IN THE COMMUNITY:

- **accomplishment** _____

- **accomplishment** _____

- **accomplishment** _____

EDUCATION:

My anticipated graduation date from _____ High School is _____ and my future plans are to _____

LESSON #24 – APPLYING FOR A JOB

SUBJECT: Applying for a Job

GOAL: Students will locate job openings and apply for them.

OBJECTIVES: Students will

1. Prepare information for job applications and take it along when applying.
2. Become familiar with various sources of information on job openings.
3. Exemplify appropriate behavior when applying for jobs in person.

SAMPLE CONTENT STANDARDS: Engage in job-seeking skills

VOCABULARY & TERMS: classified, job fair, networking, classified, application, references, recommendations, qualifications, openings, online

CONCEPT SUMMARY: The job application process includes being strategic: Know your qualifications and be able to confidently describe them.

EXPLICIT INSTRUCTION AND PRACTICE:

- Discuss the importance of actively seeking jobs and then taking the appropriate steps to apply for them.
- Develop a list of job seeking steps: What is involved from search to application.
- Review and discuss vocabulary and terms and how they are personally applicable.
- Compile the basic types of information requested on employment applications.
- Sequence employment and education history.
- Record personal information on model applications.
- Demonstrate neatness and accuracy in prepared text.
- Describe ways to become aware of current job vacancies.
- Have references and contact information available.
- View and discuss websites and videos on seeking and applying for jobs.
- Complete an online application.

POINTS TO MAKE:

- Jobs that require more qualifications in experience and training/education will often pay higher salaries.
- Job applications and resumes are thoroughly screened by employers before candidates are invited to be interviewed.

- Sources of finding out about job openings include newspapers, flyers, job wanted signs, online solicitations, and word of mouth.
- Other sources of job leads include human resources department bulletin boards, online postings of openings, personal inquiry and job/career fairs.
- One should have ready access to information that will be requested on a job application: dates and responsibilities of past places of employment, reference contact information, dates and places of education/training, and contact information of past employers.
- Honesty is important on job applications. Falsified information, if discovered by the employer, can result in job termination.
- Applications are organized into sections of specific information such as education and employment.
- Applications should be accurate, concise, and neat.
- Applications and resumes should not have errors in spelling and grammar.
- Resumes can be turned in along with job applications for the purpose of further highlighting potential, skills, and experience.
- One should be neatly dressed and groomed during any contact with a potential employer including when one comes in to fill out job applications.
- Standard English should be used when communicating with potential employers.

INSTRUCTIONAL RESOURCES:

Suggested Website(s):

Title: Best Ways to Apply for Jobs
Created or Produced by: Alison Doyle
Web Address: https://www.thebalance.com/best-ways-to-apply-for-jobs-2061599
Brief Summary: Provides pointers on best practices when considering various ways and avenues for applying for jobs

Suggested YouTube Video(s):

Title: Resumes and Job Applications: Filling Out a Job Applications With no Work Experience
Creator/Producer: Shannon Terry (EHow)
Running Time: (2 minutes 45 seconds)
Format: mini-lecture
Brief Summary: Provides examples of what to highlight on job applications with respect to accomplishments and skills.

LESSON #25 – PERSONALITY AND JOB PERFORMANCE

GOAL: Students will learn about using the positive attributes of their personalities to be successful on the job.

OBJECTIVES: Students will

1. Identify at least five positive attributes about themselves.
2. Match those attributes with how they can positively impact their performances on jobs.
3. Identify an area of their personalities that is not a strength.
4. Describe a way to compensate for that area.

SAMPLE CONTENT STANDARDS: Positively contribute to a work environment

VOCABULARY & TERMS: coping skills, strength, weakness, personality, playing to one's strengths, compensating for one's weakness, conflict, balance

CONCEPT SUMMARY: One's personality influences on what types of jobs may be compatible. It is important to realize the difference between gratifying and intolerable.

EXPLICIT INSTRUCTION AND PRACTICE:

- Introduce the concept of personality and the other lesson vocabulary and terms.
- Review and clarify samples of related traits found on lesson websites.
- Apply vocabulary and terms to real life examples.
- Connect personality traits to the world of work.
- Discuss personality traits and how they can help and/or hinder at places of employment.
- Consider coping skills to help work be more tolerable.
- Isolate jobs that are compatible with given personality traits.
- Review and discuss the suggested video.
- Identify a personal trait and address how it can be positive for a specific type of job and not be as positive for another specific type of job.
- Complete Personality and Job Performance worksheet.
- Select a personality trait that may be viewed as a weakness and dialogue on strategies that help minimize any negative effects.

POINTS TO MAKE:

- Personality has to do with how individuals are distinctly different from one another in how they react to, engage with, feel about, and perceive the world around them.
- Some personality traits are more compatible within certain work environments than in others.
- Introverted people may be good matches for working in positions where a good portion of the work day can be performed in solitude.
- Good listeners who are patient and have good problem-solving skills may do well working in customer service positions.
- Friendly people who are able to influence others may do well in sales or leadership positions.
- Those who enjoy moving around frequently instead of remaining in one place may do well with jobs requiring delivery of items.
- Those who feel more secure doing repetitive things that are highly structured may do well on jobs requiring assembling or sorting.
- Those who have outgoing personalities and are sensitive to others may do well working as public servants.
- Those who like to develop their own ways of doing things may do well in a job that is not highly structured and allows room for creativity.
- Those who do not enjoy constantly moving around may do well at jobs where employees work from desks or work stations.
- Those who are energized collaborating and working with others may find satisfaction working in teams to complete tasks and projects.
- Students should look inward to determine the type of job that might be fulfilling for them.
- Consider preferences with respect to work atmosphere, pace, physical activity required, structure vs. flexibility or creativity, and working on teams or not.
- Students should determine some situations that may aggravate them on a job and have some coping strategies or plans of action in mind to offset them.
- Jobs that allow personal strengths to be utilized are ideal.

INSTRUCTIONAL RESOURCES:

Suggested Website(s):

Title: Adjectives that Describe Personality - Elementary
Created or Produced by: ESOL Courses
Web Address:
https://www.esolcourses.com/content/exercises/grammar/adjectives/personality/words-for-describing-personality.html
Brief Summary: Basic vocabulary related to different personality traits

Title: Adjectives that Describe Personality – Intermediate
Created or Produced by: ESOL Courses
Web Address:
https://www.esolcourses.com/content/exercises/grammar/adjectives/personality/more-words-for-describing-personality.html
Brief Summary: Additional basic vocabulary related to personality traits

Suggested YouTube Video(s):

Title: Are you Emotionally Intelligent
Creator/Producer: D News
Running Time: (2 minutes 46 seconds)
Format: mini-lecture / depicts various aspects of emotional intelligence
Brief Summary: Describes components of emotional intelligence and how it impacts one's life as he/she intermingles with society

PERSONALITY AND JOB PERFORMANCE

Reflection Activity: What good habits related to your personality are preparing you for future work?

GOOD HABIT #1

_____

_____

How will this habit help you to do well on a job?

_____

_____

Is improvement needed? Why or why not?

_____

_____

GOOD HABIT #2

_____

_____

How will this habit help you to do well on a job?

_____

_____

Is improvement needed? Why or why not?

_____

_____

GOOD HABIT #3

_____

_____

How will this habit help you to do well on a job?

_____

_____

Is improvement needed? Why or why not?

_____

_____

LESSON #26 – CAREER INTERESTS VS. QUALIFICATIONS

GOAL: Students will learn more about the qualifications needed for their career interests.

OBJECTIVES: Students will

1. Identify their areas of career interest.
2. Research to find out the qualifications for those careers.
3. Devise a plan for becoming qualified to work in one of their areas of interest.

SAMPLE CONTENT STANDARDS: Seeking careers based upon personal interests and consideration of qualifications

VOCABULARY & TERMS: qualification, career, educational/training plan, aptitude, ability, compatible, interest, alternative

CONCEPT SUMMARY: Students will explore what is required to become employed in their fields of interest as well as identify alternative careers and their requirements.

EXPLICIT INSTRUCTION AND PRACTICE:

- Review and discuss vocabulary and terms.
- Distinguish between career interest vs. career qualification.
- Explain the difference between a job and a career.
- Provide examples of jobs can lead to better jobs within the same career field.
- Identify career interests and why these careers are of interest.
- Provide examples of how multiple jobs are within the same career field.
- Conduct internet research to find and document qualifications for jobs of interests.
- Develop a plan to become qualified for a career of interest.
- Research and document the career field and at least two other related careers and their qualifications.
- Document career paths for the two alternatives identified.
- Confirm continued interest or if they may also consider a related career.

POINTS TO MAKE:

- Students should be aware of the qualifications for their career interests.
- Students should think of sequences of types of jobs that will help them to move into and forward within their careers.

- A good job for one person may not be a good job for another person.
- An appropriate job is one that matches one's qualifications, interests, and needs.
- Interests and qualifications do not always match.
- Some interests can evolve to match the level of qualification on the worksheet provided.
- Most jobs are related to others that require different types and levels of qualification.
- Qualifications for different jobs can be researched online or by conversing and being enlightened by people working in those types of positions.
- Qualifications include experience as well as education/training.
- Becoming qualified is a process that evolves over time.
- One may qualify and become employed in a certain job that provides preparation for future jobs as more experience and exposure is gained.
- One can gain work experiences and invest additional time in education so that one may get promoted to jobs requiring higher levels of responsibility and expertise.
- A realistic look at one's abilities and potential helps in making career decisions.
- Becoming qualified requires investing time and energy.

INSTRUCTIONAL RESOURCES:

Suggested Website(s):

Title: List of Careers & Occupations: Find Local Jobs in 40,000 Careers
Created or Produced by: Recruiter
Web Address: https://www.recruiter.com/careers/
Brief Summary: Provides links that describe various jobs, qualifications, and average salaries

Suggested YouTube Video(s):

Title: Choosing the Most Appropriate Career: A Poptropica Experience   ???--→ Choosing Your Career Now (A Poptropica Story)
Creator/Producer: Fantic Writer Jazzy 411 / Poptropica.com
Running Time: (5 minutes 50 seconds)
Format: animated with captions (music background)
Brief Summary: Addresses things to consider and thought processes that can be utilized to help make career decision

CAREER INTERESTS VS. QUALIFICATIONS

Perform online research to identify minimal qualifications and job responsibilities for three (3) types of jobs related to your area(s) of career interest(s).

TYPE OF JOB:

_____

DUTIES RELATED TO THE JOB:

_____
_____
_____

QUALIFICATIONS TO BE CONSIDERED FOR THE JOB:

_____
_____
_____

TYPE OF JOB:

_____

DUTIES RELATED TO THE JOB:

_____
_____
_____

QUALIFICATIONS TO BE CONSIDERED FOR THE JOB:

_____
_____
_____

TYPE OF JOB:

_____

DUTIES RELATED TO THE JOB:

_____
_____
_____

QUALIFICATIONS TO BE CONSIDERED FOR THE JOB:

_____
_____
_____

LESSON #27 –SALARIES AND BENEFITS RELATED TO CAREER INTERESTS

GOAL: Students will become aware of potential salaries for their career of choice.

OBJECTIVES: Students will

1. Find salaries related to their career interest for three different companies.
2. Look up related information on the website of the United States Department of Labor/Bureau of Labor Statistics.
3. Compare and contrast the three companies as far as the type and size of the companies in comparison to the expected salaries.

SAMPLE CONTENT STANDARDS: Research and exploration of career paths

VOCABULARY & TERMS: salary, benefits, commensurate, experience, beginning salary, potential salary, deductions, taxes

CONCEPT SUMMARY: Various types of jobs have salary ranges affiliated with them that are often related to the qualifications needed for them. In addition, there are employee fringe benefits that add value to those positions.

EXPLICIT INSTRUCTION AND PRACTICE:

- Examine how the same career can yield different salaries depending upon qualifications needed, size of company, and job location.
- Review and discuss vocabulary and terms
- Look up salaries online related to their career interests using the provided website.
- Share findings with class.
- Review and discuss films regarding negotiating salary.
- Compare the salary and benefits for the same job in three different companies using the worksheet provided.

POINTS TO MAKE:

- Sick leave, vacation leave, paid holidays, health insurance, dental insurance, and retirement plans are benefits that often are provided with full time jobs.
- Jobs that require more experience and education usually have higher salaries.
- Some career fields pay more than others.
- Some jobs within the same career field pay more than others.

- Employees are paid the same salary that they would receive if being present at work when they are out on sick leave, vacation leave, and paid holidays.
- Part-time employment usually provides fewer fringe benefits than full-time employment.
- Salaries usually increase as workers successfully remain in given positions.
- Deductions such as taxes, pensions, union dues, money toward insurance premiums, are subtracted from earnings prior to employees receiving paychecks; these deductions are reflected on paycheck stubs or pay deposit stubs.
- Paper checks are given to employees at some jobs, while other jobs pay employees by depositing salary into employees' personal bank accounts through direct deposit.
- Some employee benefits provided to employees by employers include flex time, sick leave, vacation leave, personal time off, jury leave, educational leave, paid holidays, health insurance, dental insurance, tuition reimbursement, pension plans, and profit sharing plans.

INSTRUCTIONAL RESOURCES:

Suggested Website(s):

Title: Occupational Employment Statistics
Created or Produced by: United States Department of Labor
Web Address: http://www.bls.gov/oes/current/oes_stru.htm
Brief Summary: Links providing average salaries and prevalence for various types of jobs

Suggested YouTube Video(s):

Title: Human Resources: How to Negotiate a Salary During a Job Offer
Creator/Producer: Pat Goodwin, Goodwin Associates (EHow)
Running Time: (2 minutes 15 seconds)
Format: mini-lecture
Brief Summary: Best strategies on how to receive a higher pay rate than what was offered

Title: Tips to Maximize Your Employee Benefits
Creator/Producer: Eric Brotman, Financial Group (WBA-LTV 11 (NBC) - Baltimore
Running Time: (3 minutes 50 seconds)
Format: interview on news broadcast
Brief Summary: Talks about fringe benefits on a job and why one should utilize them

SALARIES AND BENEFITS RELATED TO CAREER INTERESTS

Perform online research to identify average salaries for specific types of jobs within one's career interests.

TYPE OF JOB:

_____

AVERAGE SALARY:

_____

COMPANY WITH CURRENT JOB VACANCY:

_____

EMPLOYEE BENEFITS OFFERED BY THAT COMPANY:

_____

_____

_____

TYPE OF JOB:

_____

AVERAGE SALARY:

_____

COMPANY WITH CURRENT JOB VACANCY:

_____

EMPLOYEE BENEFITS OFFERED BY THAT COMPANY:

_____

_____

TYPE OF JOB:

_____

AVERAGE SALARY:

_____

COMPANY WITH CURRENT JOB VACANCY:

_____

EMPLOYEE BENEFITS OFFERED BY THAT COMPANY:

_____

_____

LESSON #28 – PREPARING FOR YOUR CAREER IN STEPS

GOAL: Students will compare career options.

OBJECTIVES: Students will

1. Identify their short term, mid-range, and long-range career goals.
2. Compare their current qualifications to those needed to enter their choices of career.
3. Describe strategies that will keep them engaged in pursuing their careers.
4. List the pros and cons of three possible career choices.
5. Identify appropriate times to self-assess to see if they should maintain or adjust their career paths.

SAMPLE CONTENT STANDARDS: Make career decisions

VOCABULARY & TERMS: career, goal, obstacles, path, delayed gratification, perseverance, determination, self-assessment, networking

CONCEPT SUMMARY: A choice of a career is personal and should mirror one's interests as well as skillsets and willingness to complete additional training/education as necessary.

EXPLICIT INSTRUCTION AND PRACTICE: Have students

- Discuss lesson concepts.
- Review lesson vocabulary.
- Reflect upon their career choices; list pros and cons of each.
- Identify job clusters that require college, vocational/trade school, or on the job training.
- Locate specific places in their city that employ people within their career of interest.
- Consider jobs that could contribute to a successful career and also be engaging.
- Research career options that meet short, mid-range, and long-term personal goals.
- Compare preparing for and working in those careers and identify key times to reassess.
- React to or reenact internet material and/or videos on career planning.
- Prepare a plan of steps to become eligible for a realistic job using the provided worksheets.
- Conclude that knowledge about yourself and prospective careers increases the chances of getting and maintaining a rewarding job.

POINTS TO MAKE:

- One's skillsets and qualifications must match the type of job one is seeking.
- Students should look at personal career goals and what is required to move into their target positions when making decisions about courses to take and volunteer assignments to accept.
- When analyzing career choices, determine if the work atmosphere, expected outcomes, productivity level, and physical demands seem pleasant.
- Think through the steps and timelines for accomplishing steps that are needed to pursue and grow within a career of interest.
- Qualifications include factors such as skills, experience, training, and education.
- As qualifications are gradually obtained and developed, one can seek more favorable jobs that require more responsibility.
- When obstacles are met while pursuing a goal, one should consider if there are ways around the obstacle or if another goal might be more suitable and/or obtainable.
- Build a good reputation at a particular company by accepting an entry level position; developing skills, experience, competency, and credibility in that position; and then seeking promotion(s) to higher level or more preferable positions
- Being turned down for a job because of 'lack of qualifications' means you have to become more qualified and/or provide more proof of your qualifications.
- Internships help develop one's work ethics, talents, job references, and skills which can open doors to paid employment.
- Network with people who may be able to help connect you to potential employers and/or opportunities for advancement.
- Meeting challenges and solving problems help build stamina and self-confidence – traits that promote job success.

INSTRUCTIONAL RESOURCES

Suggested Website(s):

Title: Preparing for a Career: An Online Tutorial
Created or Produced by: Sheryl Burgstahler, Ph.D., Sara Lopez, and Scott Bellman
Web Address: http://www.washington.edu/doit/preparing-career-online-tutorial
Brief Summary: A list of links related to getting prepared for careers

Suggested YouTube Video(s):

Title: How to Find the Career for You With Lisa Nicole Bell
Creator/Producer: Lisa Nicole Bell / Careers Out There
Running Time: (5 minutes 51 seconds)
Format: mini-lecture
Brief Summary: Addresses staying in tune with your passions and skillsets when deciding upon an occupation and selling yourself as a potential employee

Title: Create a Career Path and Set Career Goals – Job Genius Education Series
Creator/Producer: Express Empowerment Professionals
Running Time: (14 minutes 49 seconds)
Format: mini-lecture
Brief Summary: Talks about the importance of choosing career goals to pursue and developing softs skills as one prepares through appropriate training, education, and experience; shares examples of people who explored personal career paths

STEPS FROM NOW TO CAREER SUCCESS

List your current status as one who is employed for pay or as a volunteer. Otherwise, identify the status as "student". Complete the last section on the list by specifying your career goal. Create intermediate steps and later explain the sequential connections.

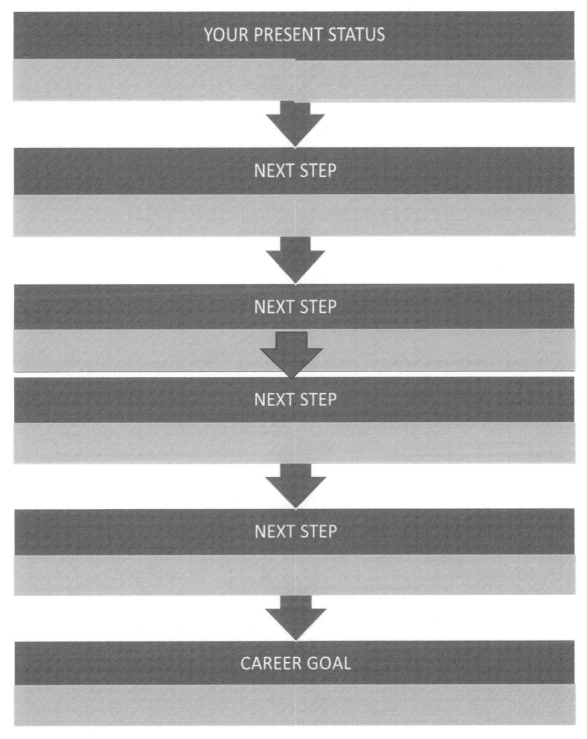

YOUR PRESENT STATUS

NEXT STEP

NEXT STEP

NEXT STEP

NEXT STEP

CAREER GOAL

MOVING TOWARD YOUR CAREER

Complete this sheet after reflecting on your career aspirations. Consider goal and qualifications. Use online research or videos to help with your responses.

1. **What do you plan to become in your career?**

   _____

   _____

2. **What qualifications do you need to get that type of job?**

   _____

   _____

3. **How will you become qualified?**

   _____

   _____

4. **Where will you become qualified?**

   _____

   _____

5. **Why do you want this type of career?**

   _____

   _____

6. **What qualities do you have that will help you do well in this type of career?**

   _____

   _____

7. **What qualities or skills will you have to develop to be considered for this career?**

   _____

   _____

8. **What other types of related jobs would you consider?**

   _____

   _____

LESSON #29 – HOW DO YOUR ABILITIES MATCH YOUR CAREER INTERESTS?

GOAL: Students will make career decisions.

OBJECTIVES: Students will

1. Indicate responsibilities and working conditions related to their areas of career interest.
2. Indicate risks as well as rewards related to their areas of career interest.
3. Explain why their careers of interest are appropriate for them.

SAMPLE CONTENT STANDARDS: Researching career paths

VOCABULARY & TERMS: aptitude, working conditions, responsibilities, performance, risks, rewards

CONCEPT SUMMARY: One's choice of career should involve seeking work responsibilities and environments that are gratifying and feeling valued for what one does.

EXPLICIT INSTRUCTION AND PRACTICE:

- Discuss and provide examples of vocabulary and terms.
- Review websites and videos.
- Discuss how the information provided within the instructional resources has personal connections with the students' lives.
- Reflect upon career interests and working conditions.
- Complete the worksheet comparing interests and abilities.
- Explain why you feel certain careers are appropriate and appealing.

POINTS TO MAKE:

- One should not choose a job or career just because friends work there if it is not the type of work that one is interested in doing.
- Research the qualifications for a job so that an informed choice can be made prior to going through the application process.
- If one is not qualified for a job that is really desired, work toward becoming qualified and apply for it or a similar job in the future provided that there is an opening.
- Working conditions should be considered and can have an effect on long-term job satisfaction.

- If job qualifications are lacking, one should take the time to develop and increase in ability or explore other jobs.
- Choose a job where ability and work responsibilities intersect.
- All jobs are important and play roles in covering various niches and needs within society.
- It is a benefit to not only make money when working but to enjoy and be fulfilled in one way or another by the work that one does.
- If a job is one that will be disliked more than liked, a different one should be sought.

INSTRUCTIONAL RESOURCES:

Suggested Website(s):

Title: Choosing a Major or Career Path
Created or Produced by: DePaul, The Career Center
Web Address: http://careercenter.depaul.edu/advice/majorcareerpath.aspx
Brief Summary: Includes links on what one can do with various majors or degrees

Suggested YouTube Video(s):

Title: Matching Your Skills to a Career
Creator/Producer: Fern Selesnick / Fern Selesnick Consulting
Running Time: (6 minutes 23 seconds)
Format: news interview
Brief Summary: WWLP 22 News conducts an interview that guides listeners in deciding what types of jobs are worth learning more about and possibly pursuing

Title: Childhood Interests Can Help You Find the Right Career
Creator/Producer: Oren Madison / Hire Story
Running Time: (3 minutes 29 seconds)
Format: changing scenery showing various worksite tasks along with interviews of people who had childhood interests related to those jobs
Brief Summary: People share stories of how they developed their childhood interests into viable jobs as adults

HOW DO YOUR ABILITIES MATCH YOUR CAREER INTERESTS?

Reflect upon your career interests to help determine if your choices are those that you are willing to invest your time in order to become qualified to do the work.

CAREER INTEREST (Plan A):

_____

What will you have to be able to do to perform your job?

_____
_____
_____
_____

Which of these things are related to things you already do and how are they related?

_____
_____
_____
_____

Are there any of these duties that you believe will be challenging to learn how to do?

_____
_____
_____
_____

Why will it be worth or not worth your time to learn how to perform the duties related to your career interest?

_____
_____
_____
_____

CAREER INTEREST (Plan B):

_____

What will you have to be able to do to perform your job?

_____
_____
_____
_____

Which of these things are related to things you already do and how are they related?

_____
_____
_____
_____

Are there any of these duties that you believe will be challenging to learn how to do?

_____
_____
_____
_____

Why will it be worth or not worth your time to learn how to perform the duties related to your career interest?

_____
_____
_____
_____

LESSON #30 – THE INTERVIEW

GOAL: Students will become aware of best practices for interviewing

OBJECTIVES: Students will

1. Describe appropriate and inappropriate ways to dress for an interview.
2. Give examples of appropriate interview etiquette.
3. Describe ways to prepare for an interview.

SAMPLE CONTENT STANDARDS: Enhance job-seeking skills

VOCABULARY & TERMS: interviewer, interviewee, etiquette, impression, appearance, appropriate, non-verbal communication, body language, marketing oneself

CONCEPT SUMMARYS: Students should be made aware of how to prepare for an interview as well as appropriately engage during the interview process.

EXPLICIT INSTRUCTION AND PRACTICE:

- Discuss vocabulary and terms and their relevance to being interviewed.
- Explain what types of things can be expected during an interview.
- Review some of the dos and don'ts that should take place when being interviewed, including attire.
- View and discuss the listed instructional resources on interviewing.
- Address the importance of finding out about the purpose and vision of an employer and be prepared to share how becoming hired will assist with its vision and purpose.
- Identify a personal weakness and then shed a positive light on it in the event that an interviewer asks about weaknesses.
- Develop a short introduction that includes a personal asset as well as how that asset could benefit a potential employer.
- Describe other steps to prepare for an interview.

POINTS TO MAKE:

- The interview **is not** the first time to try to make a positive impression upon the company that one wishes to be hired by.
- Applications, resumes, and cover letters are all marketing pieces.
- Preparation including learning about the background of the company provides the interviewee with knowledge that can be used to market oneself to the employer.

- Appropriate manners should be practiced throughout the interview process.
- Effort should be made to remain attentive, engaged, and interested in the interview subject matter as demonstrated by eye contact, body language, and dialogue.
- One should express how what he/she has to offer will benefit the employer as opposed to how working for the employer will benefit the interviewee if hired.
- Always show gratitude toward the employer for taking the time to meet with you.
- Personal body space should be honored when being interviewed.
- Don't stand or sit too close to the interviewer.
- Materials, objects, and artifacts in the interviewer's office should not be touched or interacted with unless invited to do so.
- Interview time is not the appropriate time to vent about negative aspects of a prior job.
- Compliments, if given to the interviewer, should be in good taste and not overly done in such a way that they appear phony, overwhelming, or invasive.

INSTRUCTIONAL RESOURCES:

Suggested Website(s):

Title of Document: Top 10 Interview Tips From an Etiquette Professional
Created or Produced by: Nancy R. Mitchell, The Etiquette Advocate
Web Address:
https://www.experience.com/alumnus/article?channel_id=career_management&source_page=oh_behave&article_id=article_1200586167230
Brief Summary: Best practices

Suggested YouTube Video(s):

Title: Top 3 Interview and Behavioral Interview Questions and Best Interview Questions
Creator/Producer: HowIHireYou.com
Running Time: (8 minutes 36 seconds)
Format: mini-lecture including excerpts from managers explaining what they ask and why
Brief Summary: Sample questions that are asked during job interviews, the reasons for these questions, and best practices in answering them

LESSON #31 – THE MOCK INTERVIEW

GOAL: Students will participate in role play demonstrating their knowledge of interview skills.

OBJECTIVES: Students will

1. Participate in mock interviews.
2. Critique one another and offer suggestions.
3. Demonstrate effective communication skills while interviewing.
4. Demonstrate appropriate behaviors while interviewing.

SAMPLE CONTENT STANDARDS: Use of effective verbal communication skills

VOCABULARY & TERMS: critique, attentive, self-evaluate, first impression, enthusiasm, confidence, appropriate

CONCEPT SUMMARY: Mock interviews help sharpen skills for actual job interviews in terms of interview performance and strategy.

EXPLICIT INSTRUCTION AND PRACTICE:

- Explore the vocabulary and terms and discuss their significance.
- Visit suggested website on dressing for interviews and converse about why this is important.
- Review and discuss video that advises on best practices when participating in interviews.
- Choose a fictitious job opening and participate in a related mock interview.
- Establish ground rules for mutual student feedback.
- Participate in mock interviews from greeting through closure, demonstrating appropriate behaviors.
- Record student feedback on Mock Interview Forms.
- Share feedback from student mock interview forms.
- Provide feedback regarding what went well and what may need to be improved.

POINTS TO MAKE:

- Potential questions such as "Why should we hire you?" should be thought about ahead of time so that answers are forthcoming in terms of one's strengths.
- Personal skills, experience, and aspirations related to the available job should be shared during interviews.
- Wear appropriate dress for the potential work setting during job interviews.

- Objective critique of one's practice interview will help you avoid repeating some mistakes and enable you to improve your answers.
- Positive traits to exhibit during an interview are confidence without cockiness, insight into employer needs, and competence as well as potential.
- There are no "do overs" with the actual interview and first impressions can either close doors or open doors to further consideration for a position.
- Greetings and closures are expected, so practice them for your interviews.
- During an interview one not only communicates verbally but physically through body language, so avoid negative facial expressions, fidget, or check in with your cell phone during an interview.

INSTRUCTIONAL RESOURCES:

Suggested Website(s):

Title of Document: Dress Appropriately for Interviews
Created or Produced by: Thad Peterson, Monster Staff Writer **Web Address:**
https://www.monster.com/career-advice/article/appropriate-interview-dress
Brief Summary: Best Practices

Suggested YouTube Video(s):

Title: Job Interviews (Part 1): Do's and Don'ts of Mock Interviews
Creator/Producer: Kim Costa / Snag a Job
Running Time: (4 minutes 8 seconds)
Format: mini-lecture with animated examples
Brief Summary: A list and examples of best practices

MOCK INTERVIEW STUDENT TO STUDENT FEEDBACK

The teacher or other designated person will interview individual students for a position of his/her choosing. Classmates will individually evaluate the interviewee and follow-up with verbal feedback. The number 1 will serve as the highest score and the number 5 will serve as the lowest score.

INTERVIEWEE_____ MOCK POSITION_____

GREETING	1	2	3	4	5
ETIQUETTE	1	2	3	4	5
BODY LANGUAGE	1	2	3	4	5
INTERACTION	1	2	3	4	5
SELLING ONESELF	1	2	3	4	5
CLOSING	1	2	3	4	5

COMMENTS/SUGGESTIONS:

_____

_____

_____

_____

INTERVIEWEE_____ MOCK POSITION_____

GREETING	1	2	3	4	5
ETIQUETTE	1	2	3	4	5
BODY LANGUAGE	1	2	3	4	5
INTERACTION	1	2	3	4	5
SELLING ONESELF	1	2	3	4	5
CLOSING	1	2	3	4	5

COMMENTS/SUGGESTIONS:

_____

_____

_____

LESSON #32 – CAREER LADDERS

GOAL: Students will gain further access to their long-term career goals.

OBJECTIVES: Students will

1. Provide examples of how an entry level job can evolve into target positions.
2. Design career paths for themselves.
3. Sequentially list at least three positions that demonstrate a connection between an entry level job and a desired job that requires more qualifications.

SAMPLE CONTENT STANDARDS: Create career plans that lead toward career goals

VOCABULARY & TERMS: networking, references, upward mobility, goals, objectives, professional development, experience, training, entry level position, promotion, strengths, weaknesses, window of opportunity

CONCEPT SUMMARY: Strategic planning can help meet career goals.

EXPLICIT INSTRUCTION AND PRACTICE:

- Describe the reasoning for taking a lower-level job than ideal.
- Explain the significance of a career path.
- Provide an example and illustration of a career path.
- List short-term goals and intermediate steps leading to an ideal job.
- Review and discuss vocabulary and terms.
- Explore website and video about career paths.
- Discuss what was gained from the online resources.
- Provide incremental positions between now and desired job and explain each step.
- Place the incremental steps on flowcharts.

POINTS TO MAKE:

- Jobs that are obtained build experience for future jobs.
- When a person works in a job he/she can gain insight into what might be needed to move up to higher positions related to it.
- Assume additional responsibilities so your supervisor will confidently promote you.
- Assuming additional duties that include increased complexity can help one's supervisor to visualize the possibility of promoting you to more complex positions.

- Simpler jobs are stepping stones that help facilitate movement from less to more complex jobs as one demonstrates mastery.
- Given a career goal, one should visualize possible jobs or positions that are in-between the current job and the ultimate job or career that one is aiming for.
- Strive to increase experience, skills, and education/training that are required for the target goal or position.
- Career ladders include moving to jobs that require more expertise, training, and experience.
- Careers can also move laterally to a different type of job that has the same level of responsibility but may be of more interest.
- Connect to people who can assist you in gaining leads to positions that may be more gratifying in money and/or type of work.
- Begin looking at what additional qualifications are needed to move toward target positions/jobs.

INSTRUCTIONAL RESOURCES:

Suggested Website(s):

Title: Sample Career Ladders/Lattices
Created or Produced by: Competency Model Clearinghouse
Web Address:
https://www.careeronestop.org/competencymodel/careerpathway/CPWReviewSamplePaths.aspx
Brief Summary: Includes sample flowcharts representing career ladders

Suggested YouTube Video(s):

Title: Seven Steps for Creating Your Own Career Ladder
Creator/Producer: Candice Smith, Associate Professor at Joseph's College
Running Time: (2 minutes 28 seconds)
Format: mini-lecture
Brief Summary: Addresses self-assessing and tips for taking steps to take to move to higher occupational positions

LESSON #33 – THE JOB EVALUATION

GOAL: Students will become familiar with the form and function of a job evaluation.

OBJECTIVES: Students will

1. Explain what employers are considering when evaluating their performance.
2. Identify some of their strengths and how they contribute to the organization.
3. Identify a weakness that could impact job performance and a way to improve in that area.
4. Explain the purpose of job evaluations.

SAMPLE CONTENT STANDARDS: Apply personal skills for job success

VOCABULARY & TERMS: evaluation, improvement, work ethics, skills, flexibility, reliability, compatibility

CONCEPT SUMMARY: Job evaluations are tools that can benefit both the employer and employee by assessing if the employee is meeting the occupational goals of the employer and what steps can be taken to aid in improvement.

EXPLICIT INSTRUCTION AND PRACTICE:

- Review and discuss the lesson vocabulary and terms
- Visit the website and view the video designated for this lesson..
- Review a blank job evaluation form and its sections; describe purposes for them.
- Discuss possible responses and comments that could be placed on an evaluation.
- Explain how the evaluation tool is useful for both employer and employee.
- Discuss the implications of evaluations during an employee's probationary period.
- Predict a weakness that might be cited on a job evaluation and consider ways to improve that shortcoming.
- Describe steps that can be taken by the employee if the evaluation is unfavorable.
- Create a list of best practices to receive positive job evaluations.
- Compare and contrast their responses with other classmates.

POINTS TO MAKE:

- Job evaluations are given at the end of one's probationary period and then yearly to assess how well one is performing.
- The job evaluation that is given during or at the end of the probationary period can help to determine if the employee should be retained or dismissed from employment.

- The job evaluation can be used to isolate factors that need to be improved by the employee and may include plans of action to facilitate these improvements.
- The job evaluation also acknowledges if job responsibilities are being handled well.
- Job evaluations include quality of performance, reliability, work ethic, attendance, and competence exhibited when performing job responsibilities.
- Performance ratings from unacceptable/poor to good/excellent are normally documented by the supervisor for each area of job responsibility.
- Comments are often documented related to those ratings.
- The employee has the right to add his/her comments or disagree with the evaluation prior to it being placed in his/her personnel file.
- The employee has the right to discuss the ratings given by the supervisor in order to improve them, based on merit.
- The main purpose of the employee evaluation is to determine if individual employees are on-target with their work performance.
- Evaluations also provide guidance on areas that may require improvement.

INSTRUCTIONAL RESOURCES:

Suggested Website(s):

Title: Sample Performance Comments
Created or Produced by: Southeastern Louisiana University
Web Address:
http://www.southeastern.edu/admin/hr/ee_and_mngr_info/manager_information/ppr_comments.html
Brief Summary: Explains the categories that an employer often looks at when giving a performance review for individual employees

Suggested YouTube Video(s):

Title: What to Ask Your Manager During Your Performance Review
Creator/Producer: Margaret Buj
Running Time: (3 minutes 33 seconds)
Format: monologue with questions and answers
Brief Summary: Strategies for keeping your personal performance review positive as you prepare for future performance

SAMPLE JOB EVALUATION

This an example of some of the things that you may find on job evaluation forms that your future employers may use to document your job performance:

NAME OF COMPANY OR BUSINESS

NAME:_____   EMPLOYEE#: _____

DATE OF HIRE: _____   DATE OF EVALUATION: _____

POSITION: _____   DEPARTMENT: _____

SUPERVISOR: _____   FULL or PART TIME? _____

	Excellent	Good	Fair	Needs Improvement	Unsatisfactory
Work Quality					
Flexibility					
Reliability					
Teamwork					
Attendance					
Punctuality					
OVERALL RATING					

Supervisor Comments:

_____

_____

Employee Comments:

_____

_____

_____   _____
Supervisor Signature   **Employee Signature**

_____   _____
Date Signed   **Date Signed**

LESSON #34 – ALTERNATIVE CAREERS RELATED TO PERSONAL INTERESTS

GOAL: Students will acknowledge the existence of other positions related to their interests or alternative positions that allow them to work in the company/business of their choice.

OBJECTIVES: Students will

1. Identify potential businesses or industries that may serve as alternatives in the event that they are unable to secure their dream jobs.
2. Identify multiple jobs that are within the same career field.
3. Compare and contrast the job responsibilities of at least three jobs that are within the same career field.
4. List the qualifications for the type of job that they are interested in and compare them to qualifications of at least two other related jobs.

SAMPLE CONTENT STANDARDS: Research careers to assist in personal choices

VOCABULARY & TERMS: career cluster, career field, qualifications, responsibilities, entry level position, window of opportunity

CONCEPT SUMMARY: Jobs are classified into career clusters that may include alternative jobs of interest that could be considered.

EXPLICIT INSTRUCTION AND PRACTICE:

- Ask students to identify a career field of interest as well as an alternative interest.
- Review and discuss the vocabulary and terms designated for this lesson.
- Watch short films that describe what a typical workday consists of.
- Identify local companies that employ people working within their careers of interest.
- Go to the websites of those companies and identify alternative positions for which they are hiring.
- Review lesson-related website and suggested films pertaining to changing careers.
- Look up and identify which career cluster contains their interests.
- Research and identify three other job options within those clusters.
- Complete the "Comparing and Contrasting Careers With Alternative Careers" worksheet.

POINTS TO MAKE:

- There are several types of jobs that are related to the same career cluster or field according to the United States Department of Education National Career Clusters Framework:

- Career Cluster #1   agriculture, food, and natural resources
- Career Cluster #2   architecture and construction
- Career Cluster #3   arts, audio/video technology, and communications
- Career Cluster #4   business management
- Career Cluster #5   education and training
- Career Cluster #6   finance
- Career Cluster #7   government and public administration
- Career Cluster #8   health sciences
- Career Cluster #9   hospitality and tourism
- Career Cluster #10   human services
- Career Cluster #11   information technology
- Career Cluster #12   law, public safety, corrections, and security
- Career Cluster #13   manufacturing
- Career Cluster #14   marketing, sales, and service
- Career Cluster #15   science, technology, engineering and mathematics
- Career Cluster #16   transportation, distribution and logistics
- Pursuing alternative jobs is a positive action if the amended pursuit is more compatible with one's interests, abilities, and anticipated qualifications.
- Some jobs within the same career field require more education, training, and experience than others.
- Compare and contrast job responsibilities and qualifications required for various jobs related to one's career interest when attempting to determine personal suitability.
- Some jobs within a career field may help to pave the way for acquiring jobs within that same field that are more complex or require greater responsibility.
- Working in entry level jobs related to one's career interest will help to provide perspective on the possibility of upward mobility.
- Work environment and demands may also help determine which types of jobs within a chosen career field may be most suitable.
- Employers recruit more or less for positions based on demand or lack of demand for those jobs.

INSTRUCTIONAL RESOURCES:

Suggested Website(s):

Title: The 10 Worst Mistakes Career Changes Can Make

Created or Produced by: Barbara Reinhold, Monster
Web Address: https://www.monster.com/career-advice/article/10-worst-career-change-mistakes
Brief Summary: Things to consider before changing careers

Suggested YouTube Video(s):

Title: How to Change Careers: 5 Tips From a Career Advisor
Creator/Producer: Linda Spencer, Harvard Extension School
Running Time: (3 minutes 9 seconds)
Format: mini lecture
Brief Summary: Things to consider and best practices to exercise when deciding to leave one career for another one

Title: How to Change Careers: Dealing With the Fear and Transitioning Smart
Creator/Producer: Leo (Actualized.org)
Running Time: (13 minutes 11 seconds)
Format: mini-lecture
Brief Summary: Guidance in sorting through one's feelings related to changing from one career to another

COMPARING & CONTRASTING CAREERS WITH ALTERNATIVE CAREERS

After researching your Plan A and Plan B career choices, answer the following questions:

MAIN CAREER CHOICE:

_____

How does this career contribute to society?

_____

What makes this career attractive to you?

_____

How do you qualify to work in this career field?

_____

ALTERNATIVE CAREER CHOICE:

_____

How does this career contribute to society?

_____

What makes this career attractive to you?

_____

How do you qualify to work in this career field?

_____

What similarities exist between the two choices?

_____

What major factor makes the first career choice different from the other career choice?

_____

Are you comfortable with the thought of working in either of these careers for several years? Why or why not?

_____

_____

_____

_____

LESSON #35 – MANAGING CONFLICT ON THE JOB

GOAL: Students will consider strategies to use in the event of conflict on the job.

OBJECTIVES: Students will

1. Provide appropriate steps to take in the event of conflict on the job.
2. Become familiar with the concept of labor unions and other work-related advocates.
3. Identify sources of conflict that may impact a job and should be avoided.

SAMPLE CONTENT STANDARDS: Develop personal skills for job success

VOCABULARY & TERMS: conflict, mediate, win/win, labor union, "burning bridges", compromise, tolerance, chain of command, grievance, harassment, personality conflict, conflict of interest, insubordination, mediation, damage control, confrontation, anger management, "choosing your battles"

CONCEPT SUMMARY: There are job-related situations that have the potential to cause friction between the employee and other employees as well as with the employer. There are actions that can be taken to avoid or resolve conflict while exercising damage control.

EXPLICIT INSTRUCTION AND PRACTICE:

- Review and discuss vocabulary words and terms.
- Explain how conflict is created through misunderstandings and expectations of others not being met.
- Discuss considerations when deciding whether to confront conflict, how to disengage from conflict, and best strategies for resolving conflict.
- Review and discuss suggested website and the YouTube video.
- Provide conflict-related scenarios and provide appropriate actions on the "What Would You Do If" worksheet and discuss responses.
- Discuss advocacy and the role of labor unions.

POINTS TO MAKE:

- It is important that conflicts on the job be resolved so that people on both sides of the conflict co-exist in a healthy and productive work environment.
- There is a chain of command to follow beginning with one's immediate supervisor and then working one's way up if necessary to resolve workplace problems.
- Maintaining a congenial environment and productivity in the workplace is important.

- One does not have to agree with the views of coworkers in order to harmoniously complete work tasks together.
- It is important to respect other worker's privacy, possessions, and personal space to avoid entering conflict related to those factors.
- One should consider risk vs. benefit when deciding if, when, and how to address conflict on the job.
- Differences of gender, race, background, religion, and political views should not interfere with cooperation and productivity at work.
- When one becomes angry with a co-worker, it is better to take a timeout or request one than to risk losing a job or prosecution from assaulting them.
- If as an employee, one believes that he/she has been treated unfairly by a supervisor, he/she can request to discuss his/her concerns with the supervisor.
- If discussing problems with the supervisor doesn't resolve the situation, then ask the Human Resources Department to help mediate your differences.
- A last resort would be to file a grievance with those in power to impose consequences if merited.
- Labor unions are organizations that represent various groups of workers that can assist when a conflict exists in the workplace.
- It is important to disengage from the conflict long enough to decide upon how to approach the situation without escalating the conflict.
- Impulsive reactions can often make things worse instead of better.
- Sometimes it is in the best interest of the employee to make compromises with the supervisor for the purpose of moving on and resuming the business of the company.

INSTRUCTIONAL RESOURCES:

Suggested Website(s):

Title: 8 Tips for Handling Workplace Conflict
Created or Produced by: Boston.com
Web Address: http://archive.boston.com/jobs/advice/2013/12/30/tips-for-handling-workplace-conflict/HdjGXL7AqfH4G1bQQ0JITM/story.html#slide-1
Brief Summary: Best Practices

Suggested YouTube Video(s):

Title: How to Deal with People You Don't Like at Work
Creator/Producer: Christal Fuentes (The Ladies Coach)
Running Time: (6 minutes 58 seconds)
Format: mini-lecture

Brief Summary: Provides guidance in remaining productive and effective at work while encountering co-workers with personalities that are deemed as negative

Title: Respect in the Workplace
Creator/Producer: vdhohr
Running Time: (6 minutes 59 seconds)
Format: role play that exhibits disrespect in the workplace
Brief Summary: Strategies that will help diffuse conflict at work that could escalate into the realm of disrespect

Title: How to Survive a Job You Hate
Creator/Producer: Howcast.com
Running Time: (2 minutes 3 seconds)
Format: list of strategies
Brief Summary: Examines positive ways to perceive benefit from a job that you don't enjoy until a better one is found

"WHAT WOULD YOU DO IF...?" JOB CONFLICT SCENARIOS

Respond individually to the "What Would You Do If...?" job conflict scenarios and then share your responses and feedback between your classmates who are also participating in this exercise. Consider the pros and cons of your choices.

WHAT WOULD YOU DO IF......

1. Someone keeps borrowing your work equipment and never returns the equipment without being asked

2. You are just learning a new job and each time you make a mistake, your supervisor yells at you in front of everyone

3. A co-worker is socializing so much that he/she is not getting his/her fair share of the work done that your group must complete together.

4. You review your paycheck stub and find that you have not been paid for all of the hours you worked.

5. You have been scheduled to work on a day or shift that conflicts with an important event that you believe that you should attend.

6. You want to move into a higher-level position at your job, but each time you apply, you are passed over and another employee is promoted.

7. You are pressured by a co-worker to mistreat another co-worker that he/she is experiencing conflict with.

8. You accidentally broke something that others on the job have to also use.

9. Your supervisor is giving you a task to do on your job that you don't believe you are able to satisfactorily perform.

10. Your supervisor has written you up for failing to follow rules on the job and you know that the allegations are not true.

11. You and a co-worker have a disagreement about how to perform a particular job-related task.

12. You are working at a company and begin to no longer enjoy working in the department that you are assigned to.

LESSON #36 – PERSONAL ISSUES AND WORK PERFORMANCE

GOAL: Students will manage their personal lives in a way that minimizes the potential negative impact on work performance.

OBJECTIVES: Students will

1. Identify sources of stress that may stem from personal circumstances in life.
2. Consider strategies that can help them separate personal life from work life.
3. Determine actions to avoid in the workplace so that private life won't negatively affect work life.

SAMPLE CONTENT STANDARDS: Balancing life roles; caring for personal needs

VOCABULARY & TERMS: stress, conflict of interest, counseling, support groups, emotional outlets, displaced aggression, delayed gratification, work life vs. personal life

CONCEPT SUMMARY: Stressful situations often occur during life that are separate and apart from the workplace. However, it is important that one's reactions are managed so that they do not significantly interfere with performing one's job.

EXPLICIT INSTRUCTION AND PRACTICE:

- Recall a situation at school when someone was upset about something that had nothing to do with school but behaved inappropriately because he/she was upset.
- Supply some alternatives for coping without behaving inappropriately.
- Discuss factors such as displaced aggression and withdrawal and how they affect work performance and working relationships.
- Review and discuss vocabulary terms.
- Pinpoint personal sources of stress.
- Visit suggested website and view YouTube video.
- Identify positive and negative ways to deal with stress resulting from non-work related issues.
- Identify negative things that can happen at work when overwhelmed by personal issues.
- List strategies on the provided worksheet to help minimize those personal issues from adversely affecting work performance.

POINTS TO MAKE:

- Employers expect quality work performance which requires employees to separate personal life from work life.
- Sometimes personal situations are overwhelming and one needs intervention to help cope and perform job responsibilities at the same time.
- Divulging personal and private details about situations outside of the workplace to co-workers could be harmful.
- It is important to not displace anger related to something that happened at home to co-workers who have nothing to do with the problem.
- One should seek positive activities to engage in outside of work hours such as recreation, exercise, support groups, and venting with friends/family to release stress.
- When one experiences a lot of stress in one's personal life and does not utilize positive outlets to release the stress, those factors can become overwhelming.
- Stress, if not properly coped with and managed, can be distracting and contribute to decreased work performance.
- Many places of employment have Employee Assistance Programs that provide counseling resources to help employees more effectively deal with stress.
- It is mentally healthy to take the time for personal pampering to disengage from stress during off-work time.
- Remaining task-driven at work can help take one's mind off of problems that are occurring outside of the workplace.

INSTRUCTIONAL RESOURCES:

Suggested Website(s):

Title of Document: 10 Tips for Handling a Personal Crisis at Work
Created or Produced by: Jacquelyn Smith, Forbes
Web Address: http://www.forbes.com/sites/jacquelynsmith/2013/08/07/10-tips-for-handling-a-personal-crisis-at-work/#1d6590238b5a
Brief Summary: Suggestions on what to do or not to do at work hen going through a personal crisis

Suggested YouTube Video(s):

Title: Scenario 14: Bringing Personal Problems to Work
Creator/Producer: Rachel Gomes
Running Time: (1 minute 49 seconds)
Format: role play
Brief Summary: Shows how bringing personal problems to work can be distracting.

PERSONAL ISSUES THAT CAN AFFECT WORK PERFORMANCE

Students will identify some negative outcomes that can happen at work when overwhelmed by personal issues. Students will then list strategies to help minimize how the outcomes adversely affect work performance.

****

POTENTIAL NEGATIVE OUTCOME

_____

_____

HELPFUL STRATEGY

_____

_____

POTENTIAL NEGATIVE OUTCOME

_____

_____

HELPFUL STRATEGY

_____

_____

POTENTIAL NEGATIVE OUTCOME

_____

_____

HELPFUL STRATEGY

_____

_____

POTENTIAL NEGATIVE OUTCOME

_____

_____

HELPFUL STRATEGY

_____

_____

LESSON #37 – BEGINNING A NEW JOB AND/OR POSITION

GOAL: Students will recognize best practices for beginning a new job.

OBJECTIVES: Students will

1. Identify work attitudes that are necessary for successful workplace entry.
2. Provide examples of what not to do when beginning a new job.
3. Identify behaviors that will help them integrate into an already existing work team.

SAMPLE CONTENT STANDARDS: Improve personal skills for job success

VOCABULARY & TERMS: standard operating procedures, protocol, regulations, enthusiasm, teachable, flexibility, work culture, approachability, dress code, probationary period

CONCEPT SUMMARY: Certain personal practices when beginning a new job or position helps to facilitate smooth entry and early productivity within new work teams.

EXPLICIT INSTRUCTION AND PRACTICE:

- Identify positive attitudes for beginning new jobs and/or positions.
- Review vocabulary and terms.
- Consume the websites and video suggested for this lesson.
- Provide a list of at least three best practices that should be exercised when beginning a new job and the rationale behind each.

POINTS TO MAKE:

- It is important to be observant during the beginning weeks/months of employment to receive cues about what is appropriate and/or acceptable behavior and practices there.
- Take and keep notes to refer back to when learning procedures for performing jobs.
- It is better to ask questions on what, when, where, and how to do tasks on a job than to risk making mistakes that may be difficult to recover from.
- It is better to overperform on a new job than to underperform.
- Each particular place of employment has its own procedures, priorities, and policies to become accustomed to.
- A new employee can't rely upon what was the norm at a past place of employment.
- Orientation is the initial training on job expectations, procedures, and policy.

- Probation is that period when an employer observes the new employee's performance and decides if he/she should become a permanent employee or be released.

INSTRUCTIONAL RESOURCES:

Suggested Website(s):

Title: 10 Rules for Starting Your New Job on the Right Foot
Created or Produced by: Work It Daily
Web Address: https://www.workitdaily.com/10-rules-beginning-job-foot/
Brief Summary: Best Practices

Title: 7 Things You Should Never do When Beginning a New Job
Created or Produced by: Dawn Rosenberg McKay
Web Address: https://www.thebalance.com/new-job-donts-525839
Brief Summary: Best Practices

Suggested YouTube Video(s):

Title: Things You Should Never Do When Starting a New Job
Creator/Producer: Jeff Maher (ABC – Sacramento, CA)
Running Time: (2 minutes 38 seconds)
Format: mini-lecture including videos of scenes found at workplaces
Brief Summary: Best practices for maintaining a positive impression on a new job

Title: New Job? The first 90 Days are Critical to Your Success
Creator/Producer: Smith Arnold Partners
Running Time: (4 minutes 59 seconds)
Format: mini-lecture
Brief Summary: Addresses practices to avoid when one is starting a new job and why

LESSON #38 – DIVERSITY IN THE WORKPLACE

GOAL: Students will become more aware of cultural differences in the workplace and contribute to a positive and productive work environment.

OBJECTIVES: Students will

1. Identify diverse group categories of people found in a workplace.
2. Discuss tolerance of groups of people who differ from them.
3. Recognize common goals that must be accomplished in a workplace.
4. Contemplate problems that may exist in a workplace when diversity is not accepted.

SAMPLE CONTENT STANDARDS: Demonstrate respect for diversity

VOCABULARY & TERMS: race, culture, ethnicity, nationality, gender, age, disability, socio-economic status, religion, political persuasion, prejudice, discrimination, diversity, tolerance, Americans with Disabilities Act, Equal Employment Opportunity

CONCEPT SUMMARY: People in society have distinct differences, but in the workplace, the differences should not be allowed to hinder workplace productivity.

EXPLICIT INSTRUCTION AND PRACTICE:

- Share how fellow students are similar as well as different.
- Agree that diversity in students does not detract from common goals.
- Discuss factors related to discrimination in the workplace and protective laws/policy.
- Address the value of differences and the richness difference brings.
- Review vocabulary and terms.
- Share examples of practices that could be negative in the workplace with respect to diversity.
- Discuss prejudice as not only being race related.
- Discuss steps to take if you believe they have been discriminated against.
- Review and discuss the online material that has been suggested as instructional resources.
- Identify things that help to make a workplace diverse and why diversity is important.
- Hypothesize workplace problems that could arise when diversity is not embraced.

POINTS TO MAKE:

- Embracing differences is needed if one is to successfully work with people who may differ from one's own race, culture, ethnicity, religion, or other obvious traits.

- Discrimination is against the law and can result in lawsuits.
- Differences can be assets.
- Cultural norms that differ from what one is used to does not make them wrong.
- People are more alike than different.
- Beauty is not only determined by the physical traits that are displayed on the outside, but also by distinct personalities that flow from the inside of people.
- The Americans with Disabilities Act and Equal Employment Opportunity include legal mandates to reinforce citizens not being discriminated against for employment.
- Employers pay employees to fulfill the goals of companies regardless of how employees may feel about people who are different from themselves.
- Negative energy based upon intolerance of differences in co-workers can have negative effects upon the productivity and cohesiveness of work teams.
- What unifies people in the workplace is the value of the work, per se.

INSTRUCTIONAL RESOURCES:

Suggested Website(s):

Title: Diversity in the Workplace: Benefits, Challenges, and Solutions
Created or Produced by: Josh Greenberg
Web Address: http://www.multiculturaladvantage.com/recruit/diversity/diversity-in-the-workplace-benefits-challenges-solutions.asp
Brief Summary: Explains the importance of diversity in the workplace

Suggested YouTube Video(s):

Title: Creating a Respectful Workplace Training Video, Workplace Diversity Training
Creator/Producer: CRM Learning L.P.
Running Time: (4 minutes 36 seconds)
Format: two people facilitate a mini-lecture
Brief Summary: Expresses personal roles in contributing to a respectful workplace

LESSON #39 – SOCIAL GATHERINGS AND THE WORKPLACE

GOAL: Students will learn how social gatherings with co-workers differ from social gatherings with family and personal friends.

OBJECTIVES:

1. Explain why conduct at social gatherings with co-workers should include a higher level of constraint than with casual friends and acquaintances.
2. Identify behaviors that should be avoided at social gatherings with co-workers.
3. Explain how occupational networking can be accomplished with social gatherings consisting of co-workers and associates.
4. Identify certain controversial topics to avoid when engaging in conversation with co-workers in social settings.

SAMPLE CONTENT STANDARDS: Exhibit positive workplace behaviors

VOCABULARY & TERMS: integrity, image, collegiality, privacy, professionalism, constraint, networking, controversial, social setting

CONCEPT SUMMARY: When social gatherings take place that involve coworkers, one should consider himself/herself to still be at work and behave and converse accordingly.

EXPLICIT INSTRUCTION AND PRACTICE:

- Discuss interactions that are expected to take place at social gatherings.
- Share the purpose of social gatherings and what happens at them.
- Distinguish factors that make work-related social gatherings different from other types of social gatherings.
- Explain and provide examples related to the vocabulary and terms designated for this lesson.
- Review and discuss the suggested website and video.
- Generate a list of questionable practices and topics to avoid when attending an office party.
- List questions that might help you network during office social events.

POINTS TO MAKE:

- One must take into account that he/she is possibly being morally judged from the viewpoint of "co-worker" even during social outings.
- How one behaves or dresses at social outings, if considered as negative, can have an impact upon how one is viewed upon returning to the workplace.
- How one conducts oneself at workplace social gatherings can create limiting factors in the workplace based upon the opinions coworkers form of you while observing.
- Certain responses to some controversial topics when with co-workers at social outings can have negative impacts upon cohesiveness and ability to work as teams.
- It is advisable to avoid or limit responses to topics which could trigger ongoing discord.
- Use of alcoholic beverages can contribute to limited control of what one might say or how one might behave in social settings with co-workers and could be damaging.
- Outings with personal friends and family allow more room for transparency than when going out with coworkers.
- One's boss or supervisor is still one's boss or supervisor, even when participating in social outings and respect should still be rendered.
- Social outings related to one's place of employment has the potential to create or strengthen bonds between coworkers if handled appropriately.

INSTRUCTIONAL RESOURCES:

Suggested Website(s):

Title: Smart Socializing with Co-Workers
Created or Produced by: Beth Braccio Hering, Careerbuilder.com
Web Address: http://www.cnn.com/2011/LIVING/05/25/smart.socializing.coworkers.cb/
Brief Summary: Shares pros and cons of socializing with co-workers and appropriate vs. inappropriate interactions

Suggested YouTube Video(s):

Title: Dos and Don'ts of Holiday Office Parties
Creator/Producer: Heather Monahan (WPTV News – West Palm Beach, Florida)
Running Time: (2 minutes 52 seconds)
Format: interview
Brief Summary: Addresses appropriately conducting oneself as an employee when attending office parties

LESSON #40 – WORK ETHICS

GOAL: Students will consider norms that are expected in various work environments.

OBJECTIVES: Students will

1. Identify actions that they can avoid in the workplace that may contribute to conflict.
2. Explain the concept of teamwork and provide examples of how lack of teamwork can interfere with what gets accomplished at work.
3. Describe ways to be dependable on a job and the consequences of not being dependable.
4. Recognize boundaries on conduct and positive work ethics.

SAMPLE CONTENT STANDARDS: Recognize the different roles and responsibilities people play in the family, school, and community and how these roles and responsibilities are interrelated

VOCABULARY & TERMS: confidentiality, teamwork, reliability, competence, loyalty, fairness, respect, attentiveness, productivity, personal boundaries, ethical

CONCEPT SUMMARY: Being ethical consists of doing the right thing considering the circumstances. These practices help to create and/or maintain positive work environments.

EXPLICIT INSTRUCTION AND PRACTICE:

- Explain what being ethical means – conforming through acceptable behaviors: knowing right from wrong.
- Provide positive and negative work-related behaviors and share how they are related to work.
- Define and provide examples for vocabulary and terms.
- Describe what it means to be a dependable teammate.
- Review and discuss suggested online media material that pertains to exercising strong, moral work ethic.
- Explain consequences that could occur when one behaves non-ethically.
- Complete the "Avoiding Poor Work Ethics" worksheet and identify the negative examples on the list and replace them with positive alternatives.
- Discuss the concept of boundaries in respect to belongings and space of others.

POINTS TO MAKE:

- Each employee must pull his/her own weight.
- Teamwork depends upon each person being where he/she needs to be and working on what she/he is supposed to be working on, consistently.
- Being dependable as well as competent are mandatory qualities of good work teams.
- Work teams should be sensitive about the type of information they share with people outside of the team that could be damaging to members of the team.
- Poor attendance impacts not only the employee, but other team members who must compensate for the missing employee to complete team-related tasks.
- Every employee, regardless of position or length of employment, is due respect and has a place of value.
- Work hours are designated to fulfill the tasks and expectations that have been assigned by the employer.
- Mutual respect of boundaries related to the supplies and work tools of coworkers should be practiced.
- Respect one another's work stations as well as being considerate in shared spaces.
- Work supplies and tools of coworkers that have been borrowed with their permission should be returned in a timely manner and protected from damage.
- Regardless of position in the workplace, one must remember that each position is important and has an impact on the collective success of the workplace.
- One should be sensitive to others in the workplace and avoid practices that others may find disruptive or overly distractive.
- Integrity and honesty help to build trusting relationships and bonds in the workplace.

INSTRUCTIONAL RESOURCES:

Suggested Website(s):

Title: 5 Factors That Demonstrate a Strong Work Ethic
Created or Produced by: Amelia Jenkins
Web Address: http://smallbusiness.chron.com/5-factors-demonstrate-strong-work-ethic-15976.html
Brief Summary: Identifies major work behaviors that are considered as ethical in the workplace

Suggested YouTube Video(s):

Title: The True Definition of a Strong Work Ethic – (Motivational Video)
Creator/Producer: Endless Motivation
Running Time: (6 minutes 54 seconds)
Format: changing action scenes exhibiting work ethic while narrator describes and defines work ethic
Brief Summary: Describes developing traits one should exhibit when practicing good work ethics in spite of challenges that may be faced

AVOIDING POOR WORK ETHICS

Review the list that is provided and identify the listed practices that can create a bad reputation for yourself in the workplace. For the examples seen as unethical, provide an alternative action that is ethical in the space provided at the bottom of this worksheet

_____ **(a) Arriving at work on time**

_____ **(b) Allowing a co-worker to take the blame for your mistake**

_____ **© Sharing private information from work files with your friends**

_____ **(d) Helping your co-worker to correct a mistake that took place**

_____ **(e) Staying at home when you have an illness that others can catch**

_____ **(f) Using sick leave to help extend a vacation**

_____ **(g) Doing a good job even if your supervisor has upset you**

_____ **(h) Leaving your work area orderly for the workers who have to work later**

_____ **(i) Performing actions that hinder a co-worker from properly doing his or her job so that you will have a better chance to get the promotion that is available**

_____ **(g) Posting negative things about your job on social media**

_____**(h) Asking a co-worker to sign you in on the timesheet at work when you are unable to get there by the designated start time**

_____**(i) Saying things about your co-worker at work that are not true in order to and make the co-worker look bad to others.**
■■

Create statements that show positive work ethics to use in place of the statements that demonstrate poor work ethics. Indicate by alphabet listed above, the statements that are being changed.

_____
_____
_____
_____
_____
_____
_____

LESSON #41 – UNDERSTANDING WORK CONTRACTS

GOAL: Students will learn more about the purpose, form, and function of work contracts.

OBJECTIVES: Students will

1. Describe the purpose of a work contract.
2. Explain the basic parts of a work contract.
3. Describe what happens when a contract is being negotiated.
4. Identify possible consequences of not following the contract agreement.

SAMPLE CONTENT STANDARDS: Identify and develop planning strategies to manage personal affairs

VOCABULARY & TERMS: terms, salary, wage, expectations, labor union, binding agreement, revocation, arbitration, duration, reading the fine print, services, lawsuit, breach of contract, contract, amendment

CONCEPT SUMMARY: Work contracts are binding agreements between those doing the work and those providing the work. They include specific language which define the parameters of the agreement.

EXPLICIT INSTRUCTION AND PRACTICE:

- Explain how a work contract is a formal agreement between two or more parties that documents the agreement of mutual expectations.
- Review and discuss vocabulary and terms and their relevance to work contracts.
- Review and discuss the suggested website and video.
- Role play a contract negotiation session (show give-and-take, mutual satisfaction with result).
- Create a list of examples of situations requiring contracts.
- Look at components of real contracts.
- Discuss consequences for not abiding to a contract.
- Identify and/or list major questions that need to be addressed regarding a work contract before agreeing to and signing it.

POINTS TO MAKE:

- Work contracts specify agreements related to a job including work expectations, fringe benefits, salary/payment for services, time parameters, and work-related tasks.
- A work contract is a binding agreement between employer and employee and includes the expectations of both parties.
- Employers on work contracts can be an individual, a group of individuals, or a company that is hiring someone to perform a service or task.
- Employees on a work contract can be an individual or a group of individuals that are being hired by an employer to perform a service or task.
- Some work contracts are for temporary work/short-term assignments, and some include specifications regarding long-term employment.
- Contracts should be read thoroughly and an understanding and agreement of expectations should take place prior to signing them.
- Some contracts can be renegotiated and changes made that are mutually agreeable prior to signing and implementing them.
- Some informal work contracts can be verbal, but it is best practice to have the agreement in written form for the purpose of revisiting the agreement.
- A work contract can go through procedures to be terminated by the employer or the employee if either party fails to meet the terms agreed upon.
- Payment that has already been given by the employer to the employee for services that have not been met must be reimbursed to the company or work agreed upon must be completed to avoid the possibility of lawsuit.
- A lawsuit can be filed by an employee to recover money that is owed.
- Work contracts can be revisited and possibly amended if merited and agreed upon between both parties.

INSTRUCTIONAL RESOURCES:

Suggested Website(s):

Title: Employment Contracts: Your Employee Rights Explained
Created or Produced by: The Money Advice Service
Web Address: https://www.moneyadviceservice.org.uk/en/articles/checking-your-employment-contract
Brief Summary: Covers sample components of work contracts and their significance (United Kingdom)

Suggested YouTube Video(s):

Title: Key Things to Look for in Your Work Contract
Creator/Producer: The Student Grid
Running Time: (3 minutes 22 seconds)
Format: drawn illustrations of what should be in a work contract along with explanations of those items
Brief Summary: Highlights what to look for in a work contract that should clearly describe the agreements between a worker and an employer

LESSON #42 – SELF-MONITORING TIME WORKED VS. TIME PAID

SUBJECT: Paid vs. non-paid time at work

GOAL: Students will become familiar with how time worked is translated into a paycheck.

OBJECTIVES: Students will

1. Describe what constitutes a full-time job and how differences in time worked also is reflected in pay.
2. Identify types of days when an employee does not work and is still paid for the work day.
3. Describe a method for documenting hours worked and confirming with paycheck stubs and/or direct deposit receipts.
4. Compare and contrast hours worked between full time and part-time jobs.
5. Distinguish work hour expectations for hourly jobs with salaried jobs.

SAMPLE CONTENT STANDARDS: Apply personal, ethical, and work habit skills that contribute to job success

VOCABULARY & TERMS: part-time, full time, overtime, time, time and a half, double time, deductions, time docked, hourly worker, salaried worker, comprehensive time, holiday pay, vacation pay, paid time off, sick pay, check stub, direct deposit receipt, time off without pay, gross pay, net pay

CONCEPT SUMMARY: Payment to employees are documented on paycheck stubs which also include wages earned as well as deductions. One should verify that accurate earnings taken home are reflected.

EXPLICIT INSTRUCTION AND PRACTICE:

- Introduce and discuss the concept of wages in exchange for services rendered.
- Elaborate upon the vocabulary and terms through defining and provision of examples.
- Address how methods as well as frequency of wage payments can vary based upon the employer's options that have been established.
- Distinguish methods to verify that what is owed has been paid.
- Explain how to interpret paycheck stub sections including deductions and how they equate to take home pay.

- Review and discuss the suggested websites and online videos that accompany the lesson about form and structure of check stubs.
- Observe a paycheck stub or replica (with personal information deleted) and explain how the included content leads to the net pay recorded on it.
- Discussion will follow regarding scenarios that would make the check stub inaccurate.
- Make plans of action in the event that discrepancies on paychecks need to be corrected.

POINTS TO MAKE:

- A full-time employee is usually scheduled to work thirty to forty hours per week.
- A part-time employee is one who works less than thirty hours per week.
- Overtime is when a person who has hourly wages works more than forty hours within a given work week.
- Compensatory time is when an employee works more than the agreed upon hours to work within a normal work week and is provided time off that can be later used.
- An hourly employee is one who is paid a set amount of money related to the number of hours worked.
- A salaried employee is one who is paid an annual or monthly wage to perform a job regardless of if additional hours beyond forty hours are required for duties and tasks.
- Time is related to scheduled pay per hour for a person who is paid hourly wages when time/hours worked does not exceed forty hours for the week.
- Time and a half is related to the number of hours that exceed forty hours of work for that week and additional wages are paid at one and a half times the hourly rate.
- Holiday pay allows employees to be paid for the same amount hours for holidays while off from work that would normally be compensated for if actually at work.
- Sick leave is granted to pay the employee up to a maximum number of days per year when ill or caring for ill relatives at the normal rate of pay if one were at work
- Vacation leave and paid time off (PTO time) are granted so that employees have up to a maximum number of paid days per year to use at their discretion.
- Time off without pay are days or hours taken off when an employee has no type of paid leave days/hours available to them and creates less pay for that given pay period.
- Deductions are those extra amounts of money that are subtracted from employee salaries for things such as taxes, union dues, retirement plans, and etc.
- Time docked are minutes, hours, days that have been subtracted from the number of hours normally worked and paid due to not having sufficient leave available.
- A check stub or direct deposit receipt shows the number of hours worked, how much salary vs. deductions, and up-to-date accounting of this information for the year.
- Gross pay is the amount of money employees have earned.

- Net pay is the amount of money employees have earned minus funds that have been deducted for taxes and etc.

INSTRUCTIONAL RESOURCES:

Suggested Website(s):

Title: Fact Sheet #22: Hours Worked Under The Fair Labor Standards Act
Created or Produced by: United States Department of Labor
Web Address: https://www.dol.gov/whd/regs/compliance/whdfs22.pdf
Brief Summary: Addresses what is covered and should be compensated as work time

Title: How to Read Your Paycheck Stub
Created or Produced by: Clearpoint
Web Address: http://www.clearpoint.org/how-to-read-your-pay-stub/
Brief Summary: Talks about wages and deductions and what is included on the paycheck stub

Suggested YouTube Video(s):

Title: Biz Kids: Understanding Your Paycheck
Creator/Producer: DCMP
Running Time: (4 minutes 8 seconds)
Format: short skit
Brief Summary: A skit consisting of teenagers discussing what is earned vs. received and how it appears on payroll checks

Title: How to Understand Your Paycheck
Creator/Producer: Elana / Workforce Studies
Running Time: (2 minutes 27 seconds)
Format: mini-lecture
Brief Summary: Explains and shows examples of the various sections on a paycheck stub and their purposes

LESSON #43– WORK ETIQUETTE

GOAL: Students will review appropriate behaviors for the workplace.

OBJECTIVES: Students will

1. Explain how personal workspaces have an effect on others.
2. Identify practices that can be avoided at work that could create major distractions or inconveniences for other co-workers.
3. Identify good manners that should be practiced when at work.
4. Explain why poor work etiquette can create poor relationships with co-workers and lessen the quality of the work environment.

SAMPLE CONTENT STANDARDS: Develop the understanding of work behaviors and habits that contribute to job success

VOCABULARY & TERMS: etiquette, considerate, personal space, shared space, respectful, non-critical, helpful, personal workload, invasive

CONCEPT SUMMARY: Mutual practice of good work etiquette helps to maintain a positive work atmosphere.

EXPLICIT INSTRUCTION AND PRACTICE:

- Provide examples of good manners and poor manners at home and in the community.
- Define and clarify vocabulary and terms.
- Explore examples of how poor personal work etiquette affects co-workers.
- Review and discuss workplace etiquette that is discussed on suggested website and video.
- Identify examples online or in magazines of acceptable types of clothing for non-office work settings.
- Provide positive examples of practicing work etiquette as opposed to the negative examples that are found on the worksheet.
- Think of and reflect upon at least one personal practice to improve for the workplace.

POINTS TO MAKE:

- Respect coworkers' personal belongings and do not touch or use their things without their permission.
- Maintain the neatness of one's personal and shared work space.
- Be considerate of co-workers by maintaining the volume of electronic devices at levels that are not distracting in the event that electronic devices are allowed.

151

- Extend courtesy to co-workers by greeting them.
- Avoid displaying items that are considered to be offensive.
- When borrowing tools and resources from co-workers after getting their permission, make sure the borrowed items are promptly returned in the same condition.
- When there is an issue between co-workers, try to personally work out the situation together instead of spreading the feelings of discontent around the workplace.
- Be prompt when attending work-related meetings.
- Do not extend the time of social interactions when co-workers are trying to complete duties that require their focus.
- Avoid strong smelling perfume or cologne which could trigger allergic reactions of others.
- Avoid asking co-workers to disclose private and personal information.
- When using the last of something in the office or workplace that is needed to perform assigned duties, seek to get the items restocked.
- Help one another when possible and if needed.

INSTRUCTIONAL RESOURCES:

Suggested Website(s):

Title: Skills – Workplace Etiquette
Created or Produced by: Columbia University Center for Career Education
Web Address: https://www.careereducation.columbia.edu/resources/tipsheets/skills-business-etiquette
Brief Summary: Tips for practicing etiquette in the workplace

Suggested YouTube Video(s):

Title: How to Develop a Dress Code for Work: Business Style Etiquette
Creator/Producer: Dee Marshall, Life Coach (eHow)
Running Time: (2 minutes 55 seconds)
Format: mini lecture
Brief Summary: Guidance in how employers should describe in the dress codes employees are expected to follow and the clarity that should exist

Title: What Not to Wear for Business Casual: Business Style Etiquette
Creator/Producer: Dee Marshall, Life Coach (eHow Finances)
Running Time: (3 minutes 31 seconds)
Format: showcase of examples
Brief Summary: Describes what business casual is not and shows examples of such clothing

FROM POOR WORK ETIQUETTE TO GOOD WORK ETIQUETTE

Below, you will find examples of poor work etiquette. Given the following situations, what could have been done instead to show good work etiquette? Share, compare and provide the reasons for your responses with classmates.

(1) You are in a hurry to warm up your food in your department's microwave. Since someone else's food is already in it being warmed, you remove that person's food and begin warming your own food.

_____

_____

_____

(2) A group of co-workers have gathered and are facing one another and discussing something. You walk in and need to talk to someone in the group about a totally different topic. You walk in and begin talking to that person while having your back facing the rest of the group.

_____

_____

_____

(3) You are with a group of co-workers planning an activity. Your cell phone rings and you get into a long conversation on your phone while the rest of the group is waiting on you to complete the group's planning activity.

_____

_____

_____

(4) You use the last of a certain supply that several people need to use in order to perform parts of their jobs. You then leave and go on break.

_____

_____

_____

(5) You have a scheduled meeting and find out that you need to do something else on that day. You do that other activity and arrive to the scheduled meeting very late. The person who you were supposed to meet with was unsure if you were still coming.

_____

_____

_____

LESSON #44 – BEING PRESENTABLE WHEN REPORTING TO WORK

GOAL: Students will learn more about how they should personally present themselves in the workplace.

OBJECTIVES: Students will

1. Describe the elements of appropriate work attire for various types of jobs.
2. Identify what is considered as poor hygiene and grooming and how they can affect the work environment.
3. Provide examples of inappropriate work attire for specific types of work environments.
4. Describe the purpose of work uniforms for some types of jobs.
5. Define dress code and the purpose for having one.

SAMPLE CONTENT STANDARDS: Demonstrate appropriate work attire and requisite grooming

VOCABULARY & TERMS: appropriate clothing, professional, hygiene, grooming, casual wear, business casual, business attire, party clothing, work uniform, dress code

CONCEPT SUMMARY: Personal image in the workplace includes appropriate clothing as well as good grooming and hygiene practices.

EXPLICIT INSTRUCTION AND PRACTICE:

- Discuss appropriate clothing for various settings.
- Ascertain why certain types of clothing are appropriate in some settings and not appropriate for other settings.
- Consider how the type of clothing worn to work reflects on potential productivity.
- Describe how appropriate work attire may vary based upon the type and place one works.
- Address and discuss vocabulary and terms.
- Provide examples of what good grooming and hygiene practices are and why they are necessary.
- Review and discuss suggested website and videos.
- Draft a reasonable dress code.
- Describe the significance of personal image.
- Show online pictures of people wearing clothing. Distinguish appropriate vs. inappropriate for work.

POINTS TO MAKE:

- One should be neat and clean when reporting to work.
- Good hygiene practices are critical.
- Street clothing is not acceptable when it breaks uniform policy.
- Some large tattoos that are not covered by clothing when at work are unacceptable in some places of employment.
- Assimilate into the practices and norms of individual workplaces with respect to appropriate clothing.
- Business attire differs from casual or party attire.
- Appropriate clothing can vary and is based upon the type of job.
- When in doubt, refer to the dress code policy of the job or ask a supervisor what is or is not appropriate for that specific workplace.

INSTRUCTIONAL RESOURCES:

Suggested Website(s):

Title: 20 Tips to Dress Appropriately for Work
Created or Produced by: Vivian Giang
Web Address: http://www.executivestyle.com.au/20-tips-to-dress-appropriately-for-work-2xvcy
Brief Summary: Provides advice and tips for how to personally remain presentable in the workplace for both women and men

Suggested YouTube Video(s):

Title: What to Wear: Internships (Office Casual)
Creator/Producer: wesochic
Running Time: (4 minutes 9 seconds)
Format: demonstration
Brief Summary: Female models appropriate workwear while background music is playing

Title: How to Dress Well/Work and Office Attire for Men
Creator/Producer: Alex
Running Time: (3 minutes 27 seconds)
Format: mini-lecture and demonstration
Brief Summary: Male models clothing for the job as he describes what he wears and why the look is significant

Title: Blue Collar Guide to Dressing Well at Work

Creator/Producer: New England Style Consultant

Running Time: (3 minutes 11 seconds)

Format: mini-lecture and demonstration

Brief Summary: male describes why a good impression is important at blue collar jobs and also models workwear.

LESSON #45 – COMPONENTS OF A WORKDAY

SUBJECT: Components of a Workday

GOAL: Students will increase their knowledge of work flow during a routine work day at various types of worksites.

OBJECTIVES: Students will

1. Provide three separate scenarios of routine work days and compare and contrast them.
2. Share the significance of each segment of a routine work day.
3. Identify scenarios that may temporarily change the typical routine of a work day.
4. Explain how working at one job may help to prepare them for working at the next job.

SAMPLE CONTENT STANDARDS: Assimilate into work environments

VOCABULARY & TERMS: punch-in/sign-in, punch-out/sign-out, swipe in/ swipe out, time clock, time sheet, break time, lunch time, set up/break down, routine, modify, preparation

CONCEPT SUMMARY: A typical workday has variations from one type of job to another, but at the same time, has many similarities.

EXPLICIT INSTRUCTION AND PRACTICE:

- Take a class poll to find out who works.
- Allow current student workers to provide examples of their typical work days.
- List sequences of activities on the board.
- Compare and contrast their work days to demonstrate that there are many parts of the day that are common to work places in general.
- Emphasize that there are some specific differences based upon the type of job.
- Review vocabulary and terms.
- Review and discuss website on strategies for beginning a work day.
- Watch video that shares what takes place on a typical work day.
- Complete the attached homework assignment to explore what a typical workday consists of.
- Discuss findings upon return to class.

POINTS TO MAKE:

- There are a variety of ways that employers verify employee attendance.
- Some employers confirm attendance by seeing the employee at his/her assigned work station during assigned work times.
- Identification badges are used to swipe in and out using electronic machines that document arrival and departure times.
- Sign-in sheets are signed by employees to verify arrival and departure.
- Individual employee cards are inserted into time clock machines so that arrival and departure times/dates will be stamped/punched on them.
- Offsite employees may be required to check in and out online.
- Employers usually include break time and short lunch breaks (such as thirty minutes) as part of employee working hours.
- Employers often exclude lunch breaks of an hour or more as part of employee work hours.
- Some jobs have scheduled break times and others allow employees to choose when to take allocated breaks.
- A starting point for many work shifts includes setting up materials to complete tasks.
- Others may begin work shifts picking up from where they or other employees have stopped during earlier shifts.
- Some jobs require that the same routines and set of tasks continue throughout work shifts and on a daily basis.
- Some jobs have shifting priorities which may change the order when certain tasks should be performed.
- Some jobs specify which tasks should be performed during certain times of work shifts.
- Other jobs allow employees to use personal judgment to determine how and when to get certain tasks completed and which tasks can be carried to the next shift or day.
- Jobs that require breaking things down and putting things away at the end of a work shift require allocating enough time prior to scheduled departure times.
- Employees depend upon one another to do his/her share of the work.
- Employees are expected to perform the work tasks that they have been hired to do.
- Employers expect employees to be present and functioning at work during the days/hours they are assigned to work.
- Jobs may be similar or different in terms of workday routine.

INSTRUCTIONAL RESOURCES:

Suggested Website(s):

Title: 10 Ways to Have a Good Day at Work
Created or Produced by: Daniel Wallen
Web Address: http://www.lifehack.org/articles/work/10-ways-have-good-day-work.html
Brief Summary: Strategies to jumpstart your workday on a positive note

Suggested YouTube Video(s):

Title: Why a Typical Workday is 8 Hours Long
Creator/Producer: Today I Found Out
Running Time: (4 minutes 44 seconds)
Format: mini-lecture
Brief Summary: Explains how a typical work day evolved to what it has become

A TYPICAL WORKDAY HOMEWORK ASSIGNMENT

Interview a family member or someone else in your community about his/her job and ask the following questions, fill out the information, and report your findings in class.

What type of job do you have?

_____

_____

What are your main duties?

_____

_____

_____

What are the main things that take place from arrival to departure from work and in what order? (Use as many lines as needed and additional responses can be recorded on the back of the sheet.)

1sr _____

2nd _____

3rd _____

4th _____

5th _____

6th _____

7th _____

8th _____

What conditions or events might create changes in the normal routine?

_____

_____

_____

_____

_____

LESSON #46 – THE JOB SEARCH

GOAL: Students will explain the job search and application process.

OBJECTIVES: Students will

1. Identify sources where they can find out about job openings.
2. Express the sequence of steps for pursuing open positions.
3. Assess the qualifications for job vacancies to determine if they qualify.
4. Explain the importance of learning more about the company and position prior to participating in interviews related to openings they have applied for.

SAMPLE CONTENT STANDARDS: Use appropriate job seeking skills to obtain employment

VOCABULARY & TERMS: want ads, human resources department, job fairs, vacancies, promotions, web search, inside informant, verbal inquiry

CONCEPT SUMMARY: One must be strategic in locating and pursuing open positions one is qualified for and also interested in.

EXPLICIT INSTRUCTION AND PRACTICE:

- Discuss personal experiences of becoming aware of job vacancies of interest.
- Generate a list of sources for finding jobs.
- Review vocabulary and terms.
- Share personal preparations and research that are necessary prior to pursuing a job.
- Define the roles that job applications, resumes, and interviews play.
- Perform online searches and locate job vacancies related to their chosen career fields.
- Report findings to the class including position, location, duties, and qualifications.
- Review and discuss the suggested websites and videos related to searching for jobs.
- Compare about the pros and cons of various methods to hunt for jobs.

POINTS TO MAKE:

- Job openings can be discovered by word of mouth and online research.
- Employers share openings on human resource bulletin boards, public service media announcements, company websites, want ads, and in response to verbal inquiry.

- Other avenues for job vacancy awareness are through flyers, job/career fairs, company recruiter solicitation, and hearing of promotions at current places of employment.
- Job applications should be accurate, complete, and neat.
- Resumes should be factual, relevant to the position be applied for, well organized, and concise. Additionally, they should market one's skills, expertise, experience, and related training/education.
- Job interviews are opportunities to continue marketing oneself as being a potential asset to the company if given the opportunity.
- Once job openings are discovered, application requirements and deadlines need to be followed.
- There are no "do overs" for first impressions from initial inquiry of vacancies to submission of applications and resumes.
- When desiring to be promoted within a company, one should become aware of the qualifications for the higher positions so that appropriate preparation can take place.
- Different types of jobs in different regions can be researched online regarding starting salaries.
- People you know who work in places of interest may be able to share information regarding working environments, conditions, and expectations.

INSTRUCTIONAL RESOURCES:

Suggested Website(s):

Title: 10 Ways the Job Search Has Changed
Created or Produced by: Joshua Waldman, Forbes
Web Address: http://www.forbes.com/sites/nextavenue/2013/07/02/10-ways-the-job-search-has-changed/#428cf5b2cee4
Brief Summary: Examples of how job hunting practices differ from how they were done in the past

Suggested YouTube Video(s):

Title: Job Search Tips (Part 14) Jobs Search Advice Nobody Tells You
Creator/Producer: Kim Costa / Snagajob
Running Time: (2 minutes 47 seconds)
Format: mini lecture
Brief Summary: Best practices when interviewing with a potential employer

Title: Job Search Tips (Part 1): Common Job Search Mistakes

Creator/Producer: Kim Costa / Snagajob

Running Time: (4 minutes 43 seconds)

Format: mini-lecture

Brief Summary: Addresses errors that can cause an employer to lose interest in considering a person for a job vacancy

LESSON #47 – BEST PRACTICES WHEN LEAVING A JOB OR POSITION

GOAL: Students will learn about appropriate job exit behaviors.

OBJECTIVES: Students will

1. Identify different reasons people leave jobs.
2. Compare and contrast reasonable and unreasonable reasons people leave jobs.
3. Identify appropriate and inappropriate behaviors to exhibit when leaving jobs.
4. Explain the importance of leaving jobs in appropriate ways.

SAMPLE CONTENT STANDARDS: Exhibit coping skills to manage life-changing events

VOCABULARY & TERMS: promotion, transfer, layoff, resignation, termination, two-week notice, burning bridges, unemployment compensation, severance pay, retirement, performance feedback

CONCEPT SUMMARY: One should maintain professionalism and exercise caution in one's behavior when leaving jobs and positions. The positions being left behind may be bridges to facilitate future employment.

EXPLICIT INSTRUCTION AND PRACTICE:

- Discuss reasons why people leave jobs as well as best exit practices.
- Review and discuss vocabulary and terms.
- Discuss potential ramifications for leaving a job haphazardly.
- Verbalize pros and cons of various scenarios related to leaving jobs.
- Discuss consequences to being terminated from a job for failure to perform duties or for inappropriate behavior.
- Provide examples of damage control to avoid getting fired.
- Explain the required conditions for receiving unemployment compensation.
- Consider qualifications for receiving retirement pay.

POINTS TO MAKE:

- A written two-week notice should be given to the employer prior to leaving a position in order to give the employer the opportunity to seek a replacement.
- One should avoid creating chaos in the work environment when leaving a job.

- Sometimes future potential employers may request references from previous employers.
- One should leave a job or position peacefully, orderly, and professionally.
- Promotion is when a person moves from one job/position to a higher job/position within a company.
- Transfer is when a person moves from one job/position for one located elsewhere within that company.
- Demotion is when a person leaves a job/position for a lower one within a company due to performance issues or the current position being eliminated.
- Termination is when an employer releases an employee from working due to poor performance or not following rules and regulations.
- Layoff is when an employer releases an employee from working due to no longer having enough work available for him/her to justify a salary.
- Severance pay is money that is sometimes provided to a laid off or terminated employee by the employer for a given number of weeks.
- Unemployment compensation is paid to employees who have experienced lay-offs or terminations after working the required number of weeks during a given time period.
- Unemployment compensation is not indefinite but lasts for a given number of weeks.
- Unemployment compensation is a state benefit that includes funding generated by the unemployment insurance of employers.
- If a person is not forced off a job but quits on his/her own, he/she is not entitled to receive unemployment compensation.
- Retirement is when an employee stops working for a company after a specified years of service/age requirement has been met and continues to receive a partial paycheck.
- Retirement pay is not as much as payment while on the job.
- When employees leave jobs they go to new ones, they can apply acquired experience and knowledge.

INSTRUCTIONAL RESOURCES:

Suggested Website(s):

Title: *The Best (and Worst) Ways to Transition Out of a Job*
Created or Produced By: Common Good Careers
Web Address: http://commongoocareers.org/articles/detail/the-best-and-worst-ways-to-transition-out-of-a-job
Brief Summary: Provides a list of best practices for leaving a job

Suggested YouTube Video(s):

Title: How to Know When It's Time to Quit Your Job
Creator/Producer: Howcast
Running Time: (2 minutes 3 seconds)
Format: animated presentation
Brief Summary: Things to weigh when considering a job change

Title: What to do if You Get Fired from a Job

Creator/Producer: askwilliamc.com
Running Time: (5 minutes 25 seconds)
Format: mini-lecture
Brief Summary: Relates strategies for securing a new job after being terminated from the previous one

CHAPTER THREE

QUALITY OF ADULT LIFE

Independent living involves handling life's day to day personal affairs. Self-efficacy includes making informed choices that are personally appropriate given one's abilities, skills, interests, support systems, and resources. Independent mindsets and choices are intertwined in post-secondary education and transition to employment. The lessons in this section address topics related to looking out for one's best interests while pursuing successful transition-related outcomes. Students consider scenarios of living independently and develop personal plans of action related to those scenarios.

LESSON #48 – 1040 EZ INCOME TAX FORMS

GOAL: Students will become familiar with the 1040EZ Tax Form

OBJECTIVES: Students will

1. Identify the types of information that are included on 1040 EZ tax forms.
2. Use fictitious information and fill out tax forms.
3. Explain the purpose of paying taxes.
4. Provide examples of when more than a 1040 EZ tax form has to be filled out and submitted.

SAMPLE CONTENT STANDARDS: Manage personal finances

VOCABULARY & TERMS: w2 forms, filing, deductions, refund, taxable income, 1040 EZ tax form

CONCEPT SUMMARY: Income tax forms such as the 1040 EZ form are completed annually to document taxes paid vs. taxes owed to the government as employees. Income and payment amounts are verified on W2 forms provided by the employer.

EXPLICIT INSTRUCTION AND PRACTICE:

- Describe why people are required to pay taxes.
- Discuss the purpose of 1040 EZ and other income tax forms
- Review and discuss the vocabulary and terms.
- Review suggested website related to the 1040 EZ tax form.
- View and discuss the suggested video that addresses the purpose of taxes.
- Explain what conditions must exist for the 1040 EZ tax form to be the appropriate tax form to complete.
- Examine parts of the 1040 EZ tax form and what is to be placed in each section.
- Examine other tax forms that may need to be completed.
- Provide fictitious financial information to students.
- Complete tax forms based upon the fictitious financial information that was provided.
- Review tax forms for accuracy.

POINTS TO MAKE:

- People who work in the United States have taxes taken out of their paychecks to help pay for public services.
- When a person has paid more taxes than what the government says he/she is required to, the extra tax money is given back after the employee files his/her income taxes.
- When a person has not had as many tax dollars as required deducted from his/her paycheck, he/she must submit payment to the government for what is owed.
- Federal income taxes are filed annually on 1040, 1040A, or 1040EZ Income Tax Forms.
- The type of form used depends upon how complicated the person's financial information is.
- A simple form to fill out when one has minimal deductions that lower the income tax liability is the 1040EZ.
- It is illegal to owe income taxes and not pay them.
- The government can pursue one's personal funds to recover unpaid income taxes.
- The 1040EZ form requires that income and taxes that have been paid be listed The form provides information for what the tax liability is for the individual.
- The 1040EZ form is not to be used when one has a lot of deductions that decrease tax liability.
- Tax liability is how much a person is supposed to pay the government given his/her income after tax deductions have been subtracted.
- The 1040 EZ tax form is for those with an adjusted income that is less than $100,000, when no dependents or other tax credits are claimed, and filing a single or joint return.
- Those with higher amounts of income owe a larger percentage of it to the government for taxes.
- Not only are there federal taxes, but one must also file state taxes annually.

INSTRUCTIONAL RESOURCES:

<u>**Suggested Website(s):**</u>

Title: Instructions for 1040 EZ Form
Created or Produced by: Department of the Treasury
Web Address: https://www.irs.gov/pub/irs-pdf/i1040ez.pdf
Brief Summary: Online instruction booklet from the Internal Revenue Service including what is needed on each line of the 1040 EZ form.

<u>Suggested YouTube Video(s):</u>

Title: How to do Your Taxes Explained

Creator/Producer: How to Adult

Running Time: (8 minutes 23 seconds)

Format: mini-lecture

Brief Summary: Shares how to prepare for tax time and what documents should be used to supply information on your tax form

LESSON #49 – CREATING AND MANAGING BUDGETS / LIVING WITHIN YOUR MEANS

GOAL: Students will learn more about managing the money they have.

OBJECTIVES: Students will

1. Describe the pros and cons of different types of bank accounts.
2. Provide examples of predatory lending practices.
3. Explain the importance of a credit score.
4. Identify money related fees they can avoid.

SAMPLE CONTENT STANDARDS: Manage personal finances

VOCABULARY & TERMS: ATM cards, checking, savings, predatory lending, credit score, check cashing, balancing accounts, needs vs. wants, budgeting, sales

CONCEPT SUMMARY: One's income minus ongoing expenses determines a remainder for present and future purchases and payments.

EXPLICIT INSTRUCTION AND PRACTICE:

- Describe the importance of having a bank account.
- Review and discuss vocabulary and terms.
- Discuss wise choices for handling one's own money including the pros and cons of various types of bank accounts and savings plans..
- Address ways to avoid predatory lending type practices.
- Review and discuss websites related to personal funds.
- Review and discuss suggested films that address banking and credit and the implications related to managing them properly.
- Consider opening a savings account and what is needed to do so.
- Discuss budgeting given the amount of income coming into a household.
- List probable living expenses given various hypothetical income levels.
- Predict how spending habits may tend to vary based upon income.
- Discuss credit scores and how to maintain an adequate rating.

POINTS TO MAKE:

- Bank accounts allow people to save their money in secure places that guarantee that they can retrieve their funds later.
- One must have proof of identification and current contact information when opening bank accounts.
- Savings accounts not only include the money that banking customers put into them but extra money called interest that the bank pays customers for using their money.
- Banks invest customer money to make additional money and then pays the customer interest for the privilege of borrowing from the customer to make these investments.
- Banks must maintain minimal balances and/or number of transactions required in order for customers to maintain accounts free of charge.
- Checking accounts allow customers to pay others who they owe by writing checks okaying the transferring of money from their checking accounts to who is owed.
- Debit cards are plastic and have a magnetic strip or chip which can be swiped or inserted into a card reader so that people can retrieve or forward money from their bank without personally going to the bank to get the funds.
- P.I.N. (personal identification numbers) are codes attached to accounts that permit customers to securely access their money electronically.
- Automated Teller Machines (ATMs) are bank machines where people can use their bank cards to retrieve money from their bank accounts.
- When people use ATMs belonging to a different banking chain/system than the one that their bank account is connected to, additional convenience fees are charged.
- Bank statements come out monthly and are either mailed to the customer or made available online for review of monthly money transactions.
- When one has a bank account, paychecks and other checks can be cashed at the affiliated bank without being charged check cashing fees.
- Banks are also places where people with acceptable credit ratings can borrow money that must be paid back with interest charges added.

INSTRUCTIONAL RESOURCES

Suggested Website(s):

Title: Nine Basic Financial Skills No Young Adult Should Leave Home Without
Created or Produced by: Jesse Campbell
Web Address: https://www.moneymanagement.org/Community/Blogs/Blogging-for-Change/2015/May/Nine-basic-financial-skills-no-young-adult-should-leave-home-without.aspx
Brief Summary: How to strategically utilize income (includes links)

Title: 10 Ways to Live Within Your Means

Created or Produced by: Stephanie O'Connell

Web Address: http://money.usnews.com/money/the-frugal-shopper/2015/03/27/10-ways-to-live-within-your-means

Brief Summary: Strategies to stretch money over longer lengths of time

Suggested YouTube Video(s):

Title: Understanding Credit

Creator/Producer: FCACan

Running Time: (13 minutes 8 seconds)

Format: mini-lecture

Brief Summary: Explains how credit agreements and credit reporting can vary from company to company and how these variables and one's responsible use of credit can affect one's credit worthiness

Title: CashVille Kidz Episode 17: Roles of a Bank

Creator/Producer: Cashville Kidz

Running Time: (7 minutes 14 seconds)

Format: animated presentation

Brief Summary: Explains the purpose of banks and how citizens use various banking services

LESSON #50 – BALANCING FAMILY, SCHOOL, AND WORK

GOAL: Students will develop strategies to balance their time so that their personal goals and objectives can be met.

OBJECTIVES: Students will

1. Compare and contrast a typical weekday time schedule with a typical weekend time schedule.
2. Establish priorities when arranging personal schedules and flexibility within those schedules.
3. Identify every part of the day that must be considered when planning a week's events.

SAMPLE CONTENT STANDARDS: Balance life roles

VOCABULARY & TERMS: time management, prioritize, multi-tasking, conflict of interest, responsibility, balance, schedule, personal goals and objectives, borrowed time

CONCEPT SUMMARY: Within a twenty-four hour day and seven day week, one is involved in multiple activities; some more of a priority than others. One's personal schedule should not be so overloaded that responsibilities become neglected. Daily life should exemplify some sort of balance.

EXPLICIT INSTRUCTION AND PRACTICE:

- Examine and identify what takes place in a typical day.
- Identify activities that take place during an atypical day.
- Compare and contrast a typical weekday with a weekend's usual activities.
- Create pie charts comparing weekday and weekend portions of: work, school, leisure, rest, errands, and chores.
- Discuss vocabulary and terms.
- Revisit pie charts that were created and show how percentage of time is adjusted when adding additional activities not normally occurring in one's routine.
- Demonstrate on a pie chart how time can be borrowed and repaid at a later time.
- Create a twenty-four-hour schedule, then modify it to accommodate a change in priorities.
- Review and discuss suggested websites and video that address living balanced lives.
- Give examples of shifting priorities as needed to maintain a school, family, work-life balance while handling those matters that are non-negotiable.

174

- Describe how the amount time spent in one type of activity has an impact on the others.
- Discuss the importance of including ample time for rest, leisure, and family time.

POINTS TO MAKE:

- When people work to receive income for provision of personal and family needs, they should build in time to wind down and relax.
- Clustering activities that are near one another or on the way may free up time that can be utilized to do other things that are needed.
- Priorities evolve and may require modifying personal schedules of activities for that day, week, or even a longer period of time.
- Adequate rest time should be scheduled to help increase one's energy and focus when performing work tasks.
- If one does not allow time to nurture family and important relationships, those bonds can disintegrate over time.
- If one spends so much time with family and important relationships - focusing upon them in place of performing employment tasks - the job may suffer and be jeopardized.
- It is important to separate time allocated to one's work life from time allocated to one's personal life so that they do not conflict.
- A healthy balance exists when time is allotted to participate in various activities outside of school and work.

INSTRUCTIONAL RESOURCES:

Suggested Website(s):

Title of Document: 37 Tips for a Better Work-Life Balance
Created or Produced by: The Daily Muse Editor
Web Address: https://www.themuse.com/advice/37-tips-for-a-better-worklife-balance
Brief Summary: A good oral reading/discussion about work and life apart from work

Title: School-Life Balance
Created or Produced by: John Hopkins University
Web Address: http://jhsap.org/self_help_resources/school-life_balance/
Brief Summary: A self-reflection article about school and life apart from school

Suggested YouTube Video(s):

Title: Work-Life Balance

Creator/Producer: The School of Life

Running Time: (3 minutes 13 seconds)

Format: animated illustration of concepts

Brief Summary: Explains the importance of one's life being balanced with work and other meaningful activities

LESSON #51 – DEVELOPING SHORT-RANGE, MID-RANGE, AND LONG-RANGE PERSONAL GOALS

GOAL: Students will develop personal plans in sequential stages.

OBJECTIVES: Students will

1. Identify major personal goals in the areas of post-secondary education, employment, and independent living.
2. Create sequential steps for meeting major personal goals.
3. Explain why meeting certain goals is needed to create foundations for future goals.
4. Identify potential obstacles to meeting their goals and possible ways to overcome them.

SAMPLE CONTENT STANDARDS: Develop plans for personal goal attainment

VOCABULARY & TERMS: strategy, realistic goals, objectives, time-frame, foundation, resources, capabilities, support systems, preparation, pre-requisites, personal growth, self-reflection, evaluation, altered plans

CONCEPT SUMMARY: Personal goal attainment takes time and requires planning as well as actions that connect the present with the future one hopes for.

EXPLICIT INSTRUCTION AND PRACTICE:

- Discuss the value of having long-term personal plans along with intermediate plans that help to connect the present with the future.
- Share transition-related plans and identify what needs to take place to bring these plans into fruition.
- Review and discuss vocabulary and terms.
- List short-range, mid-range, and long-range personal goals for themselves in the areas of post-secondary education, employment, and independent living.
- Sequentially document steps toward long-term plans on flow charts.
- Research and report on support, resources, and aptitudes that need to be in place in order to make the goals realistic.
- Identify factors that could cause changes in goals and why those factors should be considered.
- List interim goals that could lead to future ones on the goal planning worksheet provided.
- Review and discuss suggested website and video addressing future plans.

- Revisit goals and explain the connections between their short, mid, and long-range outcomes related to post-secondary education, employment, and independent living.
- Consider obstacles to goals and how to surmount them.

POINTS TO MAKE:

- Short-term, mid-range, and long-range goals will likely differ from one another due to increased requirements as one sequentially builds from present to future.
- Earlier steps help to facilitate future steps in post-secondary education, employment, and independent living.
- Reality checks should take place along the away to determine what is needed to reach various goals and if personal progress is being made.
- When personal goals are created, one should consider whether the goals are realistic, given one's pattern of progress.
- Personal goals should be reassessed from time to time for appropriateness and desirability.
- No matter how old a person is, personal goal creation and modification as needed are still appropriate.
- Alternatives should be considered if goals are no longer of interest or appropriate.
- Each productive step made should be assessed to see if and how the step can lead toward greater steps in life.
- Decisions should be made on if to continue current goals and for how long based upon progress or desirability.
- One should decide if or when to shift gears in another direction, what the future direction should be, and how to get there.
- When progress lags, one should assess why and ask others for advice and help.
- To increase progress one should begin considering what steps, if followed, may be more likely to bring positive results.
- It is important to pursue one's own goals instead of merely living to fulfill someone else's goals.
- Goal creation is a work in progress that evolves as life situations present themselves.
- Celebrate along the way as mini-steps are accomplished.
- Experiencing failure along the way to accomplishing a goal does not always mean abandoning the goal, but may mean finding alternative routes toward attainment.

INSTRUCTIONAL RESOURCES

Suggested Website(s):

Title: Personal Goal Setting: Planning to Live Your Life Your Way
Created or Produced by: Mind Tools
Web Address: https://www.linkedin.com/pulse/personal-goal-setting-planning-live-your-life-way
Brief Summary: Explains how to create SMART goals for oneself and how to stay on course

Suggested YouTube Video(s):

Title: Life After High School
Creator/Producer: Stephanie Rodriguez
Running Time: (5 minutes 5 seconds)
Format: mini-lecture
Brief Summary: Students speak about how life changed after high school and share advice on how to adapt to the changes

GOAL PLANNING: CONNECTING NOW WITH YOUR FUTURE

List the personal goals you are creating for yourself. Consider which early goals lead toward fulfilling later goals and how goals overlap between employment, post-secondary education, and independent living.

PERSONAL EMPLOYMENT GOALS

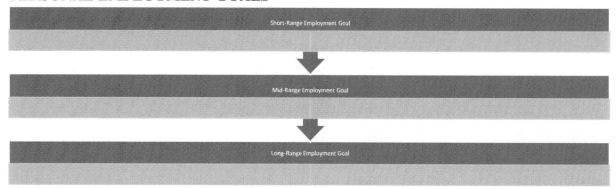

PERSONAL POST-SECONDARY EDUCATION GOALS

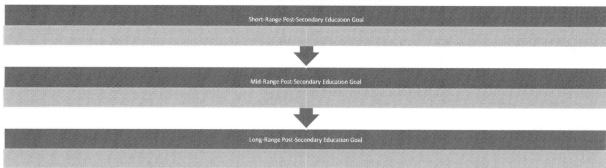

PERSONAL INDEPENDENT LIVING GOALS

How do your employment, post-secondary education, and independent living goals have an impact on one another?

_____

_____

_____

LESSON #52 – PROS AND CONS OF SOCIAL MEDIA

GOAL: Students will reflect upon the impact of social media on their lives.

OBJECTIVES: Students will

1. Identify positive and negative aspects of social media
2. Provide examples of how social media can help them.
3. Pose ways that social media can hurt them.
4. Become familiar with LinkedIn and how it can be used to help them find jobs as well as connect with others who may be vocationally helpful.

SAMPLE CONTENT STANDARDS: Develop skills for maintaining self-esteem and positive personal image; exhibit respect for others within a diverse society

VOCABULARY & TERMS: social media, transparency, vulnerability, personal image, reputation, affiliation, misrepresentation, visibility, privacy settings, account piracy, hacking, online forums, live video, password protection, internet security

CONCEPT SUMMARY: Social media is a useful tool to network without face to face meetings. However, one should use sound judgment regarding how much and what type of personal information is shared with others.

EXPLICIT INSTRUCTION AND PRACTICE:

- Describe different forms of social media they are familiar with and have been using as well as their purposes for doing so.
- Discuss how social media can be a positive communication tool.
- Share how some online practices may contribute to adverse results.
- Review and discuss vocabulary and terms as they relate to social media usage.
- Explain the importance or protecting one's image on social media sites.
- List pros and cons related to social media.
- Review LinkedIn and the types of content and sharing that take place on it.
- Create LinkedIn accounts.
- Identify practices that are considered risky when utilizing social media and why those practices can be risky.
- Review and discuss suggested websites and videos for this lesson.

POINTS TO MAKE:

- Social media is an outlet for communicating with peers and other groups of interest.
- Social media can be used to publicly share information that may be useful to others.
- Beware of personal information that is posted on social media that miscellaneous people may get to see and possibly use to engage in identify theft.
- Potential employers sometimes view social media pages of potential employees to form opinions related to character and image.
- Sharing on social media that a person is presently out of town may cue potential burglars that one's home is unoccupied.
- Posts on social media should not include personal information that you would not be willing to share with anyone who may see the post without your knowledge.
- Posts on social media can create long-term good or bad impressions about the type of person you have portrayed yourself to be.
- Be sensitive to the use of words that can be hard to take back once posted and seen.
- Some statements can be misinterpreted and create bad feelings between those communicating on social media.
- Social media can be used as a forum for seeking and sharing resources.
- Social media can be used to share information about upcoming events.
- Beware of requests to connect with someone on social media that you are already connected with as this may indicate that that person's account has been hacked.
- A hacked account is when someone is perpetrating to be the actual social media account owner.
- Revisit the privacy settings on personal social media accounts to help determine who has access to what is being posted by you.
- "LinkedIn" is a site to help connect employees with employers and those with similar business interests.
- "LinkedIn" provides an online platform for sharing personal business profiles, resumes, work skill endorsements, and career interests with other relevant parties.
- Beware of entering unfamiliar links and attachments that could potentially release viruses into one's computer system or network when on various social media sites.
- Posting "live" on social media includes the risk of showing the unexpected or potentially inappropriate behavior of others.
- Posting on one's personal social media account can impact people's opinions and impressions of you based upon the image portrayed.

INSTRUCTIONAL RESOURCES:

Suggested Website(s):

Title: List of Social Networking Websites
Created or Produced by: Wikipedia
Web Address: https://en.wikipedia.org/wiki/List_of_social_networking_websites
Brief Summary: Lists various social media sites, usership, and dates of origin

Suggested YouTube Video(s):

Title: Pros and Cons of Social Media on Teens
Creator/Producer: Heather Lin
Running Time: (4 minutes 22 seconds)
Format: animated with captions and music
Brief Summary: Shares how social media can be helpful but can also hinder teens

Title: The Pros and Cons of Screening Job Applicants Using Social Media
Creator/Producer: Employee Screen IQ
Running Time: (8 minutes 49 seconds)
Format: Interview
Brief Summary: Shares how employers can research potential applicants using social media sites

LESSON #53 – TIME MANAGEMENT

GOAL: Students will strategically distribute their time so that mandatory activities are accomplished.

OBJECTIVES: Students will

1. Review their own personal schedules and situations that have created time conflicts.
2. Provide examples of how to cluster or sequence activities in order to manage time and effort more efficiently.
3. Describe which factors make an event on their "to do list" a higher priority than another event.
4. Demonstrate ways to document and monitor the completion of mandatory tasks that are not part of their daily routines.

SAMPLE CONTENT STANDARDS: Establish priorities and plans of action needed to manage personal affairs

VOCABULARY & TERMS: prioritize, organize, multi-task, routine, non-negotiables, schedule conflict, over-scheduling, room for the unexpected, borrowed time, rescheduling, clustering, time-sensitive, reminders, deadlines

CONCEPT SUMMARY: A given time period is finite and one must find ways to effectively plan, integrate, and execute an array of activities that need to take place within that timeframe allocation.

EXPLICIT INSTRUCTION AND PRACTICE:

- Discuss the importance of prioritizing, participating in, and completing mandatory tasks and events that may not have been previously scheduled.
- Review and discuss vocabulary and terms and how they relate to time management.
- Share strategies for integrating unexpected tasks and events into pre-established routines.
- Explain how effective time management incorporates both needs and wants.
- Discuss the concept of clustering activities so they can be handled simultaneously.
- Describe how to consolidate activities within the same geographical area or route.
- Demonstrate pre-organizing tasks that require the use of multiple or complicated steps.
- Review suggested website and videos related to time management.
- Create "to-do lists" and then integrate unexpected tasks or engagements into that list and explain how the decisions on where to place the extra activities were made.

POINTS TO MAKE:

- Time management involves efficiently and effectively accomplish what has been planned.
- Priority status of doing certain required activities on schedule is based upon time-sensitivity, and if the window of opportunity is expiring.
- Activities of personal interest and importance should be given high priority on one's schedule.
- When overscheduled, one should decide which tasks can be delegated.
- Prior to taking on new tasks one should assess if he/she has resources available to complete the tasks, and if one is able, willing, and interested.
- Weekday schedules will often differ from weekend schedules.
- Some activities that can be started and left for a while to complete, can overlap with activities that require direct attention now.
- Clustering errands in sequence on a given day that are on the way to work or school helps to save time.
- When scheduling activities, always allow extra time just in case the unexpected occurs such as an earlier activity continuing longer than expected.
- Extra time may also need be scheduled when the commute requires a variable amount of travel time, and if there is a set arrival deadline to meet.
- Overscheduling oneself can result in being frustrated for not being able to accomplish everything planned within a given period of time and in a thorough fashion.
- Overscheduling oneself can contribute to increased stress, fatigue, and a sense of feeling overwhelmed.
- Schedules must sometimes be rearranged to allow room for the unexpected.
- Establishing routines can be altered as additional tasks are required and priorities require a shift of task order.
- Maintaining calendars that list scheduled activities and placing notes in strategic places help serve as reminders of activities that must take place.
- Buddy systems are helpful so those who are participating in activities together can remind one another.
- Remember to schedule some personal time to relax, rejuvenate, replenish oneself, and participate in leisure activities to balance work and business activities.
- Maintaining balance contributes to personal well-being.

INSTRUCTIONAL RESOURCES:

Suggested Website(s):

Title: 45 Tips for Staying Organized in College
Created or Produced by: Sara Laughed
Web Address: http://saralaughed.com/index.php/45-tips-for-staying-organized-in-college/
Brief Summary: A list of strategies and details to become organized

Suggested YouTube Video(s):

Title: How to Manage Time With 10 Tips that Work
Creator/Producer: Entrepreneur
Running Time: (3 minutes 27 seconds)
Format: animated illustration
Brief Summary: Demonstrates personal planning in order to manage time effectively

Title: College Survival Tips: Time Management for Beginners
Creator/Producer: MyCollegePal
Running Time: (1 minute 16 seconds)
Format: mini-lecture
Brief Summary: Includes helpful tips for remaining organized in college

LESSON #54 – PREDATORY LENDING

GOAL: Students will become acquainted with factors that make some lenders predatory lenders.

OBJECTIVES: Students will

1. Define different types of interest rates.
2. Explain credit-worthiness and how it impacts borrowing.
3. Generalize why certain lenders are considered to be predatory lenders.
4. Describe the pros and cons of using the services of predatory lenders.

SAMPLE CONTENT STANDARDS: Develop decision making skills to evaluate risks prior to taking actions

VOCABULARY & TERMS: payday loans, pawn shops, title loans, interest rate, default, collateral, risks, payment terms, repossession, balloon notes, credit-worthiness, compounded interest, variable interest

CONCEPT SUMMARY: Predatory lending activities require great risks of revenue and possessions due to exorbitant interests, fees, and high consequences for going into default.

EXPLICIT INSTRUCTION AND PRACTICE:

- Explain different types of interest rates.
- View and discuss suggested film on predatory lending.
- Review and discuss vocabulary and terms and how they relate to predatory lending.
- Predict factors that create predatory situations when money is being borrowed.
- Identify characteristics of predatory lending institutions.
- Provide examples of types of local predatory lenders.
- Explain why a person would consider borrowing money.
- Discuss the long-term adverse impact of predatory lending on borrowers.
- Hypothesize reasons why predatory lending sources are utilized.
- Discuss ways to end the cycle of using predatory lending institutions.
- Review and discuss website that addresses unfair lending practices.
- Calculate interest and fees for a set amount of money borrowed from a typical payday loan company that takes two weeks, four weeks, six weeks, and eight weeks to pay back.
- Determine how much extra money was charged in addition to the loan amounts for those calculations.

POINTS TO MAKE:

- Predatory lending consists of loaners charging excessive fees to borrowers and imposing excessive financial risk and consequences if default occurs.
- Collateral is items of financial value the borrower agrees to risk losing if money is not paid back to the lender as scheduled.
- Default is the condition of a borrower when a scheduled payment for a loan is overdue.
- Interest is the amount of extra money a borrower pays a lender in addition to the amount of the loan for the convenience of being extended a loan.
- Late fees are charges to the borrower in addition to interest and the dollar amount borrowed when scheduled payments on loans are made late.
- A fixed interest rate remains at the same percentage of the amount owed throughout the repayment period of a loan.
- A variable interest rate can change based upon the market and can go up and down throughout the repayment of a loan.
- Balloon notes are when repayment rates exceed what the borrower agreed to repay on.
- Title loans allow the lender to assume the ownership of the titled item, such as a car, if repayment agreements are not adhered to.
- Pawn shops allow the lender to gain ownership of an item that belongs to a borrower and can sell it in the event that the borrower does not meet repayment agreements. The money loaned is significantly less than the value of the pawned item.
- Rent to own stores charge excessively more over a period of time for payments of an item than what one would normally pay outright for the item and will repossess the item if payment terms are not adhered to.
- Payday loan businesses allow borrowers to borrow money with excessive interest rates that must be paid when the person's payday arrives.
- Payday loan lenders require borrowers to provide a pre-signed check that can be cashed by the lender on a certain date, or reborrowed with additional charges.
- Each time a payday loan repayment is due and can't be repaid in full, additional charges and fees are imposed on the borrower. This cycle is repeated until the entire balance plus additional fees and interest are paid.
- Borrowers sometimes are required to make major sacrifices to get out of payday loan debt including losing some of their belongings, not paying some of their bills, or doing without other personal needs.
- A person with a good credit score has a better opportunity of going through traditional means of borrowing money such as banks and credit unions.

- Traditional lending resources do not have the excessive fees and interest rates as predatory lenders do.
- A good credit score is obtained by remaining employed, showing that one pays bills on time, and not being overly indebted to several sources at the same time.
- Poor credit scores can be corrected over time by showing evidence of being able to maintain scheduled payments on money one has borrowed.
- One should avoid borrowing more money than one can manage to pay back on time.
- Maintaining a status of owing less than the maximum that specific lenders allow for the individual borrower helps to increase credit scores.

INSTRUCTIONAL RESOURCES:

Suggested Website(s):

Title: Predatory Lending: Laws & Unfair Credit Practices
Created or Produced by: Debt.org
Web Address: https://www.debt.org/credit/predatory-lending/
Brief Summary: Identifies and explains various types of predatory lending practices

Suggested YouTube Video(s):

Title: Predatory Lending Manager Speaks Out
Creator/Producer: Virginia Interfaith Center
Running Time: (6 minutes 9 seconds)
Format: a sharing of experience
Brief Summary: Predatory lending manager is transparent about how such services have a high potential to exploit customers with need

Title: The Case Against Predatory Lending
Creator/Producer: Michael Victor
Running Time: (30 minutes 17 seconds)
Format: a sharing of experience
Brief Summary: Lady discloses how she became entangled in a web of extended indebtedness to a predatory lender

LESSON #55 – SELF-ADVOCACY AND DAILY LIVING

GOAL: Students will learn more about looking out for themselves.

OBJECTIVES: Students will

1. Identify potential problems they may run into when conducting personal affairs and what can be done if problems arise in those areas.
2. Explain the main things to look for when agreeing to sign contracts.
3. Develop strategies to use in the event that they do not agree with what they will get in exchange for what they will give.
4. Identify resources to use in the event that they are unable to resolve a conflict about personal affairs, employment, or post-secondary education.
5. Develop strategies to look out for themselves instead of solely relying on others.

SAMPLE CONTENT STANDARDS: Recognize the different roles and responsibilities people play in the family, school, and community, and how those roles and responsibilities are interrelated

VOCABULARY & TERMS: second opinion, compare and contrast, risk vs. benefit, flexibility, investigate, negotiate, chain of command, bait and switch, plan of action, cutting your losses, customer service, contract, agreement, identity theft, self-incrimination, paper trail, attorney, Legal Aid Society, consultation, "reading the fine print", informed decision making, proactive

CONCEPT SUMMARY: There are many situations where one will need to play an active role in looking out for oneself. Sometimes it is a solo act, and at other times, one must know who to go to for assistance.

EXPLICIT INSTRUCTION AND PRACTICE:

- Identify business affairs of theirs that their parents/guardians handle for them and what they have done when things are not working out as planned.
- Relate situations where one must intervene to avoid receiving undesired results.
- Review and discuss vocabulary and terms that are part of this lesson and their relevance to situations that require their attention.
- Create plans of action when various needs are considered as high priorities.
- Identify additional help in the community that one can solicit when trying to get one's needs met and describe how they might be helpful.
- Describe responsibilities that students will have to begin handling for themselves.

- Review and discuss suggested website and video about developing self-advocacy practices.
- Complete the worksheet on strategies for developing self-advocacy.
- Provide examples of potential situations where one can be taken advantage of and suggest how to manage the situation to one's own advantage.
- Complete the "What Would You Do If" worksheet and discuss responses.
- Compare sample contracts and agree on which would be safe to sign.

POINTS TO MAKE:

- One should choose and pursue activities in life that bring self-fulfillment.
- Do not sign any contracts without reading through them thoroughly and understanding the content, even if this means signing them later.
- Compare the risks vs. benefits prior to making major decisions.
- When seeking advice regarding major decisions, it is helpful to talk with others who are more experienced.
- Second opinions of other knowledgeable people will provide additional perspective to make informed decisions.
- As a general rule, do not share personal information such as social security numbers and date of birth due to the risk of identity theft.
- Identity theft involves fraudulently using a person's information as if it were his/her own for transactions such as buying things and cashing checks.
- Being careless by leaving personal information where others could view it could create the same risk.
- On the job, there is a chain of command to go through when seeking to resolve conflict or situations that one considers to be unfair.
- Pursue the chain of command with one's immediate supervisor and next with the supervisor's boss if the situation is serious and has not been resolved.
- When one is a customer and there is a problem that is not being resolved appropriately ask to speak with management and express the concern.
- Customer complaints can be expressed to the manager on duty or to the customer service department of that company.
- Help from others is sometimes needed to navigate through barriers, victimization, disenfranchisement, and hardship.
- Self-advocacy involves not only looking out for oneself, but knowing when and how to reach out for help in order to get one's needs met.

- Just because a person recognizes that he/she has been mistreated or taken advantage of does not mean that this pattern has to continue.
- Self-advocacy can involve securing the assistance of the appropriate people who can provide guidance and/or connections with resources that can help resolve issues.

INSTRUCTIONAL RESOURCES:

Suggested Website(s):

Title: Definition of Self-Advocacy
Created or Produced by: Kent State
Web Address: http://www.ehhs.kent.edu/cite/CASAP/docs/SADef+tips.doc
Brief Summary: Describes and explains the elements of self-advocacy

Suggested YouTube Video(s):

Title: How to Speak Up for Yourself – Ted Talk 2016
Creator/Producer: Adam Galinsky
Running Time: (15 minutes 40 seconds)
Format: recorded speaking event
Brief Summary: Shares strategies on how to be effective when speaking up for oneself

GROWING IN SELF-ADVOCACY

Reflect upon your life and note ways that others help you to move forward with handling your personal affairs. List five examples of how others help you and then list five strategies of what you plan to do to take on these responsibilities yourself.

Example #1 of someone helping to handle your personal affairs for you:

_____

Strategy for developing independence for handling your personal affair listed in Example #1 on your own:

_____

_____

Example #2 of someone helping to handle your personal affairs for you:

_____

Strategy for developing independence for handling your personal affair listed in Example #2 on your own:

_____

_____

Example #3 of someone helping to handle your personal affairs for you:

_____

Strategy for developing independence for handling your personal affair listed in Example #3 on your own:

_____

_____

Example #4 of someone helping to handle your personal affairs for you:

_____

Strategy for developing independence for handling your personal affair listed in Example #4 on your own:

_____

_____

Example #5 of someone helping to handle your personal affairs for you:

_____

Strategy for developing independence for handling your personal affair listed in Example #5 on your own:

_____

_____

WHAT WOULD YOU DO IF.....? (A SELF-ADVOCACY EXERCISE)

Review each scenario listed below and decide upon an appropriate response to the situation. Then discuss your answers with the other classmates who also completed the assignment.

1. You are working on a job and find out that your position will be discontinued in about a month.

2. You are taking a class and believe that you were graded unfairly.

3. You have a social media account and found out that someone created a fake one and attached your name to it.

4. You bought an item at a store and discovered that it was damaged after you pulled it from the bag at home.

5. One of the bills that you received at home in the mail has charges on it for services or goods that you did not authorize.

6. You are told at your job that you will now work additional hours during a work week that were not included on your contract.

7. Your academic advisor in college creates a course schedule for you that you believe will interfere with your work schedule.

8. You must complete an assignment but did not understand the information presented in class that is needed in order to do the assignment correctly.

9. You owe for a bill that must be paid within a month and you discover that you will not have enough money to pay for it.

10. You have a roommate in college who keeps a lot of noise going on in the room late in evening which is disturbing your sleep.

11. You want a better job than the one you currently have.

12. You have a store coupon that will soon expire and the store does not have any more of the item that you wanted to purchase using that coupon.

LESSON #56 – DEVELOPING INDEPENDENCE

GOAL: Students will become more knowledgeable about assuming responsibility in stages.

OBJECTIVES: Students will

1. Recognize things in their lives that they depend upon others to manage.
2. Identify things in their lives that they plan to be able to handle for themselves after they have become adults.
3. Discuss steps or changes that lead from dependency to independence.
4. Describe multiple options for learning and practicing self-reliance.

SAMPLE CONTENT STANDARDS: Develop performance skills and knowledge to help pursue transition-related outcomes.

VOCABULARY & TERMS: informed decision, mentoring, guidance, limitations, co-dependence, responsibility, consequence, risk

CONCEPT SUMMARY: Becoming independent is a process that involves learning from others and developing personal strategies to handle one's personal affairs. Ideally, one handles affairs with less and less assistance from others.

EXPLICIT INSTRUCTION AND PRACTICE:

- Discuss some of the things that their parents did for them as younger children that they now do for themselves.
- Describe how they knew they were ready to assume some of those tasks on their own.
- Review and discuss vocabulary and terms.
- Identify additional responsibilities that have recently been acquired and challenges that were surmounted.
- Identify people who play mentoring roles in their lives and what they contribute.
- Review and discuss suggested website and videos on becoming independent.

POINTS TO MAKE:

- Independence is accomplished in stages.
- One should build independence gradually by adding complexity or frequency to tasks one is already doing.
- One person's level of independence to the best of his/her ability may differ from another person's level of independence to the best of his/her ability.

- One should be aware of his/her own personal limitations and recognize when assistance and support should be utilized to go beyond those limitations.
- Advice and support from role models should be solicited when assuming new levels of responsibility.
- When practice and repetition of responsibilities are practiced as well as mastered with the help of mentors, then more of those responsibilities can require less assistance.
- Mentors gradually ease individuals into doing more and more on their own.
- When new responsibilities arise that have greater amounts of risks associated with them, advice and counseling can help confidence and proficiency develop.
- When in doubt about how to do something, ask a reputable source.

INSTRUCTIONAL RESOURCES:

Suggested Website(s):

Title: 10 Steps to Become Independent: Learning the Basics of Essential Life Skills
Created or Produced by: Wrong Planet
Web Address: http://wrongplanet.net/10-steps-to-become-independent-learning-the-basics-of-essential-life-skills/
Brief Summary: Assuming more responsibility for one's personal affairs

Title: How to be Independent
Created or Produced by: wikiHow
Web Address: http://www.wikihow.com/Be-Independent
Brief Summary: Mindsets that help to foster independence

Suggested YouTube Video(s):

Title: My Struggle to Become Independent / College Grad
Creator/Producer: Ebony Empowerment
Running Time: (5 minutes 29 seconds)
Format: a sharing of experience
Brief Summary: Candid analysis of the speaker's journey toward living independently and the thought processes involved

LESSON #57 – BUILDING DETERMINATION

GOAL: Students will learn about strategies to help them to continue or repeat actions that lead to positive results.

OBJECTIVES: Students will

1. Create and work to accomplish goals as opposed to passively letting life go by.
2. Discuss the benefit of assessing progress toward goals and determining next steps given the amount and type of progress.
3. Provide examples of how to break up difficult or time-consuming goals into manageable and sequential smaller objectives.
4. Identify personal support groups that they can bounce ideas off of as well as receive encouragement from while trying to create and pursue personal goals.

SAMPLE CONTENT STANDARDS: Gain strategies needed to remain goal oriented in spite of obstacles.

VOCABULARY & TERMS: perseverance, goal-setting, objectives, obstacles, alternatives, limitations, realistic, plan of action, goal-oriented, support systems, accomplishment, determination

CONCEPT SUMMARY: Determination is built when one remains task oriented and seeks solutions to overcoming obstacles instead of giving up.

EXPLICIT INSTRUCTION AND PRACTICE:

- Identify areas in their lives that require overcoming obstacles without becoming discouraged.
- Label situations and obstacles that could interfere with accomplishments.
- Share if and how any obstacles may have had an impact on their thinking.
- Explain how they got past any negative thinking connected with the obstacles.
- Review and discuss vocabulary and terms as they relate to being determined.
- Discuss successful strategies to remain determined to reach personal goals.
- Reflect upon personal goals related to employment, post-secondary education, and independent living and predict possible obstacles that may be encountered in those areas.
- Break a goal down into smaller, manageable steps.
- Locate support groups that could help with goal attainment.

- Identify what will be missed if one becomes sidetracked or loses focus on goal completion.
- Identify a positive thought to focus on to break inertia or distraction and get back on track.
- Create plans of action to counteract or compensate for the possible obstacles identified.
- Review and discuss suggested website and video related to determination.
- Complete the Self Talk and Self Determination worksheet.

POINTS TO MAKE:

- A plan of action should be created for each goal that one wants to accomplish.
- There is more than one way to accomplish desired goals.
- One should consider possible obstacles and challenges that one could encounter while pursuing various goals.
- Possible plans of action to detour and/or navigate through challenges that are faced while pursuing goals should be considered ahead of time when possible.
- Failed attempts to accomplish something does not mean that it cannot be done.
- Desire plus ability plus opportunity plus resources/support systems equals a greater chance to accomplish personal goals which adds to determination.
- It is imperative that one discovers which actions are within one's power to take to increase the likelihood of success.
- The drive to be determined can be encouraged by others but comes from belief inside about possibilities when one does not give up.
- One must assess risk vs. benefits when deciding if it is in one's best interest to remain determined to fulfill certain goals, or more reasonable to replace them with alternate ones.
- As obstacles arise when seeking to accomplish goals, consider alternative paths that will still lead toward goal attainment.
- When failure arises, assess the situation to determine what actions contributed to failure and change those parts of the action plan.
- Maintain the parts of the action plan that are going well and yielding positive results.
- Surrounding oneself with support systems who not only provide encouragement, but also feedback and motivation, may improve chances for success.
- Each portion of a goal that is completed places a person closer to completing the overall goal.
- As long as a goal remains appropriate, reachable, and desirable, it is reasonable to continue moving forward towards it.

INSTRUCTIONAL RESOURCES:

Suggested Website(s):

Title: 5 Strategies for Delayed Gratification and Why You Should Do It
Created or Produced by: Brendan Baker
Web Address: http://www.startofhappiness.com/power-delayed-gratification/
Brief Summary: Addresses what things are worth waiting for and how to devise plans to reach personal goals

Suggested YouTube Video(s):

Title: Fran Kick – Fun, Good, Work
Creator/Producer: Fran Kick
Running Time: (4 minutes 9 seconds)
Format: mini-lecture
Brief Summary: Explains the interconnections between how fun, work, and becoming good at something enhance one another

Title: How to Get Determination / Become More Determined to Reach Your Goals
Creator/Producer: Rafael Eliassen
Running Time: (6 minutes 21 seconds)
Format: mini-lecture
Brief Summary: Speaker encourages self-reflection and changing strategies as needed to continue pursuing goals including aiming for smaller victories along the way

SELF-TALK AND SELF-DETERMINATION

Revisit your personal goals that you have set to prepare for life after high school in the areas of post-secondary education, employment, and independent living. Reflect upon why the goals you have set are important to you. For each goal, list what you risk if you don't follow through and continue pursuing the goal. In addition, identify two (2) positive thoughts you can focus upon to stay on track or to get you back on track if sidetracked.

PERSONAL GOAL FOR POST-SECONDARY EDUCATION:

_____

Positive self-talk statement #1 to stay on track or to get back on track with your post-secondary education goal:

_____

Positive self-talk statement #2 to stay on track or to get back on track with your post-secondary education goal:

_____

PERSONAL GOAL FOR EMPLOYMENT:

_____

Positive self-talk statement #1 to stay on track or to get back on track with your employment goal:

_____

Positive self-talk statement #2 to stay on track or to get back on track with your employment goal:

_____

PERSONAL GOAL FOR INDEPENDENT LIVING:

_____

Positive self-talk statement #1 to stay on track or to get back on track with your independent living goal:

_____

Positive self-talk statement #2 to stay on track or to get back on track with your independent living goal:

_____

LESSON #58 – BUILDING CONFIDENCE

GOAL: Students will learn more about ways to become self-assured as they face unfamiliar experiences.

OBJECTIVES: Students will

1. Identify the positive consequences of accomplishing things that they have never done before.
2. Perform a cost/benefit analysis of trying to make a new accomplishment.
3. Create safety zones for themselves in the event of falling short when trying to do something new.

SAMPLE CONTENT STANDARDS: Develop and maintain a positive self-concept

VOCABULARY & TERMS: accomplishment, practice, self-assessment, manageable steps, reflection, celebration, skill building, support system, confidence

CONCEPT SUMMARY: Practice and refining one's skills increases confidence when performing those skills or tasks.

EXPLICIT INSTRUCTION AND PRACTICE:

- Explain what self-confidence is and behaviors that are related to it.
- Identify things that are currently going on that bring a sense of self-confidence.
- Review and discuss vocabulary and terms.
- Give examples of when self-confidence is important.
- Compare and contrast the pros and cons of having vs. not having self-confidence and place responses on the worksheet that is provided.
- Discuss how lack of confidence relates to lack of knowledge or skill.
- Explain the role of support systems when seeking to build self-confidence or take on new challenges.
- Describe a competence it took a long time to develop self-confidence in, and one that took a short time.
- Review and discuss the suggested website related to building self-confidence.
- Share an instance when self-confidence was lacking but is now intact and how self-confidence evolved.
- View suggested films on building self-confidence and provide the main points that were addressed.
- List the costs, benefits, and steps to a future accomplishment.

201

POINTS TO MAKE:

- When goals are divided into smaller tasks that can be accomplished with effort and attention over short periods of time, confidence grows.
- When mistakes are made, learn and grow from them.
- Make the practice of acknowledging and celebrating success in others as well as in oneself.
- Involve oneself in tasks that one can do with ease, for the purpose of experiencing success while also tackling tasks that are more difficult.
- Confidence in oneself can be a positive source of motivation.
- Cockiness can motivate but it can also contribute to failure.
- Support systems help to build confidence by acknowledging and encouraging further success.
- Skills are built upon foundations that are in place.
- Confidence builds as fundamental sub-parts of a skill are mastered.
- When failures occur, it can either lead to loss of confidence, or renewal of confidence based upon one's ability to assess progress and adjust as needed.

INSTRUCTIONAL RESOURCES:

Suggested Website(s):

Title: Building Confidence
Created or Produced by: Skills You Need
Web Address: http://www.skillsyouneed.com/ps/confidence.html
Brief Summary: Describes a series of events that are needed to build confidence

Suggested YouTube Video(s):

Title: Believe in Yourself – Motivational Video
Creator/Producer: Ben Lionel Scott
Running Time: (4 minutes 9 seconds)
Format: motivational oration accompanied by music and video
Brief Summary: A collection of motivational thoughts that help with self-affirmation

Title: Prove Them Wrong – Motivational Video

Creator/Producer: Motivate You

Running Time: (6 minutes 19 seconds)

Format: collection of positive thoughts accompanied by video

Brief Summary: A collection of motivational thoughts to consider when pressing to overcome obstacles in life

CONFIDENCE/LACK OF CONFIDENCE PROS AND CONS

Identify some of the pros and cons of being confident vs. not being confident.

PROS OF BEING CONFIDENT	CONS OF BEING CONFIDENT
PROS OF NOT BEING CONFIDENT	**CONS OF NOT BEING CONFIDENT**

LESSON #59 – ORGANIZATION SKILLS

GOAL: Students will update their organization skills.

OBJECTIVES: Students will

1. Identify activities in their lives that require organization in order to operate efficiently.
2. Predict consequences of not remaining organized.
3. Determine ways to organize their activities to meet the needs of completing college coursework.
4. Demonstrate ways to organize their personal affairs so that they will have materials and information readily available that are needed to pay bills on time and to meet deadlines.

SAMPLE CONTENT STANDARDS: Exhibit self-management skills

VOCABULARY & TERMS: timelines, resources, prioritizing, categorizing, calendar, planner, deadlines, filing. preparation, organization

CONCEPT SUMMARY: Exercising good organization skills helps keep tasks from being overlooked or inaccessible.

EXPLICIT INSTRUCTION AND PRACTICE:

- Explain the concept "organization" and provide examples.
- Distinguish organized from disorganized and provide examples.
- Discuss and provide examples of the lesson's vocabulary and terms.
- Explain how being organized helps in the timely completion of tasks.
- Share how being disorganized wastes time that could be used to complete tasks.
- Describe the relationship between exercising organization skills and task efficiency.
- Review and discuss the suggested website and video about being organized.
- Provide examples of activities that can be sequentially clustered due to proximity, location, or type.
- Name different tasks and provide actions, such as gathering materials, that must take place prior to completing those tasks.
- Explain helpful practices to implement or continue to ensure sure that multiple assignments from different classes during a semester are submitted on time.
- Prioritize the list of tasks on the worksheet provided.
- Demonstrate methods and tools to stay organized.
- Identify areas to improve in the area of organization skills.

POINTS TO MAKE:

- Disorganization creates situations that require additional energy and time for things to be completed due to haphazard movement and lack of smooth flow.
- Calendars and other reminder tools should be used to make sure that appointments, errands, and activities are remembered and do not conflict.
- When things are routinely stored in the same place, one does not have to waste time hunting for them.
- Items related to specific activities and events should be stored together as much as possible so they can be quickly retrieved from one place and none of the items forgotten.
- Items that are needed for certain days of the week should be kept together instead of gathered from separate places prior to leaving home.
- Activities that can be clustered and flow sequentially into one another can become part of regular routines.
- Clustering helps to enforce that when one part of the routine is addressed, the other parts are also addressed.
- Supplies needed to complete a task should be acquired and assembled earlier than when they are needed so that they are available when the task needs to be completed.

INSTRUCTIONAL RESOURCES:

Suggested Website(s):

Title: 27 Great Tips to Keep Your Life Organized
Created or Produced by: Zen Habits
Web Address: https://zenhabits.net/27-great-tips-to-keep-your-life-organized/
Brief Summary: A list of strategies

Suggested YouTube Video(s):

Title: Being Organized: Organization Skills; The Importance of Organization
Creator/Producer: Career and Life Skills Lessons
Running Time: (2 minutes 27 seconds)
Format: animated illustrations accompany mini-lecture
Brief Summary: Explains the purpose and benefit of being organized

ORGANIZING AND PRIORITIZING A "TO DO LIST"

Review the "To Do List" below. Identify if the items are mandatory, optional, routine, non-routine, or time-sensitive by placing "yes" or "no" in the appropriate spaces.

	Mandatory?	Optional?	Routine?	Non-Routine?	Time-Sensitive?
Doctor's Appointment					
Going to Work					
Studying for an exam					
Shopping for a gift					
Paying bills					
Vacation					
Housework					
Socializing					
Attending a concert					
Redecorating your home					
Enrolling in classes					
Errands					
Family time					
Rest and relaxation					
Community activities					

Discuss your strategy for determining priorities with your classmates.

LESSON #60 – BEING POSITIVE THROUGH SELF-REFLECTION

GOAL: Students will maintain or regain good self-esteem.

OBJECTIVES: Students will

1. Identify admirable traits in others that they would also like to possess.
2. Pinpoint positive factors about their lives that are extremely important to them to maintain and not change, and be able to provide reasons.
3. Qualify positive things that they believe others see in them and justify why those things are important.

SAMPLE CONTENT STANDARDS: Develop strategies for maintaining positive self-image

VOCABULARY & TERMS: critique, satisfaction, goals, objectives, affirmation, improvement, regression, self-gratification, accomplishment

CONCEPT SUMMARY: It is important that one discover and acknowledge positive things about himself/herself to continue growing in those areas.

EXPLICIT INSTRUCTION AND PRACTICE:

- Supply a short list of examples of negative ways of thinking.
- Supply positive counterparts for each of those responses.
- Address the connections between the negatives and the positives as continuums.
- Review and discuss vocabulary and terms.
- Share how parts of one's journey that are viewed as unfavorable may contribute to the process of self-development.
- Review and discuss suggested website and video as a reinforcement of the lesson.
- Use concept maps as graphic organizers to dissect and clarify what positive self-reflection consists of.
- Describe how to maintain positive thoughts and outlook.
- Isolate aspect of life to maintain and describe how.
- Predict how others view them positively.
- Create lists of things that one does well or has accomplished.
- Also create a list of things to do and accomplish in the future.
- Complete and discuss the worksheet on past accomplishments and how they can propel future goals.

POINTS TO MAKE:

- Every individual has something positive to contribute to society.
- Every individual is constantly from current to future.
- Each day is an opportunity to become a better you.
- How others see you does not have to place a limit on who you are becoming.
- Positive feelings about oneself increases one's motivation to make progress.
- Negative feelings about oneself decreases one's motivation to make progress.
- Negative situations in one's life do not have to define one's destination.
- People who are secure about themselves do not need to tear others down.

INSTRUCTIONAL RESOURCES:

Suggested Website(s):

Title: 7 Ways Self-Reflection and Introspection Will Give You a Happier Life
Created or Produced by: Sara Uzer
Web Address: http://elitedaily.com/life/7-ways-self-reflection-introspection-will-give-happier-life/943309/
Brief Summary: Poses ways to maintain positive thoughts

Suggested YouTube Video(s):

Title: My Self Reflection
Creator/Producer: Morgan Pinhorn
Running Time: 3 minutes 9 seconds)
Format: music and video with captions
Brief Summary: Suggests positive ways to interpret and think of oneself

Title: Reflection / Self Care
Creator/Producer: Godzdesign
Running Time: (4 minutes 26 seconds)
Format: mini-lecture
Brief Summary: Explains how to simultaneously enjoy life and manage one's personal affairs

REMEMBERING AND PERPETUATING THE POSITIVE "YOU"

List some personal accomplishments and/or some things that you do well.

- _____

- _____

- _____

- _____

- _____

- _____

- _____

- _____

- _____

- _____

In what ways has experiencing those successes helped to prepare you for future challenges and unfamiliar situations?

_____
_____
_____
_____
_____
_____
_____
_____

LESSON #61 – KNOWING WHEN AND WHERE TO GET HELP AND/OR SUPPORT

GOAL: Students will learn how to set criteria for themselves that they will use to help determine and use others for intervention.

OBJECTIVES: Students will

1. Locate key resources in their communities where they can get assistance pertaining to living independently there.
2. Identify things that they normally would do for themselves that have the possibility of evolving into situations where they would need the help of others.
3. Determine types of assistance that can connect specific people and resources in their family and community.
4. Describe the consequences of not getting assistance in important scenarios that have gone beyond their control to manage on their own.

SAMPLE CONTENT STANDARDS: Develop ways of coping e during life-changing events

VOCABULARY & TERMS: social services, clinics, food banks, legal aid society, political representative, place of worship, law enforcement agencies, emergency medical technicians, utility companies, landlord, social worker, professional counselor

CONCEPT SUMMARY: While it is important to live as independently as possible, one should be aware of how and where to seek assistance when needed.

EXPLICIT INSTRUCTION AND PRACTICE:

- Discuss the personal implications of independence.
- Locate resources in the community that are sometimes needed to meet personal goals.
- Identify types of services that can be accessed for assistance in community living.
- Interview classmates and instructors in regard to specific places where community support systems are located. Summarize findings.
- Describe circumstances
- Predict consequences for not using available resources during crisis situations.
- Review and discuss the suggested websites and videos that address seeking assistance.
- Complete the worksheet on knowing when and where to get help; discuss and revise responses.

.POINTS TO MAKE:

- Independence not only includes what can be done for oneself, but also includes seeking the assistance of others who provide empowerment to care for oneself.
- When unsure of what to do, one should seek the counsel, guidance, and assistance of others.
- It is better to seek assistance when needed as opposed to passively awaiting outcomes, which could be negative.
- Level of urgency and potential risk along with the ability to resolve situations on one's own should help to dictate if one should involve others in times of crisis.
- Becoming familiar with resources within one's community should occur ahead of time, so that one will know of options he/she can utilize if the need arises.
- One should assess the consequences of unresolved problems when deciding to continue to work on situations himself/herself or to seek intervention.
- It is okay to not know how to solve every situation, but when significant consequences are involved, others may be able to help contribute to resolution.

INSTRUCTIONAL RESOURCES:

Suggested Website(s):

Title: 5 Reasons You Must Learn to Ask for Help
Created or Produced by: Minda Zetlin
Web Address: http://www.inc.com/minda-zetlin/5-reasons-you-must-learn-to-ask-for-help.html
Brief Summary: Describe benefits of seeking assistance to promote one's personal goals

Title: How to Ask for Help – 12 Steps (with pictures)
Created or Produced by: wikiHow
Web Address: http://www.wikihow.com/Ask-for-Help
Brief Summary: Depicts methods of reaching out to other people for help

Suggested YouTube Video(s):

Title: The Importance of Asking Others for Help
Creator/Producer: plantriotic
Running Time: (9 minutes 58 seconds)
Format: mini-lecture
Brief Summary: Explains why networking with others is helps provide insight to goal attainment

Title: How to get Great Customer Service
Creator/Producer: Bill Crawford
Running Time: (7 minutes 39 seconds)
Format: mini-lecture
Brief Summary: Shares strategies for problem resolution as a customer including examples of situations and corresponding actions

KNOWING WHEN OR WHERE TO GET HELP AND/OR SUPPORT

Respond and later share your responses to the scenarios below along with why you chose the solution that you did. (There is more than one correct answer.)

SCENARIO #1 – You need to get to your job and find out that your car won't start.
RESPONSE: _____
WHY: _____

SCENARIO #2 – You ordered and paid for an item online, gut it never arrived.
RESPONSE: _____
WHY: _____

SCENARIO #3 – Your apartment building is being sold and the new owner wants all of the tenants to move.
RESPONSE: _____
WHY; _____

SCENARIO #4 – You have gone to the doctor, a new medicine has been prescribed, but are feeling light-headed after taking your first dose.
RESPONSE: _____
WHY: _____

SCENARIO #5 – You have left your home for the weekend and when you return and open the door, there is a very strong smell of gas.
RESPONSE: _____
WHY: _____

SCENARIO #6 – You are in college and are not being provided the disability accommodations that have been agreed upon for one of your classes.
RESPONSE: _____
WHY: _____

SCENARIO #7 - You were getting ready to buy something and discovered that your ATM card was missing. You checked at home and other places and could not find it.
RESPONSE: _____
WHY: _____

LESSON #62 – STRESS MANAGEMENT

GOAL: Students will learn more about stress, its effects, and ways of dealing with it.

OBJECTIVES: Students will

1. Prepare plans of action for themselves if they experience an excessive amount of stress.
2. Identify negative ways to deal with stress along with possible positive alternative actions.
3. Determine sources of stress and ways to minimize negative effects.
4. Predict some of the effects of excessive stress over extended periods of time.

SAMPLE CONTENT STANDARDS: Develop coping skills to use during life change events

VOCABULARY & TERMS: stress, stress outlet, stressor, trigger, breaking point, displaced aggression, counseling, tolerance, venting, redirecting negative energy, relaxation techniques

CONCEPT SUMMARY: People in general experience different levels of stress. However, it is important that one employ coping skills when stress occurs to help limit the negative effects upon one's health, behavior, or personal image.

EXPLICIT INSTRUCTION AND PRACTICE:

- Discuss beliefs about what stress consists of.
- Review vocabulary and terms and explain how each of these are related to stress.
- Discuss strategies for reducing stress and results achieved.
- Review and discuss the suggested website and video on stress management.
- Take one of the Life Change Stress Tests found online for personal reference but keep the results private.
- Describe sources of stress and how to eliminate them.
- Predict consequences of high stress over extended periods of time.
- Share takeaway information gained from the lesson.

POINTS TO MAKE:

- Stress has both negative and positive effects.
- Positives stress places one in a state of readiness and engagement.
- Negative stress can create disengagement and lack of focus,
- It helps to recognize and accept the things that one cannot change and expend effort and energy toward things that one can change, manage, and improve.
- Sustained negative stress without utilizing outlets can cause illness and emotional instability.

- Outlets to release stress include venting, exercise, recreation, meditation, and redirection of the negative energy toward positive activities.
- When one is aware of triggers that induce heightened personal stress, sometimes one can avoid those situations.
- One can mentally deflect some of the potential psychological impact of stressors by focusing upon and participating in positive things rather than focusing upon triggers.
- Triggers are events that occur that cause stressful feelings and stress-related responses.
- Events that may be stressful for one person may not be stressful for another person and are based upon personal interpretation, relevance, and impact.
- The number and intensity of stressful events that occurs over an extended time period can increase the overall stress level of the person experiencing them.
- Professional help or counseling is sometimes needed when stress levels are reaching the point in one's life of being mentally consuming and destructive.

INSTRUCTIONAL RESOURCES:

Suggested Website(s):

Title: Stress Management: Tips for Better Management of Your Stress
Created or Produced by: Lawrence Robinson, Melinda Smith, & Robert Segal
Web Address: http://www.helpguide.org/articles/stress/stress-management.htm
Brief Summary: A collection of strategies to use when facing situations that could potentially cause stress

Suggested YouTube Video(s):

Title: Stress Management Strategies: Ways to Unwind
Creator/Producer: watchwellcast
Running Time: (5 minutes 5 seconds)
Format: animated illustrations
Brief Summary: Explains some of the effects of stress and strategies to help relieve or decrease the impact of stress

LESSON #63 – AVOIDING SCAMS

GOAL: Students will correctly handle or avoid offers or requests that may be scams.

OBJECTIVES: Students will

1. Describe what a scam is.
2. Identify common scams and why they are considered to be scams.
3. Identify some steps that can be taken in the event of being scammed.
4. Identify strategies to protect their identities and money when entering business transactions.

SAMPLE CONTENT STANDARDS: Develop self-advocacy strategies

VOCABULARY & TERMS: bait and switch, scam, identity theft, reputable business, personal liability, paper/electronic trail, chargeback, forgery, passwords, verification, "too good to be true"

CONCEPT SUMMARY: Scams are deceitful practices where people take advantage of other people by acquiring the victims' assets and funds for their own benefit without permission. It is important to be aware and cautious when entering transactions with those who are not considered as reputable or when background information on them is unavailable.

EXPLICIT INSTRUCTION AND PRACTICE:

- Discuss what is known about scams.
- Review and discuss vocabulary and terms and provide examples.
- Explain the difference between legitimate vs. illegitimate transactions.
- Discuss the consequences of being scammed.
- Review and discuss suggested websites and videos on scams, fraud, and identity theft.
- Collect feedback on what was learned from the online media sites and how information from them will be reflected in personal practices.
- Identify some "red flags" in how a person or group trying to run a scam may make an introduction.
- Share some sources of assistance in the event that a scam has occurred.
- Describe how to protect identity and assets.

POINTS TO MAKE:

- If it is required that a payment be made in order to receive a prize or award, it is questionable.
- Computer passwords should not be shared with others.

- Extreme caution should be exercised when making an up-front payment for work someone will complete on your behalf.
- Research businesses/contractors to find out how reputable they may be before investing your money in services from them.
- Written contracts where both parties agree on services, products involved, cost, and timelines should be created, dated, and signed prior to any work being done.
- Always read the entire service/work contract and don't sign unless it is fully understood and agreed upon.
- Keep copies of original dated and signed agreements in case you need to use them for verification in the future.
- Beware of people soliciting payment for transactions that can't be verified through official sources of the affiliated company/agency.
- Do not give personal information such as social security numbers and dates of birth to people who may misuse this information.
- Make sure that all agreements have been met before making final payments for goods and services.
- Verify dollar amount on transactions when using credit/debit cards before swiping cards or entering pin numbers for payment.
- Do not place personal/private information on unsecured websites.
- If in doubt, check it out and investigate your options before committing personal assets to offers.

INSTRUCTIONAL RESOURCES:

Suggested Website(s):

Title: Consumer Information – 10 Things You Can Do to Avoid Fraud
Created or Produced by: Federal Trade Commission
Web Address: https://www.consumer.ftc.gov/articles/0060-10-things-you-can-do-avoid-fraud
Brief Summary: Provides strategies to help avoid the risk of being scammed

Title: 15 Ways to Prevent Online Fraud and Identity Theft
Created or Produced by: Jason Cabler
Web Address: https://www.cfinancialfreedom.com/15-ways-prevent-online-fraud-identity-theft/
Brief Summary: Identifies situations to avoid being scammed

Title: Top Tips to Avoid Online Scams
Created or Produced by: Citizens Advice Organization
Web Address: https://www.citizensadviceorg.uk/consumer/scams/scams/common-scams/top-tips-tips-toavoid-onlinescams
Brief Summary: Explains ways to avoid others from stealing passwords, account information, and other confidential information online

<u>**Suggested YouTube Video(s):**</u>

Title: Top 10 Internet Scams You Should Avoid
Creator/Producer: Most Amazing Top 10
Running Time: (8 minutes 34 seconds)
Format: mini-lecture
Brief Summary: Speaker provides examples of how people are scammed over the internet and strategies for avoiding being victimized in that way

LESSON #64 – CREATING, REVIEWING, AND REVISING PERSONAL GOALS

GOAL: Students will identify what should be considered when creating and pursuing personal goals.

OBJECTIVES: Students will

1. Articulate some major accomplishments to achieve in the areas of as of employment, post-secondary education, and independent living.
2. Identify sequential steps that need to take place to move from present achievements to anticipated goals.
3. Identify alternative goals if they change their mind in regard to goals they already created for themselves; describe major reasons to change.
4. Provide examples of how some personal plans may have an impact on other personal plans.

SAMPLE CONTENT STANDARDS: Creating and pursuing personal life plans

VOCABULARY & TERMS: goals, objectives, checkpoints, resources, aptitude, support systems, priority, alternative, deterrent, delayed gratification, confirmation, personal fulfillment, personal affirmation

CONCEPT SUMMARY: Goals are not set in stone and can evolve as one's situations, access, and interests change. However, one should weigh the pros and cons of remaining on track or changing one's path.

EXPLICIT INSTRUCTION AND PRACTICE:

- Indicate personal goals in the areas of independent living, employment, and post-secondary education and sequenced steps to achieve them.
- Review and discuss vocabulary and terms and how they relate to personal goal setting.
- Explain the need for short-term goals as one moves toward goal attainment.
- Explain how to create intermediate goals.
- Discuss reasons for pursuing, maintaining, amending, or abandoning goals after completing the related worksheet.
- Review and discuss suggested website on establishing priorities.
- Review and discuss suggested video on the relationship between one's dreams and goals.
- Review processes required to create and attain goals.
- Discuss how some personal plans may influence others.

POINTS TO MAKE:

- Goals are outcomes that people desire to work toward accomplishing.
- Objectives are smaller steps that lead toward meeting goals.
- Some sets of circumstances lead to making changes in what goals to pursue.
- While pursuing goals, one should assess if the intermediate steps are being accomplished.
- If goals are not being accomplished, one should determine methods and strategies to change.
- One should periodically assess if the goals being considered are still reasonable given the available resources, ability, and support systems.
- Possible obstacles should be acknowledged along with plans of action to overcome obstacles.
- Difficulties and challenges sometimes require alternative methods of goal attainment as opposed to goal abandonment.
- Support systems are those people and/or services that are in place to assist in meeting personal goals.
- Delayed gratification is when people do not immediately receive what they desire, but are content with getting those things after waiting.
- Personal affirmation is when a person still believes in his/her worth.
- Personal fulfillment is when a person is feels content about his/her state of being and accomplishment.
- A priority is that activity or task that is considered most important to complete in comparison to other activities or tasks.
- Appropriate reasons to change goals are:
    (1) The goals are no longer desirable,
    (2) Not enough progress is being made within a reasonable amount of time,
    (3) Not enough progress is being made with an amount of time,
    (4) Alternative potentially – fulfilling goals are more easily obtainable, and
    (5) Resources are no longer accessible that are needed to help fulfill the goals.

INSTRUCTIONAL RESOURCES:

Suggested Website(s):

Title: Quotes About Priorities
Created or Produced by: Goodreads
Web Address: http://www.goodreads.com/quotes/tag/priorities
Brief Summary: Quotes from various publicly known figures about personal priorities

Suggested YouTube Video(s):

Title: Do You Dare to Dream? – Goals – Aspirations – Comfort Zone
Creator/Producer: Tom Bloom (inKNOWation)
Running Time: (7 minutes 34 seconds)
Format: mini-lecture with drawn illustrations
Brief Summary: Addresses thought processes that are involved in accomplishing goals outside of one's comfort zone and how to move forward

CHANGING PERSONAL PLANS AS NEEDED

Identify factors related to your major personal goals that would influence you to: (1) continue current path, (2) revise the current path, or (3) switch to a different goal.

MAJOR POST-SECONDARY GOAL:

_____

What factors would influence you to continue pursuing this goal?

_____

What factors would influence you to revise your path toward pursuing this goal?

_____

What factors would influence you toward changing your goal to another goal?

_____

_____

MAJOR EMPLOYMENT GOAL:

_____

What factors would influence you to continue pursuing this goal?

_____

What factors would influence you to revise your path toward pursuing this goal?

_____

What factors would influence you toward changing your goal to another goal?

_____

_____

MAJOR INDEPENDENT LIVING GOAL:

_____

What factors would influence you to continue pursuing this goal?

_____

What factors would influence you to revise your path toward pursuing this goal?

_____

What factors would influence you toward changing your goal to another goal?

_____

_____

LESSON #65 – DECISION MAKING BASED UPON HIERARCHY OF NEEDS

GOAL: Students will prioritize needs based on available resources and time.

OBJECTIVES: Students will

1. Describe the difference between needs and wants and how they relate to one another.
2. Identify situations that will cause people to temporarily shift the order of working toward getting things completed; predict and how such decisions are made.
3. Explain why some needs are more important than others.
4. Discuss factors that should be considered e made when other people are involved in helping to meet their needs.

SAMPLE CONTENT STANDARDS: Engage in making choices that are safe and healthy

VOCABULARY & TERMS: satisfaction, gratification, companionship, comfort, security, safety, affordable, compromise, healthy, consequences, accomplishment, personal assessment

CONCEPT SUMMARY: One must differentiate between wants and needs when prioritizing one's actions with limited resources and time. However, there are scenarios where wants help to define how needs are met.

EXPLICIT INSTRUCTION AND PRACTICE:

- Distinguish the differences between wants and needs.
- Create a list of personal wants and a list of personal needs and compare the two while looking for overlap.
- Review and discuss vocabulary and terms and how they relate to wants and needs.
- Observe, interpret, and explain the Maslow's Hierarchy of Needs illustration provided.
- Identify conditions that allow wants to be fulfilled and those that may require a shift in priorities..
- Imagine circumstances that may require the fulfilling of wants to be delayed or abandoned.
- Review and discuss the suggested website and video that addresses hierarchy of needs.
- Revisit the Hierarchy of Needs chart and identify examples of things in their lives that help to fulfill the needs indicated.
- Explain why one need may not be as important as another need and why the needs they supplied fit within various categories on the Hierarchy of Needs pyramid.

POINTS TO MAKE:

- Some personal needs are more critical than other personal needs.
- How one meets one's personal needs depends upon finances and resources available, personal taste, conflicts of interest, risks involved, and others who are needed to help.
- The amounts available to spend on meeting personal needs does not increase or decrease the value of the person.
- Needs are not limited to things that are tangible.
- Physiological needs; safety needs; the needs for love and belonging, esteem, and self-actualization were researched and listed in order of importance in a study conducted by Maslow.
- Personal experiences may shape how the attainment of having needs are met.
- One must find ways to validate oneself including input from others who help to provide the validation.
- People are individuals and must discover what meets their distinct needs and what they must do to have a sense of being fulfilled in life.
- Fulfillment differs from person to person.
- It is important to find ways to also have some of our wants taken care of for the purpose of personal fulfillment.
- Choices are required when deciding which wants to pursue when limited resources and opportunities are available.

INSTRUCTIONAL RESOURCES:

Suggested Website(s):

Title: Printable Maslow's Hierarchy of Needs Chart/ Maslow's Pyramid Design
Created or Produced by: Tim's Printables
Web Address: http://www.timvandevall.com/printable-maslows-hierarchy-of-needs-chart/
Brief Summary: A visual model of Maslow's Hierarchy of Needs to use as a reference

Suggested YouTube Video(s):

Title: Hierarchy of Needs in Ratatoville
Creator/Producer: Lana Loutfy
Running Time: (7 minutes 13 seconds)
Format: animated examples of illustrations
Brief Summary: Addresses what basic needs people seek to be fulfilled and how some are even more basic than others

DECISION MAKING BASED UPON HIERARCHY OF NEEDS

Some of our wants actually become needs in many cases according to a psychologist named Maslow. Identify how these types of needs that help to provide fulfillment are either being met or sought after in your lives.

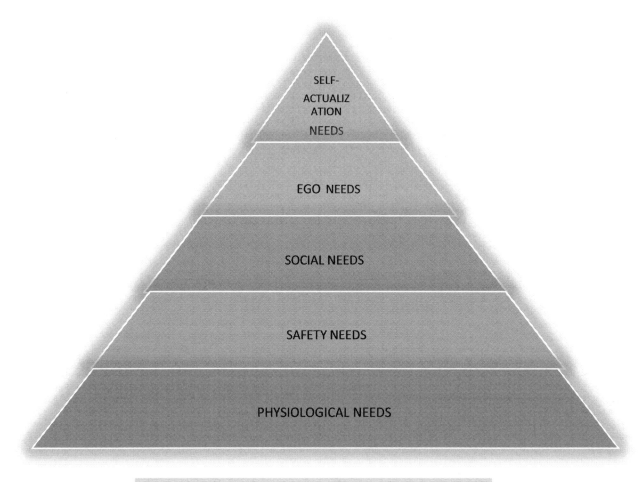

Maslow's Hierarchy of Needs Theory Concepts (1943)

Example of a need met or sought after in your life that help to fulfill self-actualization

_____

Example of a need met or sought after in your life that help to fulfill ego needs

_____

Example of a need met or sought after in your life that help to fulfill social needs

_____

Example of a need met or sought after in your life that help to fulfill safety needs

_____

Example of a need met or sought after in your life that helps to fulfill physiological (body) needs

LESSON #66 – MAINTAINING PERSONAL SAFETY

GOAL: Students will employ good practices for staying safe while living in the community.

OBJECTIVES: Students will

1. Articulate the importance of buddy systems.
2. Explain how to minimize personal risks when traveling to and from destinations.
3. Describe safety practices related to medication and other safety hazards at home.

SAMPLE CONTENT STANDARDS: Develop strategies to maintain personal safety

VOCABULARY & TERMS: expiration dates, drug interactions, medical emergency, hazard, risk-taking behavior, isolated, buddy system, attentiveness, avoidance, escape plan, accident waiting to happen, warning labels, traffic regulations

CONCEPT SUMMARY: Practicing safety on a regular basis will decrease incidents related to carelessness.

EXPLICIT INSTRUCTION AND PRACTICE:

- Discuss what the word "safety" means.
- Give examples of how safety can be practiced.
- Relate what personal practices result in staying safe.
- Record personal practices and organize them according to the type of safety practices the examples include.
- Recommend ways to lower personal risk while traveling.
- Review and discuss vocabulary and terms and how they relate to safety.
- Review and discuss the suggested website and videos about personal safety.
- Provide actions to remain safe and reasons behind those actions on the provided worksheet.

POINTS TO MAKE:

- Buddy systems rely on people looking out for and being accountable to one another.
- It is important to read the fine print on any prescriptions that one is taking to avoid adverse reactions.
- Medications taken in excess of what is prescribed can create dangers for one's body and override the potential benefits.
- Some medication combinations should be avoided because of potential negative consequences to one's body.

- Instruction sheets that are packaged with them.
- One should be aware of procedures to follow in the event of personal medical emergencies or acute illness.
- Caution should be exercised when walking to and from destinations by remaining aware of one's surroundings and avoiding areas that appear unsafe.
- One should make himself/herself aware of escape plans in the event that buildings must be evacuated due to situations becoming unsafe.
- Tools should be stored and handled with care in order to avoid accidents and injuries that may be caused by improper use and hazardous storage.
- When driving, careless behavior can cause injury or death to self and others.
- Traffic laws help citizens regulate themselves as drivers and pedestrians so that safety can be maintained and accidents can be avoided.
- Avoid isolated areas and streets because they can place individuals at greater risk for becoming crime victims.
- The appropriate first responders should be summoned if at all possible, when health and safety conditions are becoming life threatening.
- Everyone has the responsibility of doing his/her part to remain as safe as possible.

INSTRUCTIONAL RESOURCES:

Suggested Website(s):

Title: Personal Safety Tips
Created or Produced by: Montclair Safety & Improvement Council
Web Address: http://www.montclairsic.org/personalsafety.htm
Brief Summary: List of safety practices for different situations one may encounter

Suggested YouTube Video(s):

Title: Student Personal Safety and Security Video
Creator/Producer: RIT Production Services
Running Time: (4 minutes 24 seconds)
Format: mini-lecture
Brief Summary: Addresses good practices that help people to remain safe in college

Title: How to Stay Safe on the Street
Creator/Producer: Videojug
Running Time: (2 minutes 9 seconds)
Format: mini-lecture
Brief Summary: Addresses good personal safety practices to use when going down the street

STAYING SAFE

Various scenarios are listed below. You are to provide actions to remain safe.

1. **You bought some food at a restaurant but could not eat it all and brought the rest home.**

   _____

   _____

2. **You are alone, your car breaks down, and it is dark outside.**

   _____

   _____

3. **You have become ill and someone offers you medicine that he/she says will help you to feel better.**

   _____

   _____

4. **You have just gotten off the bus and have to walk home by yourself late at night.**

   _____

   _____

5. **Someone knocks on your door and asks to come in to use your phone to get a ride home.**

   _____

   _____

6. **You are trying to fry some food while you are sleepy.**

   _____

   _____

7. **You are out at a party and leave what you are drinking on the table for several minutes while you go to talk with someone across the room.**

   _____

   _____

8. **You are tired and a person you don't know offers you a ride so that you will not have to wait on the bus.**

   _____

   _____

9. **A person comes by your house and says that he works for the electric company and needs to come in and check your meter.**

   _____

   _____

10. **You are almost late for work and the stoplights are slowing you down as you drive the street.**

    _____

    _____

LESSON #67 – PERSONAL ACCOUNTABILITY

GOAL: Students will recognize the elements of personal accountability

OBJECTIVES: Students will

1. Identify things that they will assume personal responsibility for as adults.
2. Describe what they will do in the event that they have become responsible for things that they are not sure how to do or manage.
3. Explain what they will do in the event that they have taken responsibility for more things than they can properly manage.
4. Describe how accountability and time management help when handling responsibilities.

SAMPLE CONTENT STANDARDS: Recognize how roles and responsibilities relate

VOCABULARY & TERMS: time management, responsibility, follow-through, follow-up, cutting your losses, delegation, commitment, setting limits, personal limitations, reliability

CONCEPT SUMMARY: It is one's own responsibility to handle personal affairs as best as possible which may or may not include relying on others.

EXPLICIT INSTRUCTION AND PRACTICE:

- Discuss the gradual transition into adulthood and how responsibilities increase.
- Reflect on the past four years and identify some of the responsibilities that had been taken on for the first time and how they were assumed.
- Review and discuss vocabulary and terms and how they relate to assuming responsibility.
- Discuss systems of checks and balances as well as strategies for honoring one's own increasing accountability.
- Review and discuss suggested website and videos on personal accountability.
- Identify personal accountability partners and expectations of them.
- Reflect upon personal goals and how personal responsibility relates to achieving them.
- Role play how to disengage from or delegate responsibilities that are too difficult to manage.

POINTS TO MAKE:

- Part of becoming an adult includes assuming more responsibility for oneself.
- Parents and other adults can serve as role models to follow.
- Becoming independent is a gradual process.

- As adults gain wisdom they avoid repeating mistakes.
- Prior to one agreeing to roles he/she will assume, it is important that physical limitations, availability, task competence, and patience are considered.
- Pursuit of goals should be based upon personal desires and ambitions instead of the desires and ambitions of others.
- Do what will bring results that are personally desired, because you are the one who has to live with and be content with the impact of decisions and actions you take.
- Practicing good time management frees up some time that could be wasted and focuses effort on accomplishing day's objectives.
- The level of independence practiced depends upon one's ability, experience, confidence, and resources.
- Requesting help when needed is not a sign of weakness but a demonstration of engaging various support systems when appropriate.
- When working with others to get things accomplished, it is important that one does his/her part to avoid group failure and/or frustration.
- When each member fulfills his/her responsibilities within the group, the group is collectively gratified.

INSTRUCTIONAL RESOURCES:

Suggested Website(s):

Title: Taking One for the Team: 6 Tips On Developing Personal Accountability
Created or Produced by: Tedd Baldomaro
Web Address: http://tweakyourbiz.com/management/2013/11/23/taking-one-team-6-tips-developing-personal-accountability/
Brief Summary: Discusses responsibility through holding oneself accountable in the workplace

Suggested YouTube Video(s):

Title: Personal Accountability.wmv
Creator/Producer: Jeff Seren
Running Time: (1 minute 2 seconds)
Format: skit
Brief Summary: Demonstrates the importance of personal actions when one needs results

Title: Believe TV – The Power of Personal Accountability
Creator/Producer: Chad Hymas
Running Time: (2 minutes 57 seconds)
Format: mini-lecture
Brief Summary: Shares the reasons why expectations should be established and held for self and others when seeking to accomplish goals

Title: Daily Habits of Successful People: It's All About Routine
Creator/Producer: Brian Tracy
Running Time: (5 minutes 17 seconds)
Format: provision of strategies
Brief Summary: Explains the habits that contribute to success or failure and encourages one to recognize when habits need to change

LESSON #68 – ANGER MANAGEMENT

GOAL: Students will appropriately handle situations that cause anger while minimizing some of the consequences related to responding in nonproductive ways.

OBJECTIVES: Students will

1. Identify behaviors that signal when anger is not properly being managed.
2. Explain why some people become angrier about certain situations than other people.
3. Describe support systems and activities that don't harm others and will allow them to release stress related to anger.
4. Describe the importance of verifying their interpretations of actions or events to determine if anger being experienced is warranted.

SAMPLE CONTENT STANDARDS: Demonstrate positive interactions between self and others; develop coping skills when experiencing frustration

VOCABULARY & TERMS: displaced aggression, rage, conflict resolution, distorted reality, disproportionate response, counseling, problem solving skills, mediation, time-out, frustration outlet, boiling point,

CONCEPT SUMMARY: It is normal to become angry when one feels he/she is not being treated properly or if outcomes result that are unfavorable. However, we have the responsibility to ourselves and society to do no harm to ourselves or to others when angry.

EXPLICIT INSTRUCTION AND PRACTICE:

- Discuss situations that have the ability to provoke anger.
- Explain and define anger and its causes.
- Review and discuss vocabulary and terms related to anger and anger management.
- Address the idea of anger unrestrained vs. anger managed along with related consequences, both positive and negative.
- Describe the pros and cons of anger while also providing strategies to help manage it while delivering the lesson points to make.
- Review suggested website and videos and discuss implications.
- Create collages of pictures cut from magazines that represent activities that can help to alleviate stress such as that caused by anger.
- Explain how to appropriately and inappropriately manage anger.
- Describe personal tolerance in anger-provoking situations.

POINTS TO MAKE:

- Anger management does not mean that one avoids getting angry. It means one controls responses to anger in ways that avoid negative consequence.
- A person can be angry but exercise caution in how she/he reacts and resolves conflict.
- Lack of anger management can cause problems in school, at work, as well as in the community.
- If intense anger is extended over long periods of time, it can contribute to health consequences related to the mind and body and may require professional intervention.
- Temporarily remove oneself from what or who is causing the anger so that personal spontaneous responses don't make the problem worse.
- Stepping back and looking at situations objectively may improve positive actions that can bring about resolution.
- Community, school, and work resources may need to be engaged to speed up resolution of the problem.
- Sometimes anger is triggered by personal perception instead of reality.
- It is important to get clarification and understanding regarding facts that are related to the issue that one has become angry about to see if anger is merited.
- Be cautious in your reactions to anger so that you do not react by directing anger to those who are not responsible for the conflict.
- Anger due to mistreatment can constructively lead to positive solutions of the conflict.
- Interpretation of situations vary from person to person and may result in different people experiencing different intensity levels of anger related to the same situation.

INSTRUCTIONAL RESOURCES:

Suggested Website(s):

Title: Anger Management: 10 Tips to Tame Your Temper
Created or Produced by: Mayo Clinic Staff
Web Address: http://www.mayoclinic.org/healthy-lifestyle/adult-health/in-depth/anger-management/art-20045434
Brief Summary: List of strategies to control temper

Suggested YouTube Video(s):

Title: Anger Management Techniques
Creator/Producer: WatchWellCast
Running Time: (4 minutes 9 seconds)
Format: strategies with drawn illustrations
Brief Summary: Provides strategies to not only recognize anger but also to dissipate it in non-harmful ways

Title: How to Control Anger – The Shocking Truth Behind Your Anger Problems
Creator/Producer: Leo-Actualized
Running Time: (19 minutes 8 seconds)
Format: mini-lecture
Brief Summary: Shares the ill effects of maintaining states of anger and how the sources of it should be dealt with productively

Title: How to Control Your Temper with the Magic Pause
Creator/Producer: Houdini
Running Time: (3 minutes 21 seconds)
Format: mini-lecture
Brief Summary: Shares strategies of thinking through a situation before reacting to avoid additional problems.

LESSON #69 – COMMUNITY AND CIVIC ENGAGEMENT

GOAL: Students will learn about how and why to be involved in the communities in which they live.

OBJECTIVES: Students will

1. Explain the purpose of being registered voters.
2. Identify local organizations and services that work toward maintaining and/or improving their communities.
3. Describe the ways that they can learn more about issues and/or people that are on the voting ballot before going to the polls to vote.
4. Fill out voter registration cards that will be submitted onsite if they desire to register.

SAMPLE CONTENT STANDARDS: Operate as contributing members of communities

VOCABULARY & TERMS: election, precinct, ward, block unit, alderman, committeeman, ballot, voter registration, voter fraud, neighborhood, absentee voting, voice, petition, protest, boycott, nuisance, bond issue, amendment, community center

CONCEPT SUMMARY: There are various ways to get involved in community activities and outcomes including exercising one's right as a citizen to vote.

EXPLICIT INSTRUCTION AND PRACTICE:

- Provide the writing prompts, "Why do people go to the polls to vote? and Why do people not go to the polls to vote." Discuss responses.
- Provide examples of the vocabulary and terms introduced.
- Share ways to get involved in what happens to or with one's fellow neighbors and citizens, community, city, state, and country.
- View and discuss suggested website and videos about civic engagement.
- Review online sources including maps that divide one's city/community into voting precincts and wards that determine how citizens are grouped for voting.
- Identify personal precincts and wards based upon one's address.
- Discuss ways to learn more about candidates and issues.
- Complete voter registration cards or identify places to get registered in the event that students desire to and or eligible to become registered voters.
- Check voter registration cards for accuracy and completeness prior to submitting them to the local office that coordinates and oversees voting..
- Work in teams to summarize major lesson concepts and ideas.

POINTS TO MAKE:

- Registered voters go to the polls to elect political officials.
- Voting is a way to express a collective voice.
- Voting also involves making collective choices on amendments, bond issues, taxes, jurisdictional laws, tax-funded expenditures, and other local, state and federal issues.
- Registered voters have specific polling places assigned to them as determined by precincts and wards where voters reside.
- Forms of voting other than reporting to the polls on voting days include absentee voting and early voting.
- Each vote at the polls has the same weight and counts as one vote regardless of one's status.
- Voting is one way that citizens practice using a collective voice in society and is designed to influence government related decisions.
- Voters can choose to agree or disagree with proposed changes and the majority rules.
- People choose political officials to represent their stances on various issues who will conduct official business in ways that hopefully meet citizens' best interests.
- Other ways to participate civically are to participate in block units, town hall meetings, and special interest groups related to neighborhoods.
- Writing to political officials, boycotting businesses, marching in demonstrations, creating and signing petitions are additional ways to collectively voice concerns.
- Maintaining the appearance of one's community, reporting safety issues, and participating in community events are considered community engagement activities..

INSTRUCTIONAL RESOURCES:

Suggested Website(s):

Title: Voter Identification Requirements / Voter ID Laws
Created or Produced by: National Conference of State Legislators
Web Address: http://www.ncsl.org/research/elections-and-campaigns/voter-id.aspx
Brief Summary: State by state breakdown of voter requirements

<u>Suggested YouTube Video(s):</u>

Title: History of Voting
Creator/Producer: Rock the Vote
Running Time: (3 minutes 36 seconds)
Format: animated
Brief Summary: Animated illustration and explanation of how and when different populations of people in the United States were granted the right to vote and some of the obstacles they faced

Title: Unpacking "Civic Engagement"
Creator/Producer: EngageGPC
Running Time: (4 minutes 56 seconds)
Format: mini-lecture with drawn illustrations
Brief Summary: Explains how one's actions can contribute to the success of a community

LESSON #70 – MAINTAINING HEALTHY LIFESTYLES

GOAL: Students will learn more about staying healthy.

OBJECTIVES: Students will

1. Describe the importance of maintaining good health and hygiene.
2. Identify major routine health screenings, their purposes, and why they are important.
3. Explain how excessive prolonged stress has an impact on a person's physical and mental well-being.
4. Justify the purpose of having a healthy balance of work and leisure.

SAMPLE CONTENT STANDARDS: Utilize knowledge needed to remain healthy and safe

VOCABULARY & TERMS: medical screening, stress management, preventive care, substance abuse, hygiene, nutrition, abusive relationships, leisure, pleasure, dental health, genetic predisposition, health maintenance

CONCEPT SUMMARY: Remaining healthy involves making healthy choices as well as monitoring one's personal health and making changes as needed.

EXPLICIT INSTRUCTION AND PRACTICE:

- Describe how to maintain as healthy of an existence as possible.
- Identify some of the consequences due to certain unhealthy practices.
- Review and discuss vocabulary and terms.
- Explain why it is important for individuals to assume responsibility for remaining as healthy as possible.
- Address the importance of regular health and dental checkups and screening as well as prompt treatment related to situations that are time-sensitive in being addressed.
- Discuss the importance of health maintenance related to chronic conditions.
- Compare and contrast emergency medical conditions with ones not considered as emergencies and when emergency room visits vs. doctor office visits should happen.
- Review and discuss suggested website and video on maintaining one's health.
- Determine practices to add to one's routine that will assist in remaining healthy.
- Relate how prolonged stress can negatively affect health.
- Draw a scale that shows a balance between work activities and leisure activities.

POINTS TO MAKE:

- Maintaining good health has a positive effect on one's quality of life.
- Immunizations help to protect the individual from catching serious diseases.
- An immunized community helps to keep certain contagious illnesses from becoming an epidemic.
- Physical checkups with one's doctor can help to detect and identify health conditions for the purpose of treating and managing them.
- Treatment of health conditions helps to either restore health, to slow the progression, or to make people comfortable.
- A balanced diet, exercise, and sufficient rest help a person to remain healthy.
- Drug, alcohol, and tobacco abuse can have a negative effect on one's physical and mental health.
- Excessive stress sustained over extended periods of time and not diffused and diverted into positive energy, can contribute to both physical and mental illness.
- Taking care of one's body and practicing good hygiene habits are important when one seeks to remain as healthy as possible.
- Mentally, physically, and emotionally abusive relationships involve perpetrators and victims.
- Victims of abuse exist in unhealthy states of being and may be gradually destroyed both inside and out (e.g., loss of self-esteem, confidence, and self-worth).

INSTRUCTIONAL RESOURCES:

Suggested Website(s):

Title: Healthy Living in Your 20s
Created or Produced by: Remedy's Health Communities
Web Address: http://www.healthcommunities.com/healthy-aging/healthy-living-tips-20s.shtml
Brief Summary: Healthy practices

Suggested YouTube Video(s):

Title: Five Basic Rules to Maintain a Healthy Lifestyle HD
Creator/Producer: Zock Escorpian
Running Time: (2 minutes 20 seconds)
Format: music – video - captions
Brief Summary: Provides examples that demonstrate strategies for remaining healthy

LESSON #71 – PERSONAL DIRECTION, EFFORT, AND SATISFACTION

GOAL: Students will review ways that people work on improving themselves.

OBJECTIVES: Students will

1. Compare personal growth with remaining stagnant.
2. Develop plans for facilitating their improvement.
3. Identify potential obstacles to their self-improvement.
4. Determine ways to overcome some of their obstacles.

SAMPLE CONTENT STANDARDS: Develop strategies for maintaining a positive self-concept

VOCABULARY & TERMS: recreational reading, informed decision making, open-mindedness, support system, weighing the facts, self-improvement, interest groups, regression, stagnancy, self-fulfillment

CONCEPT SUMMARY: There is always room for improvement and one must determine his/her best way to improve in ways that are personally gratifying.

EXPLICIT INSTRUCTION AND PRACTICE:

- Identify accomplishments one plans to make that will most likely bring satisfaction.
- Distinguish active vs. passive behaviors and how both play roles in achieving satisfaction.
- Review and discuss vocabulary and terms and how they can relate to one's well-being.
- Discuss how positive results from one's own actions can be gratifying and encouraging.
- Describe how obstacles and lack of direction can decrease the effect of one's effort.
- Agree that obstacles don't have to cause one to quit making progress on accomplishments.
- Provide strategies for getting guidance when one is experiencing a lack of direction while trying to make accomplishments.
- Relate the importance of not only having plans that can lead to accomplishment but also having back-up plans just in case problems and unforeseen circumstances arise.
- Analyze the relationship between effort and accomplishment.

- Write a short essay about an accomplishment that took effort and the feelings experienced after the accomplishment.
- Articulate desire for future growth and create plans of action to facilitate growth and eliminate foreseen obstacles..

POINTS TO MAKE:

- When striving for personal growth, it is important to focus upon improving by using one's prior performance as a baseline.
- Personal growth differs from person to person in terms of type and amount.
- Age, by itself, does not guarantee maturity.
- As one develops and sustains responsible behaviors, one becomes more mature.
- Utilizing mentors while transitioning into adulthood provides checks and balances to confirm that appropriate decisions are being made
- Personal growth and development may have to shift in direction and/or speed depending upon life changes and crisis situations.
- Obstacles do not require abandoning life's desires if they are overcome or circumvented.
- Personal satisfaction comes from doing what is personally important and gratifying.

INSTRUCTIONAL RESOURCES:

Suggested Website(s):

Title: 5 Barriers to Achieving Your Dreams and How to Overcome Them
Created or Produced by: The Huffington Post
Web Address: http://www.huffingtonpost.com/tanuja-ramchal/5-barriers-to-achieving-your-dreams-and-how-to-overcome-them_b_6658300.html
Brief Summary: Encouragement and empowerment

Suggested YouTube Video(s):

Title: Michael Jordan's Top 10 Rules for Success
Creator/Producer: Evan Carmichael
Running Time: (9 minutes 11 seconds)
Format: mini-lecture including film slips of Michael Jordan
Brief Summary: Michael Jordan's strategies that he used as he sought success

LESSON #72 – USING PUBLIC TRANSPORTATION

GOAL: Students will use public transportation more independently.

OBJECTIVES: Students will

1. Navigate online sites to determine which buses and/or light rail lines go between various destinations.
2. Demonstrate the ability to read and interpret bus schedules.
3. Distinguish the direction of travel required to get to various destinations.
4. Compare and contrast different routes and combinations of routes that go to the same destination for efficiency, location of transfer points, and frequency of service.
5. Access public transportation information to get verbal and/or online directions to and from destinations using public transportation.

SAMPLE CONTENT STANDARD: Developing self-sufficiency

VOCABULARY & TERMS: schedules, fare, transfer points, routes, origin, destination, pass, transfer, zones, ticket, ticket dispenser, passenger rules, light-rail, bus, subway, shuttle, taxi, airplane, train, depot, limousine, security checkpoints, departure gates

CONCEPT SUMMARY: Effective use of public eliminates the need to depend upon others to drive you from place to place.

EXPLICIT INSTRUCTION AND PRACTICE:

- Request information about riding public transportation.
- Define the vocabulary and terms.
- Discuss the pros and cons of using public transportation.
- Identify the public transportation options near one's home and/or school.
- Explain how to use online schedules and routes for regional public transportation options.
- Search for and identify fare structures.
- Consider the different transportation options based on convenience, cost, payment of fare, and transfer procedures.
- Compare and contrast online fares, schedules, and time involved to travel between one's city and another city of choice riding the train, airplane, and a bus using online information.
- Review and discuss suggested websites and videos.
- Review public transit maps, locate the area of residence, and then trace the paths to school and at least two other places in the community.

POINTS TO MAKE:

- Public transportation includes buses, trains, airplanes, ferries, subways, light rail, shuttles, taxis, and car services such as limousines and Uber.
- Limousine rides are costly and are sometimes used when extra money is available for transportation for a special occasion.
- Larger cities have more public transportation options than smaller cities.
- Some forms of public transportation require that you change vehicles at various hubs and transfer points on the way to the destination.
- Hubs are places where multiple routes of a given form of transportation meet and transfers can take place.
- Fare can vary between travel points based upon the type of public transportation used.
- Airplanes, trains, and inter-city buses in larger cities often have departure and arrival gates.
- Law enforcement agents are assigned to help keep public transportation safe.
- Scheduled departures and arrivals can be obtained by contacting airlines, inter-city bus services, shuttles, and trains or by checking printed or online schedules.
- Fare on inter-city buses, trains, and airplanes are often more expensive when purchased closer to the date of departure.
- Fares on local bus lines, subways, ferries, and light rail are usually fixed and longer-termed passes (weekly or monthly) will often cost less than paying per ride.
- Customer service agents for local forms of public transportation can often be reached by telephone to provide guidance in utilizing the transportation systems.

INSTRUCTIONAL RESOURCES:

Suggested Website(s):

Title: How to Ride a Public Transportation Bus
Created or Produced by: Wikihow
Web Address: http://www.wikihow.com/Ride-a-Public-Transportation-Bus
Brief Summary: Suggested practices for riding public transportation

Title: Public Transport
Created or Produced by: Wikipedia
Web Address: https://en.wikipedia.org/wiki/Public_transport
Brief Summary: Pictures and explanation about various modes of public transportation and some of the historic origins

Additional Regional-Based Websites:

(Use local transit system website to review routes, schedules, connections, and fares.)

Suggested YouTube Video(s):

Title: Record Number of Americans used Public Transportation in 2013
Creator/Producer: Geobeats News
Running Time: (1 minute 11 seconds)
Format: data presentation
Brief Summary: Action video and ridership stats

Title: How to Ride the Bus – General Public
Creator/Producer: goldcasttransit
Running Time: (5 minutes 29 seconds)
Format: procedural presentation
Brief Summary: Illustrations of how to prepare for catching and using the bus

LESSON #73 – SELF-AWARENESS OF DISABILITIES AND STRENGTHS

GOAL: Students will analyze the category of disability that they receive services for.

OBJECTIVES: Students will

1. Identify practices that they should avoid in order to increase their chances of success at school.
2. Explain what they need to do in order to get accommodations in college.
3. Identify situations where they may need assistance in handling their personal affairs.
4. Predict situations where they may need to ask for reasonable accommodations at work

SAMPLE CONTENT STANDARDS: Consider current strengths and limitations when creating personal goals.

VOCABULARY & TERMS: 504 plans, Individualized Educational Plans (IEPs), formal evaluations, challenges, strategies, support systems, accommodations, accessibility, vocational rehabilitation, disability

CONCEPT SUMMARY: One should be aware of personal challenges and apply coping and compensation skills to overcome the, relying whenever possible on their strengths.

EXPLICIT INSTRUCTION AND PRACTICE:

- Introduce the concept of the ability/disability continuum and that all people fit somewhere within this continuum.
- Review personal Individualized Education Plans or 504 Plans and identify strategies that have been included for success at school.
- Reflect upon the information read in the Individualized Education Plan or 504 Plan and suggest personal strategies one will apply as a young adult.
- Review and discuss vocabulary and terms.
- Recognize when assistance and support is needed in order to meet personal goals and where to seek assistance.
- Provide examples of resources, support, and assistance that could be accessed to handle personal affairs independently.
- Share how disability protections are covered and protected by the law.
- Review and discuss the suggested website and video that address living with disability.

POINTS TO MAKE:

- Reasonable accommodations can be requested at work to help individual employees with disabilities.
- Accommodations provide access to workplace environments and related tasks and should not create undue hardship for the employer.
- Vocational Rehabilitation can be accessed by qualified individuals with disabilities who have signed up and have open cases.
- Vocational Rehabilitation services can be used throughout adulthood by qualified recipients seeking various forms of assistance and guidance for independent adult living.
- Support systems include family, friends, specific agencies, faith based communities, organization memberships, and community resources.
- An Individualized Education Plan (IEP) is a legally enforceable document that is provided to students who meet disability eligibility criteria for special education.
- IEPs are written for students in kindergarten through grade twelve up to the age of twenty-one to help document how disability impacts individual students.
- IEP content includes academic and school performance, strategies, accommodations, and in what way special education services will be utilized.
- The purpose of the IEP is to help individuals with disabilities succeed in school, and it includes plans to help individuals with successful transition outcomes.
- IEPs are made possible by federal regulations that are included under the Individuals with Disabilities Education Act (IDEA).
- Becoming familiar with what is in one's own IEP will help with self-advocacy by serving as a reminder of strategies that have helped with academic success.
- A 504 Plan is a legally enforceable document for students with documented disabilities through the Americans With Disabilities Act (ADA).
- A 504 Plan provides accommodations to help facilitate access to the educational process but does not include special education services.
- The Americans with Disabilities Act (ADA) was legislated through the Office of Civil Rights.
- When accessibility is provided, barriers are being/have been removed not only in school, but at work, and in public places used by those who have disabilities.
- Facilities are modified or constructed according to ADA regulations to accommodate citizens with disabilities in the general public.
- A disability substantially limits life activities: ability to eat, speak, walk, process information, see, or hear.
- As one transitions into adulthood, responsibility increases to advocate for himself/herself to get reasonable accommodations.

INSTRUCTIONAL RESOURCES:

Suggested Website(s):

Title: How to Become a Successful Adult with LD
Created or Produced by: Raskind, M.H., Goldberg, R.J.; Higgins, E.L.; & Herman, K.L.
Web Address: http://www.ldao.ca/introduction-to-ldsadhd/articles/about-issues-specific-to-adults-with-lds/how-to-become-a-successful-adult-with-ld/
Brief Summary: Includes major factors that contribute to the success of a person who has experienced a learning disability

Suggested YouTube Video(s):

Title: How My Learning Disability Didn't Limit Me with Joey Graceffa
Creator/Producer: Pretty Unfiltered
Running Time: (5 minutes 4 seconds)
Format: interview
Brief Summary: Interviewee shares how to remain inspired and to move forward and remain positive

Title: Famous People with Disabilities
Creator/Producer: n3nany
Running Time: (3 minutes 32 seconds)
Format: showcase
Brief Summary: Pictures of famous people, the disabilities they experienced, and their major accomplishments

LESSON #74 – NAVIGATING A CITY

GOAL: Students will plan how to get from one place to another.

OBJECTIVES: Students will

1. Use major intersections and streets as points of reference for finding unknown locations.
2. Locate online sources to get directions for navigating from one place to another.
3. Become familiar with the location of major communities and subdivisions around them.
4. Compare and contrast alternative routes to places based upon convenience, intermediate stops for resources or services along the way, degree of isolation or safety, and accessibility.

SAMPLE CONTENT STANDARDS: Use transportation within a community

VOCABULARY & TERMS: major intersections, neighborhoods, public transportation, directions, distance, traveling time, peak travel time, rush hour traffic, route, transfer points

CONCEPT SUMMARY: Independent adults travel from place to place to handle business and participate in leisure activities. It is important to be able to effectively commute.

EXPLICIT INSTRUCTION AND PRACTICE:

- Review and discuss the vocabulary and terms.
- Study maps of the cities or neighborhoods where they live.
- Point out major thoroughfares and intersections as well as their relative proximities to where they reside.
- Use online sources to get directions.
- Locate all of the public transportation stops near their homes and schools.
- Determine the major places one visits in the community and the nearby public transportation stops.
- Identify public transportation options that connect one's home with major places one visits with no more than one transfer.
- Express the importance of allowing enough time to reach destinations on time just in case the scheduled public transportation is delayed or missed.
- Identify multiple routes to the same place, choose the best one and explain why.
- Discuss the pros and cons of driving a car or ride sharing in lieu of using public transportation.
- Conclude that public transportation schedules may fluctuate and be less frequent when it is not peak travel time including nights, holidays, and week-ends.

POINTS TO MAKE:

- Google Maps and MapQuest are online programs that help provide directions connecting places of origin to destinations.
- Bus, subway, and light rail schedules list the days of the week and times that sources of transportation run and provide locations and times to board, get off, and transfer.
- When managing time, one should catch scheduled transportation early enough so that if it is missed, doesn't run, or is delayed, one can still get to his/her destination on time.
- Becoming familiar with major intersections and streets in cities helps to provide points of reference in relation to direction or distance from various destinations.
- During rush hour when many are traveling to and from work, streets are usually more crowded and more time is needed to get from point to point.
- Local buses, subways, ferries, and light rails often run more frequently in order to help service the increased amount of ridership during rush hour.
- Taxis may cost more during rush hour due to their meters continuously running while not flowing as quickly as when the streets are not as crowded.
- People often share travel expenses by riding together in carpools to get to and from work when their homes are on the way to the place of employment.
- Money is provided to carpool drivers in exchange for the rides in the drivers' personal vehicles to help cover travel expenses such as gas and maintenance..

INSTRUCTIONAL RESOURCES:

Suggested Website(s):

Utilize local public transportation website to review the use of routes, timetables, transfer points, and schedules.

Suggested YouTube Video(s):

Title: Do You Actually Need to Own a Car
Creator/Producer: Think Tank
Running Time: (6 minutes 24 seconds)
Format: monologue
Brief Summary: Addresses how to navigate through town without owning a car

Title: Chicago Travel – How to Get Around – 5 Ways
Creator/Producer: Lizzy Fay
Running Time: (3 minutes 43 seconds)
Format: tour and demonstration of transportation use
Brief Summary: A tour showing and explaining the use of public transportation

Title: Getting Around New York City: Street Layout, Bus, Subway, Ferry
Creator/Producer: MuchoHop
Running Time: (9 minutes 18 seconds)
Format: tour and demonstration
Brief Summary: Provides a sample of how transportation systems operate within a city, how they are used, and how awareness of how a city is geographically set up is helping in deciding the method of getting around

LESSON #75 – FINDING HOUSING

GOAL: Students will assess housing options based upon their budgets, needs, and preferences.

OBJECTIVES: Students will

1. Establish categories of expenses related to various housing options.
2. Identify the pros and cons of sharing apartments with other people.
3. Name sources of finding out about housing vacancies.
4. Determine factors that are important to them when selecting housing.

SAMPLE CONTENT STANDARDS: Use decision making skills to secure and maintain housing.

VOCABULARY & TERMS: rent, mortgage, deposit, landlord, lease, insurance, foreclosure, eviction, maintenance, renovation, remodeling, neighborhood, apartment, rooming house, house, condominium, accommodations, utilities, taxes, subsidized housing

CONCEPT SUMMARY: Living in one's own home is an independent living goal chosen by many. There are alternatives to consider based on what is affordable, accessible, and desirable.

EXPLICIT INSTRUCTION AND PRACTICE:

- Inquire about housing plans as adults and why the interest in the expressed option.
- Review vocabulary and terms.
- Distinguish between various housing options.
- Identify sources where people can find out about available housing.
- Research online the monthly costs for various forms of housing; make a chart for reference.
- Discuss what is needed to maintain one's personal area in an apartment or other housing option.
- Review and discuss suggested website and video that addresses finding affordable housing.
- Prioritize a list of what is important when deciding upon where to live.
- Visit sources of information that will help them make decisions regarding housing.

POINTS TO MAKE:

- Housing decisions should be based upon a budget that include mortgage or rent payments and other housing expenses.
- When determining what is affordable housing, one must also consider food, clothing, debt obligations, family needs, transportation, and other monthly expenses.
- When one's budget cannot cover all anticipated expenditures, then changes in the amount of expenditure for each category must take place.
- It costs more to live in some areas than in other areas.
- It often costs more to live in places that have more conveniences available for residents than places that offer fewer conveniences.
- Rental agreements are signed contracts covering a designated amount of time that indicate the monthly rent as well as expectations related to residing in the property.
- Rental agreements can be renewed or revoked at the end of the listed housing agreement term.
- When residents agree to share the expenses of rental units, if one leaves before the lease has expired, those remaining are responsible for the total cost of the agreement.
- When rental agreements are renewed, there is always the possibility of the rent increasing.
- Housing deposits are designated amounts of money that must be given to landlords prior to moving into rental units.
- Deposits confirm that the unit will become the renter's place of residence; this money is held by the landlord or rental company to cover damages that occur and have not been repaired prior to moving out.
- If there are no damages and rent is up to date, the renter is entitled to be reimbursed the housing deposit that was submitted.
- Evictions from rental units take place if the rent remains unpaid or if the renter breaks rules agreed upon such as becoming a nuisance or conducting illegal activities within the residence.
- Landlords must uphold their ends of the agreement with housing contracts or else renters may sue or take other legal actions for damage recovery.
- Subsidized housing options are rental agreements where rental payment is based upon socio-economic variables and residents provided government rental assistance .
- Those who have less income are responsible for smaller percentages of the rental costs in subsidized housing units.
- Mortgages are payments that are due over a period of time to pay the cost required to own homes.
- Mortgages usually consist of money that has been loaned to home buyers through banks and other financial systems.

253

- Mortgage payments not only include the cost of the home, but interest payments that are accrued as a result of borrowing money to finance housing purchases.
- When mortgage payments are not paid on time, late fees are added to the costs the home owners must pay.
- When mortgage payments are repeatedly not paid, the home buyer goes into default and runs the risk of losing the property and forfeiting any money already paid.
- Homeowners who default and lose their homes can be sued for the balance of the mortgage expenses that the lender can't immediately recover from the home owner.
- Renter's and homeowner's insurance are paid in addition to rent and mortgage payments to help provide recovery for losses such as theft or disaster.
- Homeowner's insurance is required by the lender while the buyer is still paying a mortgage to protect the lender in case of disaster to the property.

INSTRUCTIONAL RESOURCES:

Suggested Website(s):

Title: Steps to Find Affordable Housing
Created or Produced by: East Bay Housing Organization
Web Address: http://www.ebho.org/resources/looking-for-housing/steps-to-find-affordable-housing
Brief Summary: Tells how to explore different forms of housing and various subsidies that can assist with housing expenses

Title: Help Finding an Affordable House
Created or Produced by: USA.gov
Web Address: https://www.usa.gov/finding-home
Brief Summary: Explains various programs that are available for securing housing and includes links to various agencies that can assist with the process

Suggested YouTube Video(s):

Title: Renters Survival Guide: How to Find an Apartment/Flat
Creator/Producer: How to Adult
Running Time: (4 minutes 11 seconds)
Format: mini-lecture
Brief Summary: Suggests factors that should be considered when choosing where to live

Title: 5 Things to Know Before Moving Out

Creator/Producer: Engineered Truth

Running Time: (7 minutes 41 seconds)

Format: mini-lecture

Brief Summary: Things to think about when deciding upon living locations and arrangements

LESSON #76 – TAKING RESPONSIBILITY FOR ONE'S OWN ACTIONS AND CHOICES

GOAL: Students will remain focused upon their own actions when seeking certain outcomes.

OBJECTIVES: Students will

1. Explain the concept of making choices and owning the outcomes.
2. Recognize that negative consequences may result when one loses self-control.
3. Provide examples of how risks sometimes bring positive outcomes.
4. Explain the process of thinking through anticipated actions before deciding to perform these actions.

SAMPLE CONTENT STANDARDS: Apply problem and conflict-solving skills.

VOCABULARY & TERMS: risks, consequences, personal accountability, available options, cost/benefit analysis, discipline

CONCEPT SUMMARY: One's actions have an impact upon results that must be lived with including positive and negative consequences.

EXPLICIT INSTRUCTION AND PRACTICE:

- Define what responsibility means; what it means to be responsible.
- Discuss why adults are held accountable for their own actions unless the law has declared them as incompetent.
- Review and discuss vocabulary and terms about being responsible for one's own actions.
- Explore the concept of cost/risk vs. benefits/gains with respect to personal accountability for choosing certain actions.
- Review and discuss suggested websites and videos related to being responsible for oneself.
- Provide both a positive and a negative way to interact with each of the scenarios.
- Invent additional scenarios depicting negative and positive ways to deal with situations, and supply reasoning and consequences.

POINTS TO MAKE:

- Costs/risks vs. benefits/gains must be considered when making decisions.
- Taking the time to assess potential outcomes of actions to increase the likelihood of making rational choices.

- Although others can influence the choices one makes, it is important that one considers what he/she is willing to live with.
- Results from personal choices impact one's personal status or state of being.
- Blaming others for results does not repair the problems that result from making poor choices.
- Self-control and discipline help one avoid impulsive actions that can bring negative outcomes.
- Thinking through and evaluating plans of action before they are implemented provides the chance to amend one's actions if needed to avoid related problems.
- Some positive outcomes require that risks be taken, but one should consider the cost of potential risks and whether potential benefits outweigh those risks.

INSTRUCTIONAL RESOURCES:

Suggested Website(s):

Title: Quotes About Personal Responsibilities (115 Quotes)
Created or Produced by: Goodreads
Web Address: https://www.goodreads.com/quotes/tag/personal-responsibility
Brief Summary: Collection of quotes from various people about personal responsibility

Title: Accountability – I am Responsible for my Own Actions
Created or Produced by: Positive Inspiration Today.com
Web Address: http://www.positiveinspirationtoday.com/accountability.html
Brief Summary: An author reflects on gaining personal responsibility

Suggested YouTube Video(s):

Title: Oprah on Taking Responsibility for Your Life
Creator/Producer: Oprah Winfrey Network
Running Time: (2 minutes 5 seconds)
Format: mini-lecture
Brief Summary: Addresses how to grow from one's mistakes and move forward

Title: Profound Choices: Inspiration and Motivation to Help You Make the Best Choices
Creator/Producer: Go Bigger Seminars
Running Time: (4 minutes 10 seconds)
Format: scripted message accompanied by pictures and music
Brief Summary: Motivation accompanied by music and pictures

SHOWING ACCOUNTABILITY THROUGH YOUR ACTIONS

For each scenario listed, provide an action that may contribute to positive results as well as an action that may contribute to negative results. Compare and contrast your responses with your classmates.

SCENARIO #1 – A friend drove to your home to visit you during a party that you were hosting. He started becoming dizzy at the end of the evening and wanted to go home and go to bed.

Your positive action to Scenario #1 and reasoning behind it:

_____

_____

A negative action you could take and possible consequences related to it:

_____

_____

SCENARIO #2 – You went out with a group of friends to eat and discovered something on the menu that you really wanted but did not bring enough money for.

Your positive action to Scenario #2 and reasoning behind it:

_____

_____

A negative action you could take and possible consequences related to it:

_____

_____

SCENARIO #3 – There is a major event taking place out of town, but you are already scheduled to work on that weekend.

Your positive action to Scenario #3 and reasoning behind it:

_____

_____

A negative action you could take and possible consequences related to it:

_____

_____

LESSON #77 – THE POWER OF NETWORKING

GOAL: Students will become better acquainted with the concept of connecting with others in order to meet personal goals.

OBECTIVES: Students will

1. Define what networking consists of.
2. Describe the types of networking that may be beneficial as they prepare to enter their career fields.
3. Compare and contrast networking with socializing.
4. Identify factors that may interfere with as well as assist with positive networking.

SAMPLE CONTENT STANDARDS: Engage in activities and experiences involving other people that help to facilitate successful outcomes in regard to personal goals

VOCABULARY & TERMS: networking, personal branding, insider knowledge, personal impression, "guilt by association", circle of influence, advocate, window of opportunity

CONCEPT SUMMARY: Networking facilitates connections both negative and positive with others that include others previously unknown. Networking can help facilitate attaining personal goals.

EXPLICIT INSTRUCTION AND PRACTICE:

- Relate prior knowledge in regard to networking.
- Explain the purpose of networking.
- Provide examples of how networking can help facilitate personal goal attainment.
- Review the purposes of networking.
- Review vocabulary and terms as they relate to networking.
- Discuss consequences related to ineffective or inappropriate networking.
- Provide strategies for initiating positive networking experiences and determining if various networking experiences should be continued, modified, or discontinued.
- Review and discuss suggested websites and video.
- Create personal lists of the types of people and resources that can help with transition-related goals and /or overcoming Differentiate networking from socializing.
- Share how networking will be used to one's advantage.
- Summarize the advantages of networking on the worksheet provided.

POINTS TO MAKE:

- Some people can help you get the attention of others that you are not in direct contact with for the purpose of moving forward with meeting personal goals.
- Other people who you associate with in certain circles can interfere with others assisting you in meeting personal goals.
- Networking must sometimes be strategic and intentional when seeking to accomplish certain goals.
- One should be careful about his/her personal image that is portrayed when around people who are within the circle of influence that one wants to make a positive impression upon.
- There are times when personal networking should be delayed or temporarily discontinued in order to interact when both parties appear to be available and approachable.
- Networking is a work in progress that can change based upon circumstances and interests.
- Be cautious about what one posts on social media that could be deemed as negative by unknown viewers.

INSTRUCTIONAL RESOURCES:

Suggested Website(s):

Title: The Underestimated Importance of Personal Networking
Created or Produced by: Career Cast
Web Address: http://www.careercast.com/career-news/underestimated-importance-personal-networking
Brief Summary: Addresses the variety of networks people are involved in and how these connections may be helpful when pursuing personal goals

Title: The Dos and Don'ts of Student Networking
Created or Produced by: Alexa-Jane Moore
Web Address: https://www.theguardian.com/education/2014/jun/18/student-guide-to-networking-graduate-jobs
Brief Summary: Best practices for networking

Title: 5 Things Every Student Should Know About Networking
Created or Produced by: Joel Delgardo
Web Address: https://news.fiu.edu/2014/12/5-things-every-college-student-should-know-about-networking/83523
Brief Summary: Addresses how to navigate the networking process successfully

Suggested YouTube Video(s):

Title: Networking Basics: 8 Tips to Networking Without Being Fake
Creator/Producer: Marie Forleo
Running Time: (6 minutes 26 seconds)
Format: mini-lecture
Brief Summary: Sharing of best practices for meaningful networking experiences

THE ADVANTAGES OF NETWORKING

Identify people who can help you to meet your goals and overcome obstacles in each of the three major areas of transition.

Who can help in your personal network in the area of post-secondary education?

_____

_____

_____

Who can help in your personal network in the area of employment?

_____

_____

_____

Who can help in your personal network in the area of independent living?

_____

_____

_____

Provide an example of a personal network in action where they not only help you, but you help them as well.

_____

_____

_____

Provide an example of how your personal networks extend beyond those who you are already familiar with.

_____

_____

_____

Provide an example of when conditions related to a personal network between you and someone else should be discontinued.

_____

_____

_____

Competencies, Standards, Expectations, and Quality Indicators are used to specify skills to be taught and acquired. Transition-related subject matter is useful for students in general, both with and without disabilities. Everyone needs for adults in society to be as productive and self-sufficient as possible. Various standards are in place, and there are more standards being created that address transition-related instruction. The special education profession is identifying standards, as are career and technical education providers, and school guidance counselors. A sample standard is provided for each lesson plan and perhaps one that is related can be used from what your school district has adopted. A few of the online sources of standards are provided below.

Competencies, Standards, Expectations, and/or Quality Indicator Examples Related to Transition from Various States

Alabama Transition Standards
https://www.alsde.edu/sec/ses/Transition/Alabama%20Transition%20Standards-2014.pdf

Career Development Occupational Studies (used by state of New York)
Commencement Core Curriculum
http://www.p12.nysed.gov/cte/cdlearn/documents/CDOS-Commen-CareerandUniversa.pdf

Life Centered Education (LCE) Curriculum Matrix (Council for Exceptional Children)
https://www.cec.sped.org/~/media/Files/Publications/LCE/LCE_Matrix_4.pdf

Missouri Comprehesive School Counseling Program Career Development GLEs
https://dese.mo.gov/sites/default/files/cnsl-curr-gle-cd-9-12.pdf

National Standards & Quality Indicators for Secondary Education and Transition
http://www.nasetalliance.org/docs/NASET_8-pager.pdf

South Carolina Guidance and Counseling Curriculum
Standards and Competency Indicators - Grade Nine through Twelve Standard Competency
Indicator (pages 47-49)
https://ed.sc.gov/scdoe/assets/File/agency/ccr/Career-and-Technology-Education/documents/Ann4SCCDGCPM062308Finalpostedaug2011.pdf

Wisconsin Department of Public Instruction
Model Academic Standards for School Counseling
https://dpi.wi.gov/sspw/pupil-services/school-counseling/models/state-standards

Each lesson plan includes a Vocabulary and Terms section. The definitions provided pertain to the topics addressed and are intended for instructor reference. In the book titled *Building Academic Vocabulary*, the authors make the following connections between vocabulary and knowledge:

> People's knowledge of any topic is encapsulated in the terms they know that
> Are relevant to the topic. The more students understand these terms, the
> Easier it is for them to understand information they may read or hear about
> The topic. The more terms a person knows about a given subject, the easier
> It is to understand and learn new information related to that subject.
> (Marzano & Pickering, 2005).

There are a variety of ways that the Vocabulary and Terms section can be used to repeatedly expose students to terms that they will possibly encounter as young transitioning adults. For example, some terms could be discussed as a lesson ice-breaker and others used to summarize a lesson concept. Vocabulary has been included in each lesson plan to help students learn the terms in transition-related context rather in isolation.

HIGH SCHOOL AND BEYOND VOCABULARY & TERMS

ability – the state of being able to do something

abbreviations – a shortened form of writing a word

absentee ballot - a form that a person completes to send in his/her vote

absentee voting – the process of which a citizen formally documents his/her choice of someone running for public office, changes in public policy, and/or decisions on how taxes are spent without actually being at the polls on the day set aside for the public to officially submit these choices

abusive relationship – a situation in which a person regularly spends personal time with someone who mistreats him/her

academic advisor – a person in college who helps students to determine appropriate options for completing degree and certification programs when enrolling in coursework

academic support – people who are designated to help students with successfully completing coursework

accessibility – ease with which one can get in and out of a rooms and buildings (lack of obstacles)

accident waiting to happen – a state of careless behavior that has a high risk of damage or injury resulting because of it

accommodations – conditions and supports that are in place to help people in various environments given personal limitations that exist

accomplishment – a goal that has been completed successfully

account piracy – when someone other than the legitimate owner of an account takes over the account is if it were his/her own

acronym – a group of words that are abbreviated by using the first letter of each word and combining them into a pronounceable expression

acrostic – a form of writing where the first letter of each phrase or word, when combined sequentially, spells out a word

admissions counselor – a person on a college campus that reviews student records and interests to help determine if a student qualifies to attend the school as well as if the programs offered match the needs of the student

265

advocate – to speak up in behalf of; to help to get someone's needs met

affiliation – a connection with another person or group

affirmation – when a person or group of people shows approval for that person or group of people or their actions

affordable - when a person has enough money to pay for things and services that they want to have and still be able to take care of their needs

age discrimination – when someone is treated unfairly due to how old the person is

agreement – when two or more parties share the same decision on what should be done

airline travel – the process of arranging to, preparing for, and engaging in going from one place to another on an airplane

alderman – a person who is elected in a certain region in a city by those living in that region to help make sure that that city's government looks out for the unique needs of that community

alliance – people who you are connected with others to help fulfill certain purposes

altered plans – when changes have taken place in regard to what one was going to do at first

alternative – a choice other than one's original choice

amendment – formal change in policy

Americans with Disabilities Act (ADA) – a civil rights law that helps to protect the rights of citizens with disabilities regarding employment opportunities, public accommodations, access to services in the community, access to education, and access to telecommunication

anger management – the process by which a person controls the intensity of anger to lessen the possibility of physical or emotional harm to self or others

apartment – a living space that is not a complete house

appearance – how something or someone looks

application – paperwork that is filled out in order to be considered for receiving employment, services, or goods

application deadline – the last day that a specific form can be turned in for the purpose of being considered for certain services, considerations, and/or benefits to be received

apprenticeship – a work experience where a person is assigned to someone with experience to learn how to perform a job by watching and being guided by that person who already has experience

approachability – the state of a person being receptive to others coming to them for things

appropriate - acceptable behavior or appearance for a particular setting

aptitude – the ability of being able to learn how to do something

arbitration – the act of an outside party assisting other parties to come to an agreement

asset – possessions and abilities a person has that has the ability to create a positive impact

assistantship - when one is helped with tuition in graduate school in exchange for his/her serving as a helper to an instructor

athletic scholarship – when one receives money from a college to help pay tuition in exchange for his/her representing the college by participating on a sports team

athletics – sports

ATM card – a plastic card that can be inserted in an automated teller machine for the purpose of doing financial transactions

atmosphere – the pace, demeanor, and vibes of an environment including the people and the normal day to day activity

attendance – when one is present at a particular place

attentiveness - the state of spending time focusing on what is being done or what is being spoken about

attorney – a person who practices law by representing others in court or other legal situations

auditory learner – a person who learns best by hearing the lesson content

authority figure – a person who is seen as being in charge

autonomy – the level of which a person controls his/her decisions and makes actions on his/her own that impact of her/his life

available options – choices to choose from

average class size – the number of students that would be in a class if the populations of classes within that school or college were equalized

avoidance – staying away from people, things, or situations

bait and switch – when an advertiser invites customers to buy certain items and when the customers arrive to purchase, the advertiser does not offer what was advertised but attempts to get the purchase to buy something more expensive

balance – the amount of money remaining in an account; the amount remaining in a debt that is owed; a state of living where there are a variety of types of activities that take place in one's schedule; not too much of any one activity in one's life

balanced course load – the state of a student having the number of and combination of classes that can be managed successfully given the amount of time available and level of personal functioning

balanced workload – the state of having enough to do but not too much to do given the the available time and ability

balancing accounts – when one counts what is being spent or withdrawn from an account vs. money that is being added to an account and identifies the specific cash flow leading to the current amount of money that remains

balloon notes – when payments that have been made to pay off a loan increase to extreme prices per payment and must be paid in order to avoid being delinquent

ballot – a form that is used to cast a vote

bank account – a set of funds belonging to an individual or group and held by a financial institution where a person or group of people can add money to their own funds or take money out of their own funds

banking – the process of doing money transactions with a financial institution

beginning salary – the amount of money people make when they first start working on particular jobs

benefits – extras that a person is granted by the employer such as vacation time, sick leave, and insurance

bibliography – a list of books and/or articles used to help increase understanding about a topic that is being written about

binding agreement – a situation where both parties who decided upon something that is to be done are committed to perform his/her part or possibly face consequences

blend – to mix in smoothly with others

block unit - an organization within specific neighborhoods in a city where citizens come together to express the needs of that area as well as seek solutions to challenges of the area

body build – the structure of an individual person's size and shape

body language – movements or positions that a person makes that may reveal feelings about a situation, self, or another person

boiling point - how much intensity in an angering situation that a person can tolerate before it turns into a situation of rage or uncontrollable anger

bond issue - a thing that is placed on a voting ballot related to choices on how tax dollars should be spent

borrowed time – when a person takes extra time during a given period and pays it back later

boycott – not using certain businesses or services due to disagreeing on factors related to them

breach of contract – when a person or group of people fail to do the part agreed to as indicated on a formal documentation of the agreement

break time – time period during a work day when an employee is free from performing job responsibilities

breaking point – the amount of stress that a person can tolerate without striking out at others or shutting away from others

buddy system – going to places and participating in activities with someone else so you can look out for one another

budgeting – when a person or group of people plan on when and how to spread available funds around in such a way that as many needs are met as possible

burning bridges – actions that might destroy a positive connection with a person who might be needed in the future

bus transportation – the process of arranging to, preparing for, and engaging in going from one place to another using the bus

business attire – the type of clothing that is normally worn in an office setting that is somewhat conservative and not considered party or casual clothing

business casual – a category of clothing that is in-between business clothing and leisure clothing

calendar – a document used to list dates, times, and places of planned activities

campus community – people who live, work, and study on colleges grounds and those places where the various college activities take place

campus life – activities both academic and leisure that take place in college settings

campus security – people who work at colleges to help assure the safety of faculty, staff, students, and visitors while on the premises

capabilities – what one is able to do

career – jobs that are inter-connected to an area of interest over a given period of time

career cluster – groups of jobs that are related

career field – a category containing related jobs

career placement office – a department on a college campus that helps to facilitate students connecting with job openings related to their degrees based upon companies that have advised them of these openings

casual wear – clothing that one wears when not at work that is not conservative enough to wear to work

categorizing – breaking things, people, and events into groups depending upon similar characteristics

celebration - an event where people come together to enjoy an accomplishment or status of an individual or group

chain of command – from the person one reports to on a job, to the person that person reports to, and so on up to the top person at a place of employment

challenges – things that make it difficult to accomplish or complete goals

chargeback – when purchases that have been made without the credit card owner's approval are removed from being expenses that the card owner has to pay back to the credit card company

check cashing fee – a service charge that a person must pay in order to receive money in exchange for the official bank note provided to that person by an individual or business that represents a specific amount of money to be received

check stub – the part of an official bank note that is retained after cashing it that provides specific details about the money amounts represented

check-off sheet – a list where one marks items one by one as they are included removed, or completed

checking account – an arrangement made with a bank or credit union where a person's money is held and can be transferred to people that they owe by the owner of the account writing on and signing a bank form known as a check that authorizes who, when, and how much money will be paid

checkpoint – a location where authority figures observe and confirm approval of individuals regarding behavior, conditions, and possessions that are deemed as acceptable before the individuals are allowed to move past that current location

choosing your battles – deciding what to fight for after weighing the pros and cons of taking those actions

circle of influence – those people that a person has an effect upon in regard to those people's choices or actions

citation – written acknowledgement of written thoughts and expressions made by another author that are transported into a new piece of literature by way of listing the original author, the location of the thought or expression from the original literature, and when these thoughts or expressions were written

class presentations – an activity where students are required to formally share information with their classmates on particular topics

class project – an activity that students do together to increase as well as provide a platform for sharing gained knowledge on a particular topic

classified – grouped based upon common elements

classified advertising – a section of a newspaper that includes goods and services that are sought or being sold and includes job openings

clinics – a place where healthcare is provided; a structured activity where an experienced person or group of people guide learners toward developing a greater understanding or competency regarding a process of hands-on activities

clustering – grouping things and ideas based upon common traits

co-dependence – when a person makes it difficult for someone to break self-destructive habits due to helping the person to make excuses for or providing easy access for the continuation of those self-destructive habits

collaboration – working together to get things done

collateral – something belonging to the borrower that a lender can keep in the event that the debt is not repaid

college application – a form that is filled out and submitted for the purpose of seeking acceptance to a post-secondary school

college essay – a writing sample on a specific topic that is submitted when competing for certain scholarships

college work study – when a student supplies a service to a school in exchange for that school covering some of the student expenses

collegiality - the existence of two people engaging with one another when they both share a similar status

comfort – the act of being relieved or providing relief from emotional or physical pain

commensurate – the amount or intensity of a state of being that is considered as normal when another certain amount or intensity of another state of being exists

commitment - the act of sticking to an action that one has agreed to do

committeeman – an elected official who represents residents who live in a certain section of a city to help maintain a positive environment in that area

community – a particular region consisting of people, places, and activities

community center – a public building or sets of buildings in a region where residents of that area can come for meetings, recreation, exercise, and various scheduled events

community resources – things, places, and services that people can use in their neighborhoods that are provided to help meet their needs

commute – travel to and from

companionship – the status of people coming together to enjoy one another's company

comparable program – an activity or service provided to people that is similar to another activity or service

compare and contrast – analyzing and making note of how things are alike and different from one another

compatibility – people who are able to harmoniously do things together due to common interests and values

compatible – getting along well with those in working and/or social relationships

compatible scheduling - a condition of which things that are to be done do not conflict with the time allocated for other things that are desired to be done or to participate in

compensating for one's weakness – the condition of which a person performs another action well to make up for an action that he/she is not able to perform well

compensatory time – time off that is granted due to having already worked enough extra hours ahead of time to cover for the time off

competence – the ability to perform certain actions

compounded interest – extra money due that is added to the fees that one already has to pay for borrowing and paying back money over an extended period of time

compromise – when a person decides to settle for some of what they wanted but also less than what they wanted

computer technology services – a department within a company or organization that maintains its operating systems that access online functions

concept maps – a graphic representation that shows how information and thoughts are connected to help provide understanding about specific topics

conclusion – at the end of something; thoughts that integrate information that has been based upon observations, information shared, or review of something

condominium – a residence owned or leased by an individual or group of individuals where the funds paid for the property include the owner of the overall complex being responsible for maintaining the property and grounds

confidence – a state of being where one is sure about being able to perform a particular task or maintain a particular status

confidentiality – the state of maintaining the privacy of a person or group of people

confirmation – when something happens or is said that helps to verify one's beliefs

conflict – a strong disagreement within working or social relationships

conflict of interest – when an activity or a status of a person or group has the potential to interfere with another activity or status of that person or group if both exist at the same time

conflict resolution – finding ways to eliminate or reduce problems between two or more parties who disagree with each other

confrontation – when one party goes to another to advise them about his/her perspective regarding friction and misunderstanding that has occurred between both parties

connecting concepts – when relationships between multiple topics and thoughts are discovered and help to clarify meaning for one another

consequence – something that takes place as a result of an action

considerate – thinking about how one's actions affects others and avoiding creating negative situations for them

constraint – the act of holding back personal aggressive behaviors and expressions

consultation – sharing or receiving information with another relevant party for the purpose of making informed choices

contract – a binding agreement between two or more parties, usually in writing, to provide goods or services in exchange for payment or receipt of other services

controversial – an action or status that is highly disagreed upon by substantial amounts of people

cooperative – working together to get things accomplished

coping skills – positive ways that people behave and/or think in order to maintain success with situations that they are in

Cornell notes – a specific two-column style of organizing, collecting, and documenting information that has been provided for later review

cost/benefit analysis – a comparison of the positive and negative potential related to certain actions that are being considered or have been taken

counseling - the process where a person shares his/her thoughts with a person who strategically listens, reflects on what is being said, and assists the person is making personal choices

course catalog – an organized listing of college courses including brief overviews that are found in book form or electronic form

course offerings – classes that are available during a specific semester or academic year

course preference – classes that a student would rather take in comparison to other available classes

course scheduling – officially choosing the times and days of the week that certain classes will be taken

course sections – multiple listings of the same course indicating different instructors and/or times that the course is offered

course substitution – using an alternative class in exchange for a required class to meet a portion of the academic requirements needed to complete a degree or certificate

courtesy – being polite, using good manners

crash studying – preparing for classroom tests and exams over a very short length of time

creating connections – finding people with common interests and/or related goals and arranging to spend time interacting with them due to the common elements

credit card – a piece of plastic issued by a bank or a store that is used to pay for services or make purchases that are recorded on the card holder's account that must be paid back later

credit hours – the amount of time that a student spends per week receiving coursework instruction

credit load – the amount of scheduled classroom hours for coursework being taken

credit score – a number that indicates how well a person pays back money and is able to handle debt that is based upon the combination of companies reporting payment patterns of individuals to a central source and based on income status

credit worthiness - when a person has a pattern of regularly paying his/her debt and shows the potential for being able to maintain this practice with a new debt is added

critical – extremely important

critique – look and analyze details regarding a person, place, thing, or event

culture – a combination of a common set of beliefs, mannerisms, and practices associated with established groups of people

customer service – a department at a business or company that assists the public in resolving issues and receiving requested information in regard to the company's products and/or tasks

cutting your losses – the act of stopping to do things that have continued to bringing negative results in order to avoid additional negative results

damage control – when a person or group of people take certain actions to avoid allowing a situation to become worse

deadlines – the specific date or time that a person has to complete a task in order to avoid being penalized

dean – an administrator in a college who is responsible for the smooth operation between faculty and students for the division of the school that they are assigned to

debit card – a piece of plastic issued by a bank that is attached to bank account(s) and allows the cardholders access to their money through a bank machine or by authorizing deductions from the account(s) to purchase goods and/or services

debriefing – sharing information and insight about an event or series of events that have taken place

deductible – the amount a person must pay before their insurance begins to make payment toward insurable losses or services

deduction – an amount of money that is subtracted from a larger amount of money due to meeting certain required conditions that can lessen the amount of taxes a person is responsible for

default – failure to make payments for money that is owed

delayed gratification – waiting for a positive result to take place instead of immediately receiving that result

delegation – giving someone else a task to complete instead of doing it oneself

demographics – a description of people based upon distinguishing characteristics that classifies them by social status such as age, ethnicity, income level, gender, and etc.

demotion – to be moved to a lower paying or lower level position within a company

dental health – the status of one's teeth, gums, and mouth

departure gates – the places where one boards various forms of transportation that are designated to go to specific destinations

deposit – placing money into an account

depot – a place where one accesses various transportation options

destination – the place that one plans to travel to

determination – a state of mind when the mind has been made up to pursue and complete goals regardless of things that may get in the way of success

deterrent – something that is present that makes a person desire to avoid taking certain actions

development – the state of something or someone growing or gradually getting better at doing certain things over time

direct deposit – the condition of one's pay going directly to one's bank account instead of being provided as a check that has to be cashed

directions – steps that are provided to help someone complete a task

disability – a physical, emotional, or mental condition that significantly limits a person in one or more major life functions such as seeing, speaking, hearing, thinking, moving, concentrating, eating, or major body systemic functioning

Disability Access Office – a department at a college or university that functions to help insure that students who qualify to attend the college or university and have disabilities are provided appropriate accommodations in order to help them fully participate in college coursework, activities, and college living

discipline - the ability to self-direct and remain on task in order to accomplish certain goals

disclosure – the process of a person sharing personal private information

discretion – a person's individual ability to make decisions based upon his/her own logic and interpretation of events

discrimination – a process by which a person has been treated unfairly due to race, gender, age, culture, language, sex, or some type of minority status

displaced aggression – an action when someone reacts in anger physically or verbally toward an individual who did not cause the anger

disproportionate response – when a person's reaction is exaggerated in comparison to what that person experienced

distance – how far away one place is from another

distorted reality – not interpreting circumstances and events that one has experienced accurately

diversity – a state of existence in an environment where there are distinct differences within the population including race, gender, age, sex, culture, and/or language.

divided focus – when a person is trying to pay attention to more than one thing at a time

dorm supplies – things that students need in order to enjoy the comforts of home as much as possible while living in student housing

double time – working twice the number of hours that one normally works at his/her place of employment

draft – a written document that one authors that is not the final one but is created for the purpose of adding to or amending prior to completing a final copy of that document

dress code – how people are expected to dress to fit into the culture of a school, business, or other establishment within society

drug interaction – problems that can happen in a person's body due to taking certain combinations of medications or drugs

duration – a length of time that an activity lasts

editing – reviewing something that has been written for the purpose of improving the quality of the writing

education – the collection of experiences and/or coursework that contribute to knowledge; activities that can lead to learning

educational/training plan – a goal that has been created that involves what learning experiences to venture into along with a potential sequence, timing, and engagement of resources that are needed to engage in those experiences

efficiency – the state of being able to do things well, smoothly, and with minimal waste in time, resources, or effort

effort – action that one tries to engage in

election – the process of people voting for who will represent them in the political region where they live that is based upon who most people choose; the act of choosing the leadership of various groups or organizations based upon the choice of the majority of the people who belong to that group or organization

elective course - a class that grants credit hours but does not address specific content area requirements

electronic trail – creating or submitting a series of communications that take place online that includes the responses of others and can be retrieved for later reference

emergency medical technician – a person who works in an ambulance and serves those who are sick or injured

emotional outlet – a place or positive activity that serves as a way for a person to release bottled up energy related to unfavorable things that are being experienced

employee tuition reimbursement – when a job pays an employee back for all or part of the money that the employee paid to take coursework after the successful completion of those courses

employment goal – the type of position or company that a person is trying to eventually become placed in

employment objective - what a person plans to accomplish as it pertains to getting jobs

engage - to get involved

enthusiasm – the status of being excited and yielding positive energy toward an activity or action he/she performs

entrance requirements – a certain level of accomplishment or experience that has to exist in order to be admitted into certain college programs

entry level position – a position in an organization or business that requires less experience and/or education and is taken to prepare for higher-level positions

Equal Employment Opportunity – laws and regulations that make it illegal to deny the opportunity to work solely upon the person's demographic affiliation

escape plan - what one has thought out ahead of time in regard to getting out of a place or situation safely

ethical – the status of an action or lack of action providing benefit as opposed to harm

ethnicity – cultural and physical characteristics that distinguish groups of people from one another

etiquette – good manners

evaluate – a process where a person or group is rated to see if satisfactory performance is taking place as well as to determine factors that help or hinder success

eviction – a process where a person is forced to move out of a property due to lack of making payments or committing violations related to the housing contract

exemption – a status of which a decreased amount of tax will be owed (due to conditions such as having dependents) when annual income taxes are filed

expectations – what a person believes will happen; what a person determines to be acceptable behavior or acceptable levels of performance

expenses – those goods and services that a person must pay out of their income

experience – the amount of time and intensity of exposure that a person has had pertaining to doing certain types of work or participating in certain types of activity

expiration date – the last day that something one eats, drinks, or swallows, is predicted to remain in a state of not being broken down or spoiled such as medication or food; the last date that a contract is in force

faculty – people who provide educational experiences at a school

faculty office hours – the scheduled time that teachers make themselves available to meet with students in regard to academic concerns and clarity

FAFSA – (Free Application for Federal Student Aid) – a document that must be completed annually to be considered for assistance in paying for college through grants, loans, and work study

fairness – handling matters in such a way that the parties involved do not feel cheated or taken advantage of

fare - the amount of money a person has to pay in order to utilize transportation options

feasible – can be done due to certain abilities and sets of circumstances

fee waiver – a formal arrangement where a person does not have to make a payment that is normally required when submitting certain applications

filing – organizing and placing documents in a place for later retrieval; completing and turning in paperwork that is required in order to have certain business affairs processed and acted upon

final exams – a test that is given at the end of a class semester to assess mastery of course content

finance charge - the extra money that is charged by the lender in addition to the money or cost of things purchased that will be paid back over time

financial aid – grants, loans, work study, and scholarships that help to pay for college

first impression – an opinion formed about a person based upon the first time a person is exposed to them including appearance, behavior, and etc.

flexibility – the state of being able to change what one does or thinks in the event that the need arises

flexible scheduling – a situation where it is permissible to change the time or day that certain things will take place

flow chart – a graphic organizer that illustrates sequential order

follow-up – to check on progress to complete the intended goal

follow-through – when someone continues to work on completing something that he/she has started

follow-up – check up on and perform next steps based upon information that has been provided

food banks – places where people can go and get food that people and organizations have donated as a form of assistance to others

foreclosure – the process by which a person can lose and no longer own a home that she/he is in the process of making monthly payments on due to extensive missed payments

forgery – when a person pretends to be another person and signs the other person's name on a document

formal evaluation – an organized set of tests and assessments that are given to help determine the current status of a person or group of people

foundation – situations or things that must be completed or in place before other things or actions can take place or be added

Frayer Model – a graphic organizer that provides an explanation and examples of what a particular piece of vocabulary is and is not

freshmen orientation – an event scheduled to show new college students the location and function of various offices and activities on campus as well as to share expectations with them regarding regulations and academic progress

frustration outlet - an activity that someone engages in to relieve stress related to unresolved challenges

full time employee – a person who works at least thirty hours per week at a given place of employment

full time student – a person who attends college and takes at least twelve credit hours of coursework during a semester

gender – the status of being male or female

genetic predisposition – the state of being likely to inherit certain traits based upon the traits of one's ancestors

goal – a thing that a person wants to accomplish

goal oriented – actions that take place for the purpose of making progress and accomplishments

goal setting – the process of deciding what one will attempt to accomplish

grant – money that is received for things such as school that does not have to be paid back

gratification – the state of something bringing pleasure to someone

Greek life – activities that often take place when one is affiliated with a fraternity or sorority

grievance – a process when a person formally expresses a disagreement to those at a higher level within an organization, school, or company, when he/she believes that unfair treatment has taken place

grocer – a person or place that sells unprepared food

grooming – the process of taking care of one's appearance

gross pay – the amount of money that employees earn from their jobs prior to taxes and deductions being taken out

group affiliation-based scholarship – money that one receives to help pay for college due to who the person knows and/or is associated with

grouping concepts - establishing relationships between ideas

guidance – giving direction and/or examples to someone who is attempting to learn when, where, or how to do something

guilt by association – the concept of a person believing negative things about a person based upon who that person spends time with

hacking – the action where a person who maliciously goes into the online accounts of others and gathers personal information or misinforms others by pretending to be the owner of the accounts

hands-on learner – a person who gains understanding of new material by performing activities that help to demonstrate concepts

harassment – excessive behaviors by a person directed toward an individual that make the person feel picked upon or uncomfortable

hazard – something that can cause an accident

healthy – the status of not being sick and one's body working properly

health maintenance – the process of keeping oneself from developing or increasing illness

health screening – examinations and physical checkups that determine if the patient has any health issues that need to be addressed

healthcare – the process of engaging professional medical personnel with one's well-being to avoid or recover from illness as well as decrease the chances of an illness becoming worse

healthy – the absence of illness

highlighting – underlining or marking written material so that those things that are deemed as important stand out

holiday pay – money that an employee receives as if he/she were working due to the hours that would have been worked falling on a day that is a holiday

hourly worker – a person who gets paid based upon the agreed upon amount for each hour that is worked

housing – where a person lives while attending college; the place where a person resides in the community

housing accommodations – things that make a home accessible for those with various physical limitations and challenges

housing deposit – a down payment that is given to hold a spot at a future place of residence

housing regulations – rules that one must follow when living in certain places in order to remain living there

Human Resources Department – the department within a company that is responsible for posting job openings and securing employees to fill positions

hybrid class – coursework that consists of a combination of meeting online and meeting in a classroom

hygiene – the process of keeping one's body clean and presentable

idea clustering – grouping thoughts that are similar

identity theft – a situation in which personal information has been stolen and is being used to get goods and services as well as misrepresenting the person in other ways that can be harmful to that person

image – how a person appears when one observes them and/or interprets their actions

implementation – the beginning stage of taking an action

impression – how a person thinks and has an opinion of other people based upon their experiences with that person or group

improvement – doing better

income tax filing – the process of completing and submitting an annual document to local, state, and federal government that helps to verify if taxes have been overpaid or underpaid

independence – the degree of which a person operates on his/her own

indifference - not caring one way or the other

Individualized Educational Plan – (I.E.P.) a legal document created for students who receive special education services that includes their challenges, how well they perform, the types and amounts of services agreed upon that are to be provided to them, and personal specific goals that educators who work with them are to implement while providing services to them

informed decision making – learning about the pros and cons of certain things one will do prior to actually making a choice on what to do

inside informant – a person who shares what is happening inside of an organization that the public is generally not aware of

insider knowledge – having information about activities within an organization that the public is not generally aware of

installment Plan – making scheduled partial payments until the entire balance that is owed has been met

instructor feedback – the process where a teacher shares how well or poorly a student has performed and provides advice on how to improve

insubordination – refusing to do what one's supervisor has requested him/her to do

insurance – a service that is purchased and scheduled payments are made so if a related event involving loss or need of services occurs, some of the major costs involved are paid by the service

integration of ideas – collecting thoughts that support one another from different sources and blending them

integrity – the status of maintaining honesty and good will when participating in affairs that involve others

interest – extra money that must be paid to the lender in addition to the money that was borrowed for the privilege of being able to borrow money from them

interest groups – people who have similar concerns and come together for the purpose of discussing possible actions or solutions related to those concerns

interest rate – the percentage amount of a loan that is charged by the lending institution to the customer for the amount of money that was borrowed

interests – activities that a person likes

internet security – a system that helps to prevent others from invading online accounts that do not belong to them

internship – working at a job without being an employee for the purpose of learning about the potential responsibilities, demands, and atmosphere of that type of job

interview – an activity that involves an employer speaking with someone who has applied for an opening and asking them questions to help determine if this is who they should hire

interviewee – a person that an employee speaks with to determine if this person is one who should be considered for a job opening

interviewer – a person who represents a company or business who speaks with those who express interest in open positions to determine if that person should be considered for an open position

introduction - the part of a piece of literature that informs the reader about what type of information will follow later in the literature; the first sharing of identity between individuals or groups

invasive – trying to find out more about a person than that person is comfortable sharing

investigate – the process of checking out things to uncover unknown information of interest

isolated – the status of a place having few present at a given time

job – an activity or service that is performed in exchange for earning a wage

job evaluation – a process where the employer rates how well an employee has performed her/his duties during a given time period

job fair – an event where multiple employers or managers are available to share information regarding jobs and careers with those who are seeking employment

job skills – abilities that a person has that can be used at a place of employment

journal – a collection of scholarly writings that have been published based upon a common subject area or interest

justify – to provide an acceptable reason for an action or situation

lab class – a course that involves hands on activities

labor union – an organization that helps look out for the rights of people who work within that particular trade or profession

landlord – the person who owns a residential property that people are able to lease or rent

late fee – extra money that must be paid to a lender when a regularly scheduled payment does not take place on time

lateral move – getting a different job that is at the same level or status as the prior job

law enforcement agencies – places that employ public servants/police who ensure that people are not breaking the law and intervene when they are

lawsuit – the action where a person uses an attorney to collect for damages or money that is owed

layoff – the status of being released from a company or business due to decrease in the number of positions or jobs within that company or business

lease – a written contract for using a residence or car for a given period of time which includes the costs and conditions of use

lecture class – a course where the instructor speaks and students take notes

Legal Aid Society – an organization that helps to provide people who have limited income with legal counsel for the purpose of handling certain types of personal affairs

legal assistance – help from an attorney

leisure – activities that one does when trying to relax or have fun

leisure time – the periods where one can have rest, fun, and relaxation due to not having to engage in handling personal affairs

letter of recommendation – a written introduction that shares positive things about an individual that is based upon personal experience with them to help a college or company judge their application

liability – state of having a legal responsibility for various potential actions that may cause harm to others

library – a place that houses books and other forms of literature that can be borrowed for a given period of time

lifestyle balance – having a well-rounded life where not too much or too little of an activity takes place

light rail transportation – public transportation consisting of trains that have regular routes within metropolitan areas

limitations – things that one is not able to do

limousine – a luxury car driven by a hired chauffeur that is sometimes used for special occasions

LinkedIn – a social media site where job related information is shared

live video – a moving picture that is being broadcasted at the same time that the events on it are being recorded

living arrangements – how, where, and with who one resides

loans – money provided by another party that must be paid back

location – where a person, place, or thing is

loyalty – the status of beholding an individual or group that one will maintain support for that individual or group

main idea – the major thesis behind a story or other form of expression

maintenance – keeping things in working order and repairing them when they stop working

major – the main subject area that a student focuses upon and takes courses related to when completing credit requirements for a college degree

major intersections – places where larger well-known streets cross one another

major points – the main things

manageable steps – doing a little bit at a time with the purpose of completing an entire larger task

mannerisms – the way a person behaves and/or expresses himself/herself

marketing – presenting a person, service, and/or product in such a way that others will want to benefit from the use of the person, service, or product

math lab – a place on a college campus where there are people who help students who are having difficulty in math courses

mediation – the process of helping two parties who have a disagreement come to an agreement considering the beliefs of both parties

medical emergency – a situation when a person needs immediate care from a healthcare provider to avoid serious harm from coming to them

medical screening – a process where people in the healthcare profession collect information about a person's health

mentoring – the process where a more experienced person guides a person who is less experienced to learn what and how things must be done to be successful at completing tasks and procedures in his/her new position

merit-based college funding/scholarship – money that is given to help pay for college expenses due to a person's prior performance in school

mid-terms – a test that a person takes in school during the halfway point of that course to assess progress toward mastery

minimum payment – the smallest amount of money that a person who owes must pay for the current bill in order to avoid becoming late or delinquent

minor – a subject of personal interest in college that requires multiple courses being taken but not as many as are required for the main area or major for a specific college degree

misrepresentation – sharing an inaccurate picture or meaning that can give the listener the wrong ideas about something

mnemonic – a memorization technique that involves using the first letters of key terms to create sentences that can be remembered and then resupplying the key terms to each of those first letters

modification – the act of changing something

modify – to change something

mortgage – the amount of money that is owed for a house being purchased

motive – a reason for doing something

multi-tasking – working on more than one task during the same time period

nationality – the demographic that denotes the country from which one was born

need-based college funding/scholarship – money that is given to a person for college expenses based upon that person's limited income

needs vs. wants – what is required for survival vs. what is desired and not needed for survival

negotiate – the process making a shared agreement while both parties give consideration to the perspectives of each other

neighborhood – a given area where people live within a city or county

net pay – the amount of money issued on a paycheck after taxes and deductions have been subtracted from the total pay

networking – sharing information that can be helpful as well as providing assistance between groups of people who have common interests and have chosen to be in contact with one another

non-critical – not needed in order to survive or function

non-negotiable – an event that a person requires to take place and conditions that are required to exist in order to be acceptable for that person

non-verbal communication – sharing thoughts through gestures and other means that don't include speaking one's thoughts

norms – usual behavior, dress, and/or activity for a given group of people

nuisance – actions, conditions, or things that bother others and make them uncomfortable

nutrition – the condition of eating and drinking healthy food or drink

objective – specifically planned outcome requiring action to meet a goal

obligation - an expected behavior that should be done due to a written or unwritten agreement

obstacle – something that gets in the way and makes it difficult to accomplish goals

off-campus housing – places where students live that are not located at the college they are attending

Office of Student Affairs – a department on college campuses that has personnel who advocate for student needs and concerns

online – accessed through internet connection

online class – coursework that can be completed through interactions and assignments that are internet based

online forums – groups of people who meet and share ideas and comments about particular topics while logged in on the internet

openings – positions that are available for new hires within a company or business

open-mindedness – the ability to think about and consider ways that other people do things that may differ from how one usually does things

organizations - groups of people who interact, network, and have common interests

organize – putting things or events together in a way that makes sense for those who must use those things or participate in those events

orientation – a period of time when a person or group is informed about processes, rules, procedures, and locations of places related to performing an on-going task such as working on a new job or attending a new school

origin – where something came from or started

outline - a listing of what things will be grouped together and sequentially organized when drafting a paper or document

over-scheduling – having more things to do than can be done properly within a given period of time

overtime – the additional hours worked by an hourly employee that go beyond forty hours per week

pacing – how quickly one progresses through tasks

paid time off – work hours that are designated to be paid without requiring presence at the job

paper trail – keeping and maintaining receipts and written communications to help verify transactions that have taken place

paraphrasing ideas – finding alternative ways to express the same idea

part-time employee – a person who works less than thirty hours per week

part-time student – a person who is taking less than twelve credit hours per academic semester

party clothing – apparel that one would wear for evening entertainment and is considered as too flashy and not conservative enough to be worn to work

pass – a sort of voucher that represents that payment has already been made to cover public transportation expenses during a given time period

passenger rules – a list of behavioral expectations for anyone who uses specific forms of transportation

password – a private code that has been created to access various computerized and online functions

password protection – keeping personal information away from others that would allow them to access personal computerized and online functions

path – the direction that one takes to get from one place to another

pawn shop – a place where one borrows money in exchange for a possession being held and the person loses the possession if all money and fees are not repaid

payday loans – places that charge high interest for money that is borrowed and has agreed to be paid back on the day the person receives his/her paycheck

payment terms – an agreement of when, how much at a time, and how often a borrower is to pay back increments of money that have been borrowed from a lender

peak travel time – periods when the majority are commuting from one destination to another

pending – when something cannot happen until another thing happens first

performance – how one functions when completing tasks and assignments

perseverance – the act of not allowing hardships and setbacks to stop one from trying to accomplish his/her personal goals

persistence – the act of continuing to do something instead of giving up

personal academic plan – a thought out sequence of steps and coursework that will be taken in the process of completing graduation requirements

personal accountability – being responsible and making sure that one has done what has been agreed upon

personal affirmation – convincing oneself that he/she has value

personal application – finding ways to make information relevant and using what has been learned in one's life

personal assessment – when one makes decisions about goals based upon one's own abilities, desires, schedules, progress, and qualifications

personal boundaries – a range of behaviors and expectations that individuals are comfortable operating within

personal branding – sets of actions, behaviors, style preferences, and preferred images that a person has established as a representation of himself/herself and his/her values

personal compatibility – how well an individual gets along with and enjoys engaging in activities with another individual

personal deadline – the time boundary one creates for himself/herself to complete a task

personal fulfilment – the status of being content with oneself, what one has, and what one has accomplished

personal goal – things a person decides he or she wants to accomplish

personal growth – the state of improving and becoming better

personal image – the impression a person makes and how that person appears to others

personal impression – how one feels about another person or situation based upon experiences with that person or situation

personal liability – the status of someone being held responsible for damages that they cause to another individual

personal limitations – actions that one is normally able to perform

292

personal reference – a person who can vouch for another person in regard to being worthy of consideration for an opportunity of job or admittance into an organization

personal space – the distance surrounding a person that a person needs between himself/herself and another person without feeling invaded

personal strengths – things that a person does well

personal workload – the number of tasks that a person has decided to take on during a given period

personality – the traits of a person including how she/he thinks, behaves with others, feels about the world around him/her, and emotional make-up

personality conflict – a situation that exists when two people have difficulty getting along due to differences in values and opinions about acceptable behaviors and tastes

petition – a written and signed form expressing the desire that a certain action takes place or stops taking place

pharmacies – places where medications can be purchased and prescriptions are filled

place of worship – a church, synagogue, temple, or other place that is used as a designated location to collectively participate in organized religion

placement test – an exam that is given before college courses are taken to help determine what level of courses the student should begin with

plagiarism – the act of including wording, phrases, or ideas from another author's writing within a newly drafted piece of literature without also including the source and author of that information

plan of action – steps that one takes when trying to accomplish something

planner – a booklet or other item that allows a person to list planned activities and their dates and times to help a person organize his/her time and accomplish the plans that have been agreed upon

pleasure - the condition of enjoying something

plan – a future goal and steps that are to be taken to accomplish it

Plan B – a set of steps and/or goal that a person tries to do in the event that he/she is not able to do what was desired at first

playing to one's strengths – using skills that one already does well

pleasure – the condition of happiness or well-being related to an activity that is taking place

political persuasion – affiliation through shared values of people who are parts of certain alliances

political representative – a person who has been elected and represents the citizens of the region where one lives

portfolio – a collection of examples of one's work as well as other items that help to validate one's qualifications to perform a particular type of work

potential – the possibility of being able to perform certain tasks

practice – doing things repeatedly in order to improve performance

precinct – a political voting division including people who live in a certain area of a ward within city or county

predatory lending – loans that charge an extraordinary amount of interest

prejudice – the act of judging people based upon the demographic group that they are part of without really knowing about them, their status, or actions

premium – the amount that must regularly be paid in order to keep insurance

preparation – activity that takes place that helps make a person ready for the next step in what they are trying to accomplish

prerequisite course – classes that must be taken before other more difficult classes

presentation – how a person and the information that he/she shares appears to others

preventive care - taking care of and monitoring one's body for the purpose of remaining healthy

prior knowledge – things that a person knows already before new information is provided

prioritize – deciding upon the sequence of tasks or what should be done based upon importance and/or urgency

priority – things that are more important and should be done before other things

privacy – the status of information being restricted from those who it does not directly involve; the status of restricting others from being able to personally observe the actions and affairs of others

privacy settings – a level of restriction that is personally placed on social media sites so that one can control who sees what one posts

proactive – the state of avoiding or doing things for the purpose of preventing negative results

probationary period – the time when a person has just begun a job and the employer observes to see if the person is a good fit for becoming a long-term employee in that position

problem solving skills – actions that one takes when exploring what is causing something to be wrong and how to fix it

process of elimination – to find out what is right by first identifying what the wrong answers are

productive – the status of getting things accomplished

productivity – the condition of getting tasks completed

professional – doing things in a business-like manner; a type of job that is done for a career and requires post-secondary education to prepare for it

professional counselor – a person whose occupation involves listening to others to help them to sort through their feelings

professional development – learning opportunities that help employees increase their knowledge about things related to their jobs

professionalism – acting in a business-like manner

promotion – moving from one job in a company to a better job within that company

proofread – looking through a document that has been written to make sure that there are no mistakes and is appropriate for the audience that will read it

protest – the formal act of making it known to others and/or to those in control that one disagrees with was has been taking place

protocol – the appropriate actions to take when trying to complete specific tasks

public transportation – available means of traveling from one place to another that does not include one's personal vehicle

punch-in / sign-in – using a time clock or time sheet to document the start of one's work day

punch-out / sign-out – using a time clock or time sheet to document the end of one's work day

punctuality – being on time

qualifications – skills, experience, and education that is required to be considered for certain scholarships, jobs, entry into organizations, and positions

race – ethnicity such as Caucasian, African American, Latino, and Asian

rage – extreme anger

reading the fine print – looking at and analyzing all of the writing on a contract or agreement before agreeing to sign it

realistic – expectations that bear the likelihood of being able to be fulfilled given the conditions that exist

reasonable – actions that one agrees with as making sense and being fair

recommendation – the process of sharing agreement that a person is worthy of consideration for a job, position, or membership in an organization

recording – creating an audio, written, or visual representation of what is being heard or seen

recreation – fun activities

recreational reading – exploring literature for the purpose of enjoyment

redirecting negative energy – choosing to move from the realm of investing energy being negative to finding ways to engage in the positive

reference – a person who can share information with others about how well a person performed while in a position that was under his/her observation

reflection – when behaviors and habits of people are influenced by a memory of what they have experienced in their environments

registrar – the position at a college or university that is responsible for maintaining records verifying participation in coursework and completion of certification and/or graduation requirements for that institution

registration – the process that a person must complete to begin attending a school or class

regression – going backward with accomplishing goals instead of moving forward

regulations – rules

relaxation techniques – methods used for relieving anxiety or tension

reliability – when a person can be counted upon

religion – **shared** practices and beliefs related to creation and inspiration

remedial course – a class, usually math or English, that helps to provide the foundations needed to be successful in college-level coursework

remediation – classes that help a person brush up on skills that are needed for college-level coursework

reminders – things that are put in place to help a person remember that something is scheduled to take place

remodeling – changing the look of a place

renovation – giving a place a newer look

rent – the amount of money a person must pay on a regular basis to stay in an apartment or home owned by another person

repetition – performing an action multiple times

repossession – the act of taking property back from someone

reputable business – a place where one can trust his or her affairs being handled properly because of its history or who the place is affiliated with

reputation – believed characteristics about a person or place based upon past experiences with that person or place

required course – classes that must be taken to help meet graduation requirements

requirements – things that a person has to have or accomplish that are needed to complete or enter certain processes

research assignment – a task that is required by a class that includes having to look up and report on information that is found about a particular topic

rescheduling – setting up an event or appointment for a different time from the original time

resignation – the process of voluntarily separating oneself from employment

resource – people, places, or things that are used to help accomplish something

respect – maintaining and showing honor for another person by treating the person as a person of value

respectful – the manner of which a person maintains and shows honor for another person as a person of value

responsibility – the condition of being in a position where one's actions can impact the well-being of others

resume - a document that is created to share an applicant's experience and other qualifications with potential employers for the purpose of being considered for a position in a company or organization

retail – a place where goods are purchased

retirement – the act of leaving a job after working enough years to qualify for continued monetary benefit from having worked there

review – to look at again for the purpose of accepting what is seen or making or requesting changes

revise – to make changes to something that is being made or is already completed

revocation – the act of taking a privilege away

rewards – benefits or good things that happen because of a status one is in or an action one has taken

right – something that a person is entitled to

risk – the status of taking a chance

risk vs. benefit – the potential for something to cause harm as opposed to helping

risk-taking behavior – when a person involves himself/herself in actions that have the possibility of causing a problem

room and board – the cost of living and eating meals on a college campus

room for the unexpected – leaving enough space or breaks in one's schedule or personal arrangements so that other things can be added if need be

rooming house – a place of residence where a person rents a room that is part of a home containing multiple rooms that are rented

route – the path that a person takes to get from one place to another

routine – the usual order and/or method of things that are done on a regular basis

rush hour traffic – the situation when streets and highways are the most crowded due to the majority of people traveling to and from work or school

safety – the condition of staying away from harm

salaried worker – a person is paid a set amount on a contract during a given year of employment instead of being paid based upon the number of hours worked

salary – the amount of money a person makes for performing services

sales – a type of job where the required task is to convince someone to purchase goods or services

satisfaction – the condition of being happy or content with what has happened

savings account – a collection of money that is placed in a bank or credit union for safekeeping until the money is needed by the owner of the money

scaffolding – a form of teaching that uses small increments of information as a foundation for learning more complex content

scam – an activity that involves tricking people out of their resources

schedule – when and where certain events are supposed to take place

schedule conflict – a period of time when more than one event that a person is to attend is to happen at the same time

scholarship - money that a person receives to pay for college that has been provided based upon the performance and/or status of the one who has applied

scholarship application – a form that is filled out to solicit consideration from a person or organization who has agreed to help finance part of one's educational expenses

school culture – the appearance of and the normative behaviors within an institution of learning

school supplies – things a student needs in order to perform academic study and academic tasks

second opinion – getting the advice of an additional person prior to taking certain actions

security – the condition of keeping people and/or things safe from others

security checkpoints – specific locations where people are checked to make sure that they are not bringing certain pre-determined things into or out of an environment that may create dangerous situations for others

self-advocacy – speaking up for oneself in an effort to make sure that personal needs are being met

self-assessment – reflecting upon one's own needs and abilities to determine further needs and appropriate actions

self-care – actions related to maintaining one's physical appearance, health, and hygiene

self-evaluate – thinking about one's status and actions to decide if any changes need to be made

self-fulfillment- doing things that help one to feel good about meeting personal goals

self-gratification – doing things to make one feel content

self-improvement – the condition of one becoming better than before

self-incrimination – doing or saying things that make oneself appear guilty or at fault

self-reflection – thinking about and evaluating the status of oneself

seminar – a setting where one interacts with others as information is provided, shared, and discussed

service charge – an extra amount that a person must pay for the delivery of goods and/or services

services - things that are done for other people

self-disclosure – the act of sharing one's personal information with others

setting limits – deciding upon how much time or how much of an action that one will allow for events that will take place

set-up / break-down – putting items in place that are needed to perform a task or service and then removing them once finished

severance package – money and/or benefits that an employer gives to someone that is being separated from employment for a given period of time to help him/her as he/she adjusts to losing a job

shared space – a location where one works, visits, or lives that has others who also are located in that place

shuttle – a vehicle that runs people back and forth between a set of destinations

sick pay – money that is paid by an employer for a maximum amount of days per year as if you were at work when taking off because of medical reasons

skill building – developing the ability to do things and then improve upon how well those things are done

skills – things that a person is able to do that can be used to perform tasks on a job

social media – forums on the internet where people can share their thoughts and experiences with one another

social services – a government controlled set of agencies that help to provide assistance in meeting basic needs for those who qualify

social setting – a place where people gather to enjoy themselves

social worker – a person who works to help people solve problems by connecting them with appropriate resources

socialization – the act of intermingling and doing things with other people

socio-economic status – groupings of people that are based upon their incomes and standards of living

solution – a way to fix a problem

staff – people who work at a place

stagnancy – remaining in a state of being where no improvement is being made

standard operating procedures – the way that a company or business normally performs tasks

strategy – the method of which a person attempts to accomplish something

status - the state of how one currently stands within a situation

strategy – a method of doing things

strengths – things that a person does well

stress – the status of experiencing different things that one becomes uneasy about

stress management – doing what is needed to help provide physical and emotional balance when managing several things that cause pressure and displeasure in life in order to avoid becoming physically or emotionally ill

stress outlet – an activity that helps a person decrease the feeling of being overwhelmed

stressor – things that cause a person to feel uneasy

student activities – events that take place at school for the purpose of students enjoying positive time together

student advising – a department found on campus that has people who help students in the selection of coursework needed to fulfill academic requirements

student counseling – a department on a campus that has people who serve students by helping them sort through their feelings and assist with some mental health issues

student demographics – classifications related to the culture, social class, ethnicity and socio-economic status of students

student health services – a department found on campus where healthcare activities take place

student housing – places where students live that are affiliated with the school they are attending

student loan - money that a student borrows to cover the costs of attending college

student population – the number of people who take classes at a specific school

student support services – a department at a school that helps students with academic difficulties

study buddy – someone who is teamed up with another student in order to prepare for tests and assignments that are due

study group – people who agree to review course content with one another for a collective understanding of the material

study time – a period of the day where students take the time to review course content

subsidized housing – a place where people live and part of the cost of living there is paid for by the government

substance abuse – taking drugs for recreational instead of medical purposes

substance dependency – the status of a person physically needing to use certain chemicals to keep from feeling ill

substitute coursework – classes that students take that serve in place of other required classes needed for a particular degree

subway system – the collection of different routes which subway trains use to carry people from place to place in a region

supplemental learning – additional experiences for gaining knowledge outside of what is gained when doing coursework

support groups – people who come together and have common interests for the purpose of helping one another through situations

support system – those people and services that are available to help a person accomplish his/her personal goals

supporting ideas – thoughts that go along with an original thought that have been shared for the purpose of creating a better understanding

swipe-in / swipe-out – the act of using an identification card that has a magnetic strip on the back of it to run through a machine and document time when arriving at work and departing from work

syllabus – a written document provided to students from the instructor that indicates what to expect, what is needed to make satisfactory progress, and the order in which topics will be covered in a course

talent based scholarships – money that a student receives to help pay for academic expenses that was provided due to a school or organization investing in one's education because of activities that a student participates in and excels at

task completion – finishing something that one has set out to do

tax forms - paperwork that must be filled out every year to help determine the amount that a person is responsible for giving to the government and if that amount has been met or overpaid

tax refund – something that a person receives if he/she has overpaid too many dollars in taxes for a given year

taxable income – the amount of money that has been earned that exceeds the maximum amount that can be earned without having a tax responsibility attached to it

taxes – money that is taken out of a person's paycheck to help pay for government services and materials

taxi – a form of public car or van transportation that requires people to pay per trip and is based upon the distance traveled

teachable – ability to learn about information that is presented

teamwork – working together to accomplish something

tenacity – the ability to bounce back after a failure or disappointment

tenant – a person who lives in a rented or leased dwelling

term paper – a written assignment that is due prior to the ending of a semester for a particular class

termination – losing a job due to not meeting the standards for maintaining the job or due to the job no longer needing one's services

terms – the agreed upon conditions of which a certain thing can take place

therapeutic counseling – the act of providing a service designed to help a person feel better mentally by allowing them to discuss their issues while being guided toward solutions

thesis - the main idea that is explained more thoroughly in a paper or oral presentation

thoroughness – the act being complete and not leaving anything undone

ticket – a voucher that represents what has been paid for and is to be used when actually acquiring the goods or services that one has paid for

ticket dispenser – a machine where transportation costs are paid and is followed by giving a voucher or paper representation of that payment for a specific mode of transportation that is to be used during specific time periods

time and a half – the amount that is paid per hour plus half of that for each worked hour that goes beyond forty hours per week

time clock – a machine at a place of employment that stamps the beginning and ending time of being at work for an individual

time docked – when a person is not paid for his/her scheduled number of hours during a pay period due to circumstances that interfered with him/her being present or able to perform his/her duties

time management – assigning amounts of time to different activities that must be accomplished so that all with higher priorities are completed and some additional non-mandatory activities can also be completed

time off without pay - having permission to not be at work on a scheduled work day not receiving any financial compensation for it

time sensitive - things that must be completed by a certain deadline

time sheet – a document that has the hours that have been worked during a given payroll period recorded for further processing

time-frame – when something took place

time-line – specifically when, along a sequence of events, various things took place

time-out – when one is temporarily removed from an environment or situation

time-sensitive – things that have time limits and restrictions on when they should start and end

title loans – money that is borrowed and the lender keeps the borrower's car or house title until the money is paid back

to do list – a series of things that have been written down or voice recorded that need to get done

tolerance – living in harmony with those considered as having different practices or belonging to a different culture than one's own practices and culture

too good to be true – when things happen that are so unrealistically easy that the expected results gave false hopes

traffic regulations – rules that drivers must legally follow to avoid accidents

train transportation – a vehicle that has multiple cars attached to one another and travels on a track

training – the provision of experiences that help a person learn how to do something

transfer – a move from one position to another within a business

transfer credits – verified coursework completion that qualifies to be shared with a new school and is to be counted toward the total amount of course hours that the student needs for meeting graduation requirements

transfer point – a place where a person switches trains, buses, or airplanes to continue traveling to a certain location

transition – a change from one to another activity or phase in life

transparency – the status of being able to see through something; the action of sharing one's inner thoughts with another person or allowing them to purposely witness one's actions

transportation – a form of getting from one place to another using a vehicle such as a car, bus, airplane, or train

traveling time – how long it takes to get from place to place

trigger – an action that happens and often is followed by another specific action or reaction

tuition – the amount of money that a person has to pay to take coursework

tuition installment plan – a method for paying the cost of college coursework by making a down payment and then paying the remaining balance in increments prior to the semester ending

two-week notice – formally letting an employer know that one is leaving a job after the conclusion of two weeks

undivided attention – listening to a person or group of people during a specific period of time without having to also focus upon another activity or person

unemployment benefits – money that is funded by the government to pay someone for a short period of time who has lost his/her job

unemployment compensation – government money that is temporarily provided to someone who has worked the required quarters and has recently lost his/her job

university administration – those who hold top level positions at a university who are responsible for facilitating the effective and efficient running of that institution

update – a provision of the latest information in regard to a particular situation

upward mobility – moving from one job to another one of higher status

utilities – companies that consistently are in place to provide different forms of power and resources that are needed for homes and businesses

vacancies – positions at places of employment that need to be filled; apartments within an apartment complex that do not have anyone currently living in them

vacation pay – continued payment of salary to an employee for a specific amount of days to take off from work that are allowed per year within the work contract

values – those things that are considered to be important and respectable

variable interest rate – when the amount of money a person is charged for borrowing money does not stay the same until the debt is paid but changes at different points within that time period

Venn diagram – a graphic organizer containing overlapping circles that show comparisons and contrasts between the characteristics of two or more things with the overlapping parts showing what things are alike between the two or more things

venting – an activity where a person expresses his/her frustration to an active listener

verbal inquiry – gathering information by talking to the appropriate people

verification - something or someone who confirms the accuracy of information that has been provided

visibility – the state of being able to be seen

visual learner – a person who grasps new information better when he/she is able to see illustrations and examples of what is being taught

visuals – things a person is shown that helps to demonstrate what is being explained

Vocational Rehabilitation – an agency funded by the government that assists people who have disabilities with becoming connected to resources as they continue in their adult lives

voice – an expression of a person's choice or desire

voter fraud – when one votes illegally by using another person's voter registration identity

voter registration – a process where people fill out and turn in the proper forms that are needed so that they can legally voice their choices on future ballots when elections take place

vulnerability - a status that one is in where he/she can more easily be harmed or taken advantage of

W2 forms - an annual form provided by the employer that lists wages, taxes paid, and deductions that must be used when filing income taxes

wage – the amount of money that is paid to an employee

want ads – the place in the newspaper that lists job openings

ward – a political division of a city

warning – a spoken/written statement or a sign that lets people know that dangers or bad outcomes can happen as a result of certain actions

warning labels – information written on packages of products that advise of potential dangers related to the products

weaknesses – things that a person is not good at

web search – looking on the internet to find sources of meeting one's needs

weighing the facts - analyzing available information about a situation to form one's own perception about what has happened or may possibly happen

window of opportunity – the beginning and ending time of being able to have access to something that is desired

win/win – when both sides who do not agree with one another get some of their needs and desires met and neither is a complete loser

work atmosphere - the usual behaviors, environment, mood, and types of actions that take place at a place of employment

work culture – social behaviors, customs, levels of energy, ways of dressing, noise levels, and styles of decoration at a specific place of employment

work ethics – how a person upholds requirements and expectations as an employee

work life vs. personal life – expected norms, behaviors, ways of dressing, and respect of privacy when at the place of employment that differ from when one is away from work and with friends and family

work quality – how well one performs his/her tasks that are required at his/her place of employment

work study – a form of student financial aid that requires a student to perform work on campus in exchange for some of the costs of attending school

work uniform – specific clothing or style of clothing that an employer requires employees to wear

working conditions – the physical and psychological atmosphere that exists at a place of employment

writing lab – a department located on college campuses that provides assistance with major papers due in classes

zone – a specific area that includes where something is located

BEST WISHES AS YOU CONTINUE TO EMPOWER YOUR STUDENTS!!!

"No two flowers bloom in exactly the same way." – Author Unknown

Dr. Annette Diane Anderson Fields, Author

Transition Ahead: Lesson Plans for Life Beyond High School © 2019

"Empowered for Life Through the Acquisition of Knowledge"

Made in the USA
Las Vegas, NV
23 February 2021